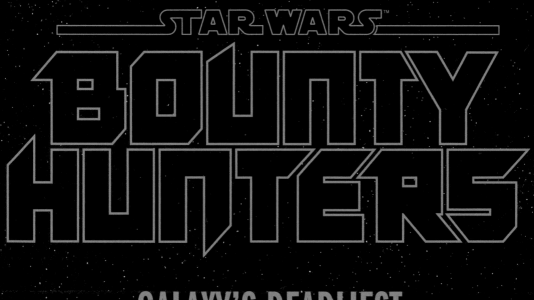

STAR WARS™
BOUNTY HUNTERS

GALAXY'S DEADLIEST

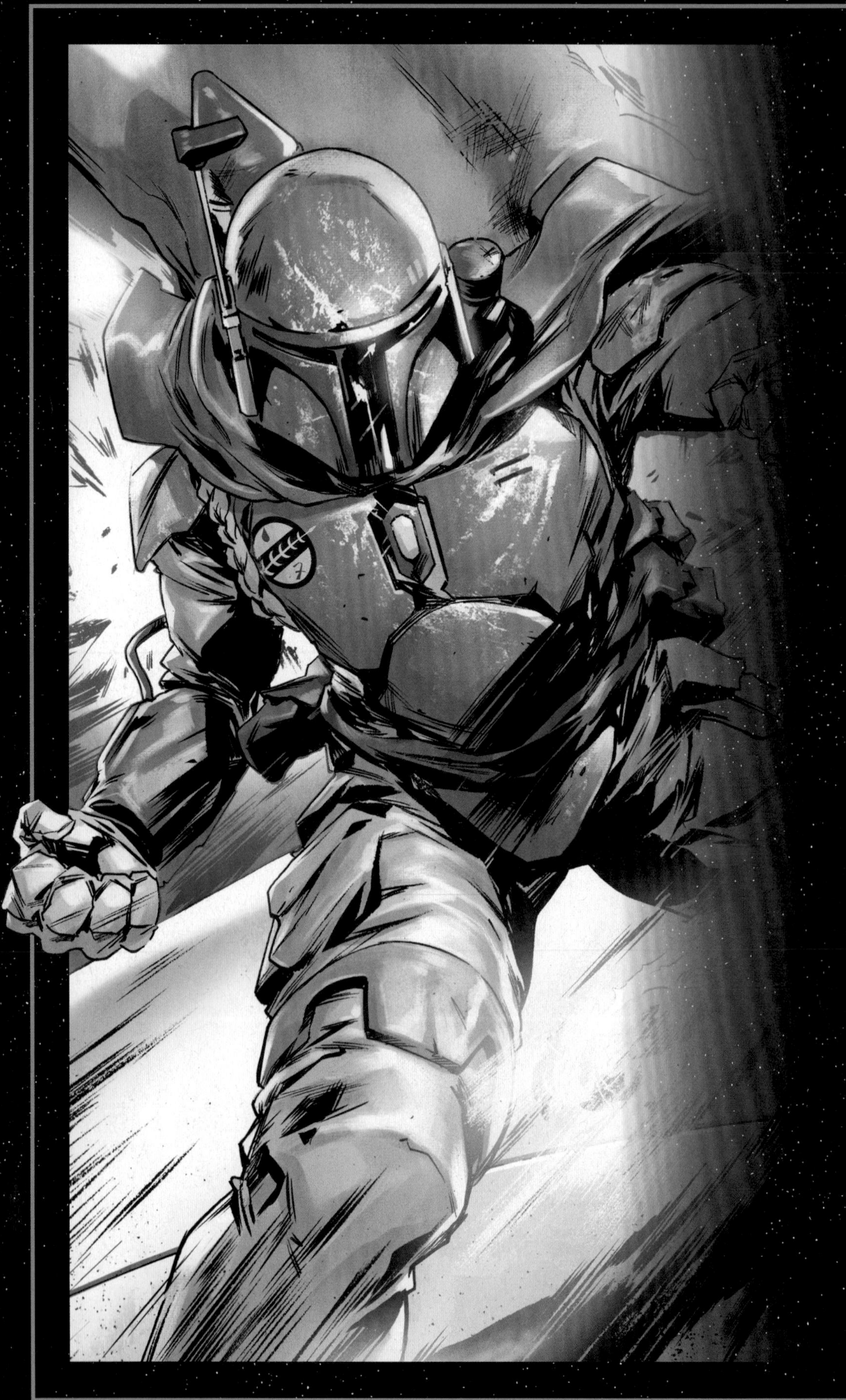

STAR WARS™
BOUNTY HUNTERS

GALAXY'S DEADLIEST

Writer
ETHAN SACKS

Artist
PAOLO VILLANELLI

Color Artist
ARIF PRIANTO

Letterer
VC's TRAVIS LANHAM

Cover Art
LEE BERMEJO

Assistant Editor
TOM GRONEMAN

Editor
MARK PANICCIA

		For Lucasfilm:	
Collection Editor	**JENNIFER GRÜNWALD**		
Assistant Editor	**DANIEL KIRCHHOFFER**		
Assistant Managing Editor	**MAIA LOY**	Senior Editor	**ROBERT SIMPSON**
Associate Manager, Talent Relations	**LISA MONTALBANO**	Creative Director	**MICHAEL SIGLAIN**
VP Production & Special Projects	**JEFF YOUNGQUIST**	Art Director	**TROY ALDERS**
Book Designer	**ADAM DEL RE**	Lucasfilm Story Group	**MATT MARTIN**
SVP Print, Sales & Marketing	**DAVID GABRIEL**		**PABLO HIDALGO**
Editor in Chief	**C.B. CEBULSKI**		**EMILY SHKOUKANI**
		Lucasfilm Art Department	**PHIL SZOSTAK**

STAR WARS: BOUNTY HUNTERS VOL. 1 — GALAXY'S DEADLIEST. Contains material originally published in magazine form as STAR WARS: BOUNTY HUNTERS (2020) #1-5. Third printing 2022. ISBN 978-1-302-92083-8. Published by MARVEL WORLDWIDE, INC., a subsidiary of MARVEL ENTERTAINMENT, LLC. OFFICE OF PUBLICATION: 1290 Avenue of the Americas, New York, NY 10104. STAR WARS and related text and illustrations are trademarks and/or copyrights, in the United States and other countries, of Lucasfilm Ltd. and/or its affiliates. © & ™ Lucasfilm Ltd. No similarity between any of the names, characters, persons, and/or institutions in this magazine with those of any living or dead person or institution is intended, and any such similarity which may exist is purely coincidental. Marvel and its logos are TM Marvel Characters, Inc. **Printed in Canada.** KEVIN FEIGE, Chief Creative Officer; DAN BUCKLEY, President, Marvel Entertainment; JOE QUESADA, EVP & Creative Director; DAVID BOGART, Associate Publisher & SVP of Talent Affairs; TOM BREVOORT, VP, Executive Editor; NICK LOWE, Executive Editor, VP of Content, Digital Publishing; DAVID GABRIEL, VP of Print & Digital Publishing; MARK ANNUNZIATO, VP of Planning & Forecasting; JEFF YOUNGQUIST, VP of Production & Special Projects; ALEX MORALES, Director of Publishing Operations; DAN EDINGTON, Director of Editorial Operations; RICKEY PURDIN, Director of Talent Relations; JENNIFER GRÜNWALD, Director of Production & Special Projects; SUSAN CRESPI, Production Manager; STAN LEE, Chairman Emeritus. For information regarding advertising in Marvel Comics or on Marvel.com, please contact Vit DeBellis, Custom Solutions & Integrated Advertising Manager, at vdebellis@marvel.com. For Marvel subscription inquiries, please call 888-511-5480. **Manufactured between 1/7/2022 and 2/8/2022 by SOLISCO PRINTERS, SCOTT, QC, CANADA.**

10 9 8 7 6 5 4 3

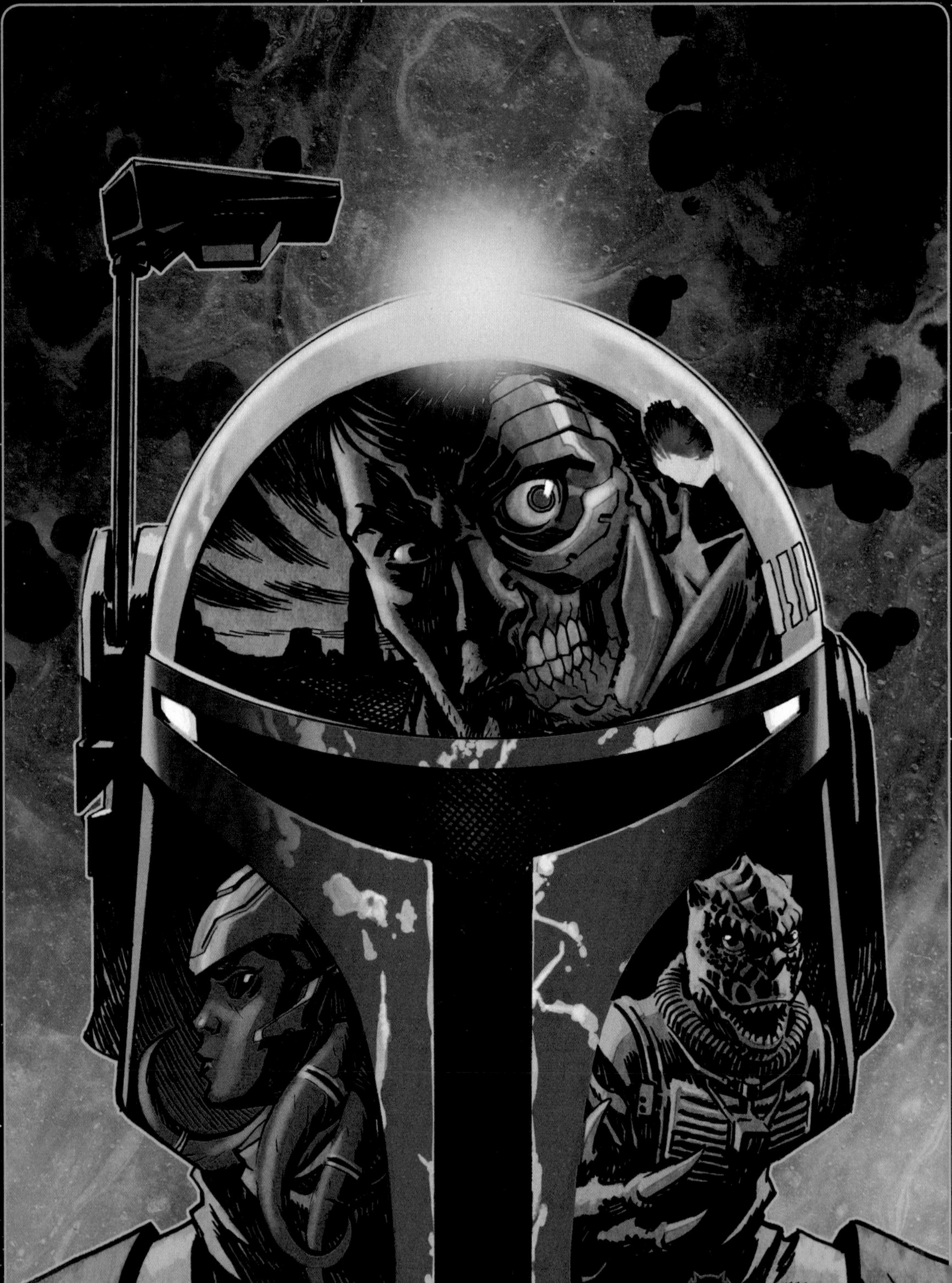

#1 Variant by
DAVE JOHNSON

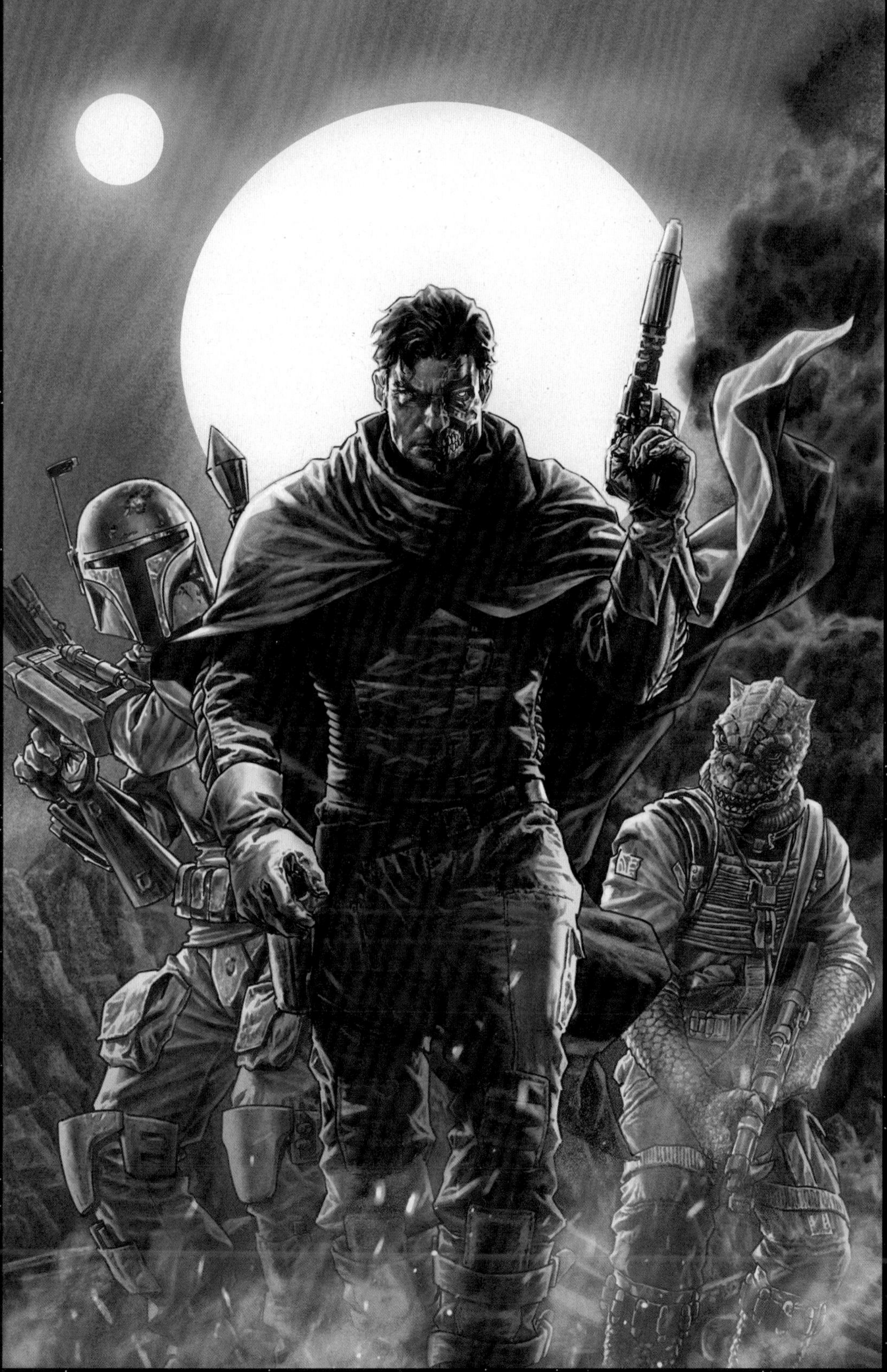

1

VALANCE **BOSSK** **BOBA FETT**

STAR WARS
BOUNTY HUNTERS

The Rebel Alliance is all but defeated after the Battle of Hoth. The Empire has redoubled their efforts to crush the scattered freedom fighters.

While the civil war consumes the galaxy the underworld thrives. Smugglers, mercenaries and thieves serve crime syndicates and cartels that vie for influence, territory and profit.

Skilled and ruthless bounty hunters-some of the most dangerous killers in the galaxy — scour systems to track down wanted criminals for the highest price. Three of these hunters — Valance, Bossk and Boba Fett — are considered some of the best. And they have a history with each other...one that's about to put them on a deadly collision course.

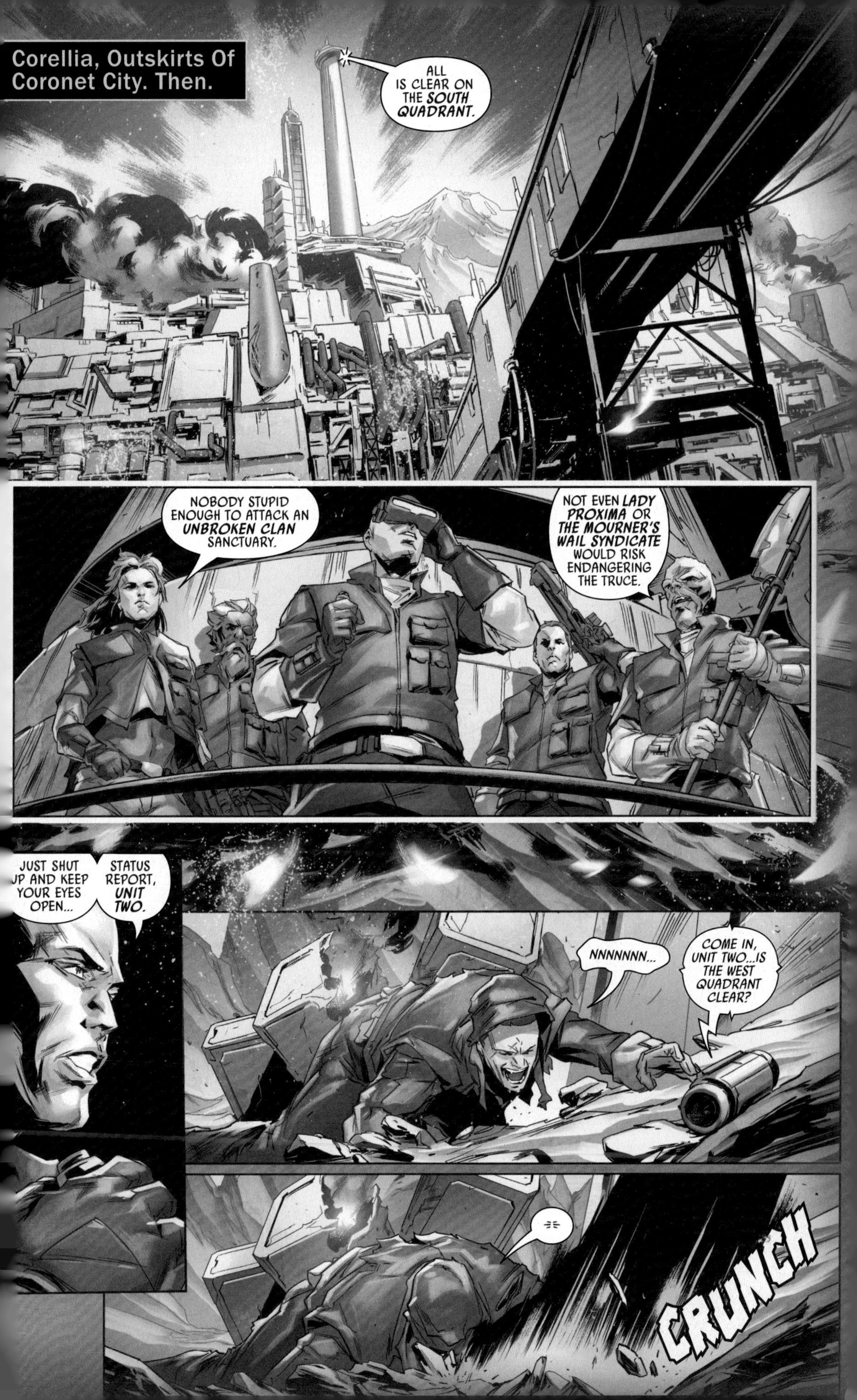
Corellia, Outskirts Of Coronet City. Then.
ALL IS CLEAR ON THE SOUTH QUADRANT.
NOBODY STUPID ENOUGH TO ATTACK AN UNBROKEN CLAN SANCTUARY.
NOT EVEN LADY PROXIMA OR THE MOURNER'S WAIL SYNDICATE WOULD RISK ENDANGERING THE TRUCE.
JUST SHUT UP AND KEEP YOUR EYES OPEN...
STATUS REPORT, UNIT TWO.
NNNNNNN...
COME IN, UNIT TWO...IS THE WEST QUADRANT CLEAR?
CRUNCH

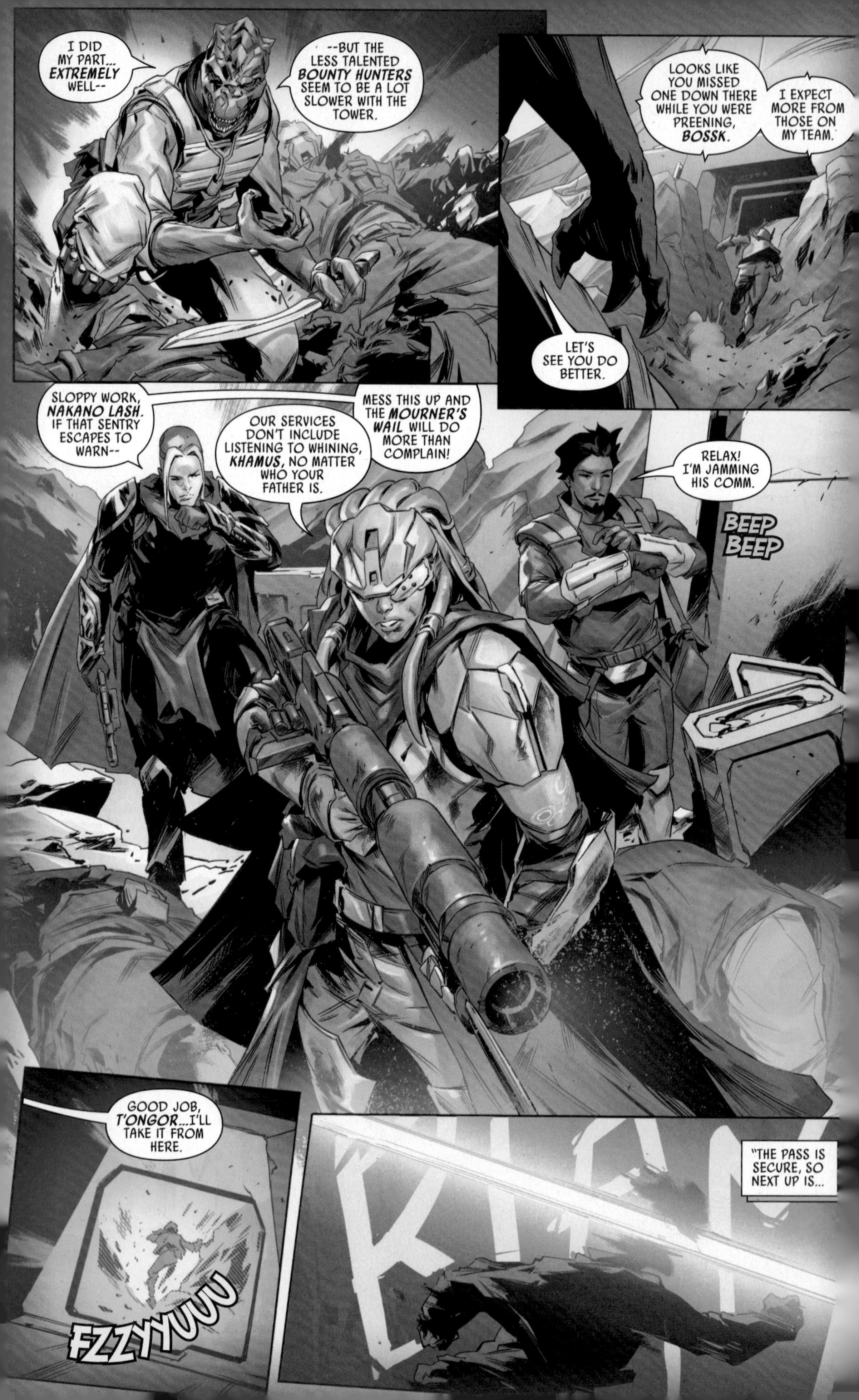

I DID MY PART... **EXTREMELY** WELL--
--BUT THE LESS TALENTED **BOUNTY HUNTERS** SEEM TO BE A LOT SLOWER WITH THE TOWER.
LOOKS LIKE YOU MISSED ONE DOWN THERE WHILE YOU WERE PREENING, **BOSSK**.
I EXPECT MORE FROM THOSE ON MY TEAM.
LET'S SEE YOU DO BETTER.
SLOPPY WORK, **NAKANO LASH**. IF THAT SENTRY ESCAPES TO WARN--
OUR SERVICES DON'T INCLUDE LISTENING TO WHINING, **KHAMUS,** NO MATTER WHO YOUR FATHER IS.
MESS THIS UP AND THE **MOURNER'S WAIL** WILL DO MORE THAN COMPLAIN!
RELAX! I'M JAMMING HIS COMM.
BEEP BEEP
GOOD JOB, **T'ONGOR**...I'LL TAKE IT FROM HERE.
FZZYYUUU
"THE PASS IS SECURE, SO NEXT UP IS...

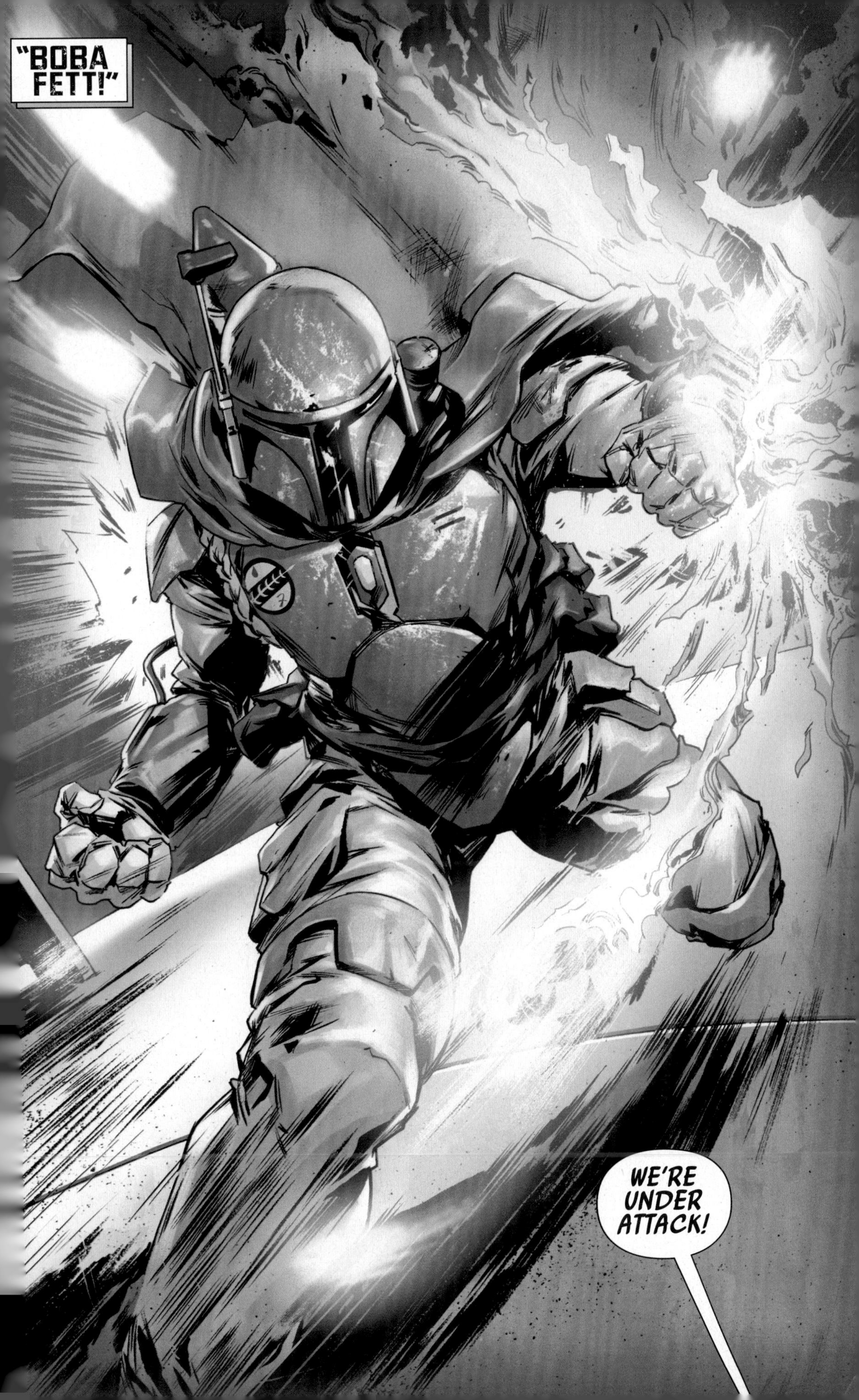
"BOBA FETT!"
WE'RE UNDER ATTACK!

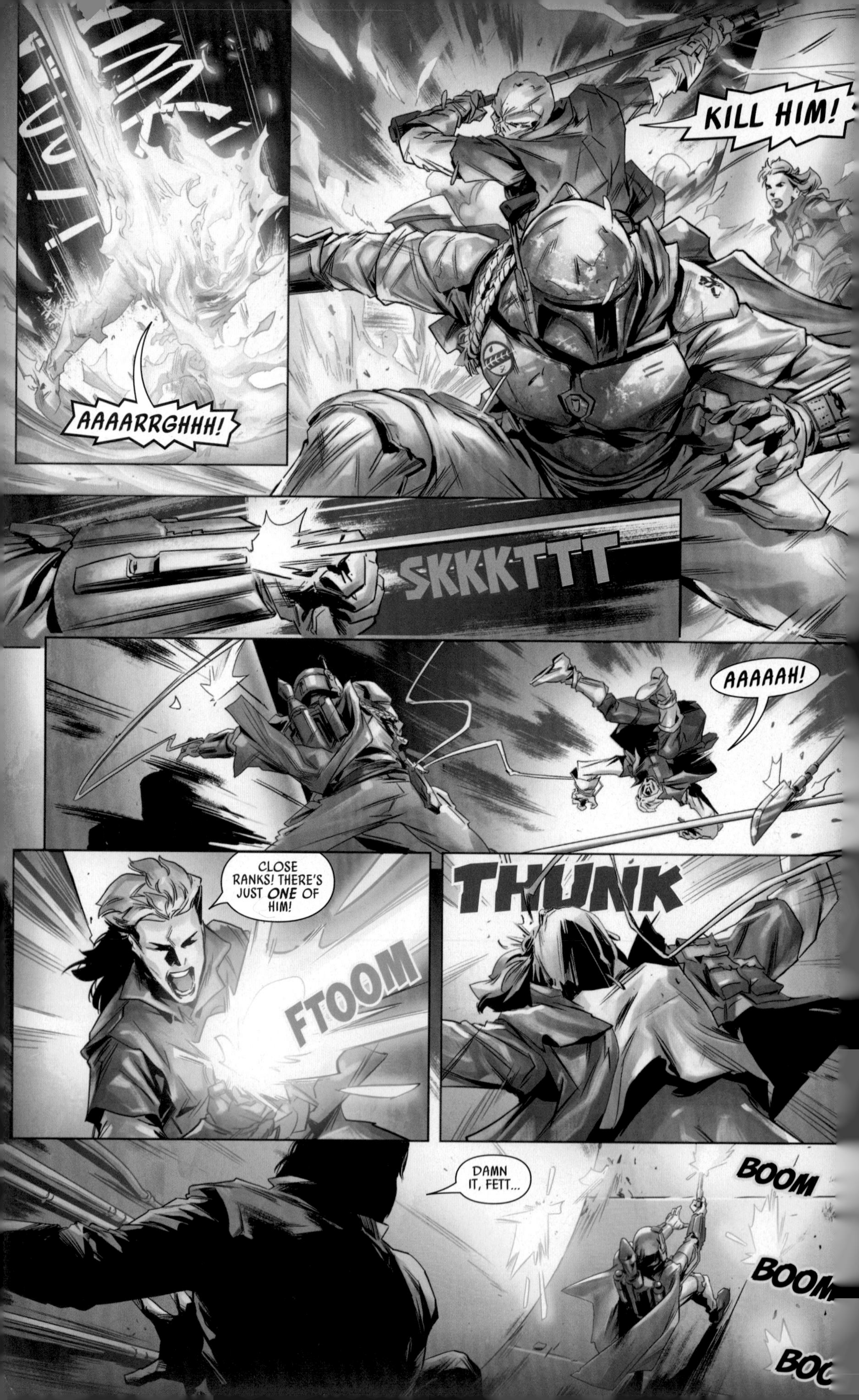

AAAARRGHHH!
KILL HIM!
SKKKTTT
AAAAAH!
CLOSE RANKS! THERE'S JUST ONE OF HIM!
FTOOM
THUNK
DAMN IT, FETT...
BOOM
BOOM

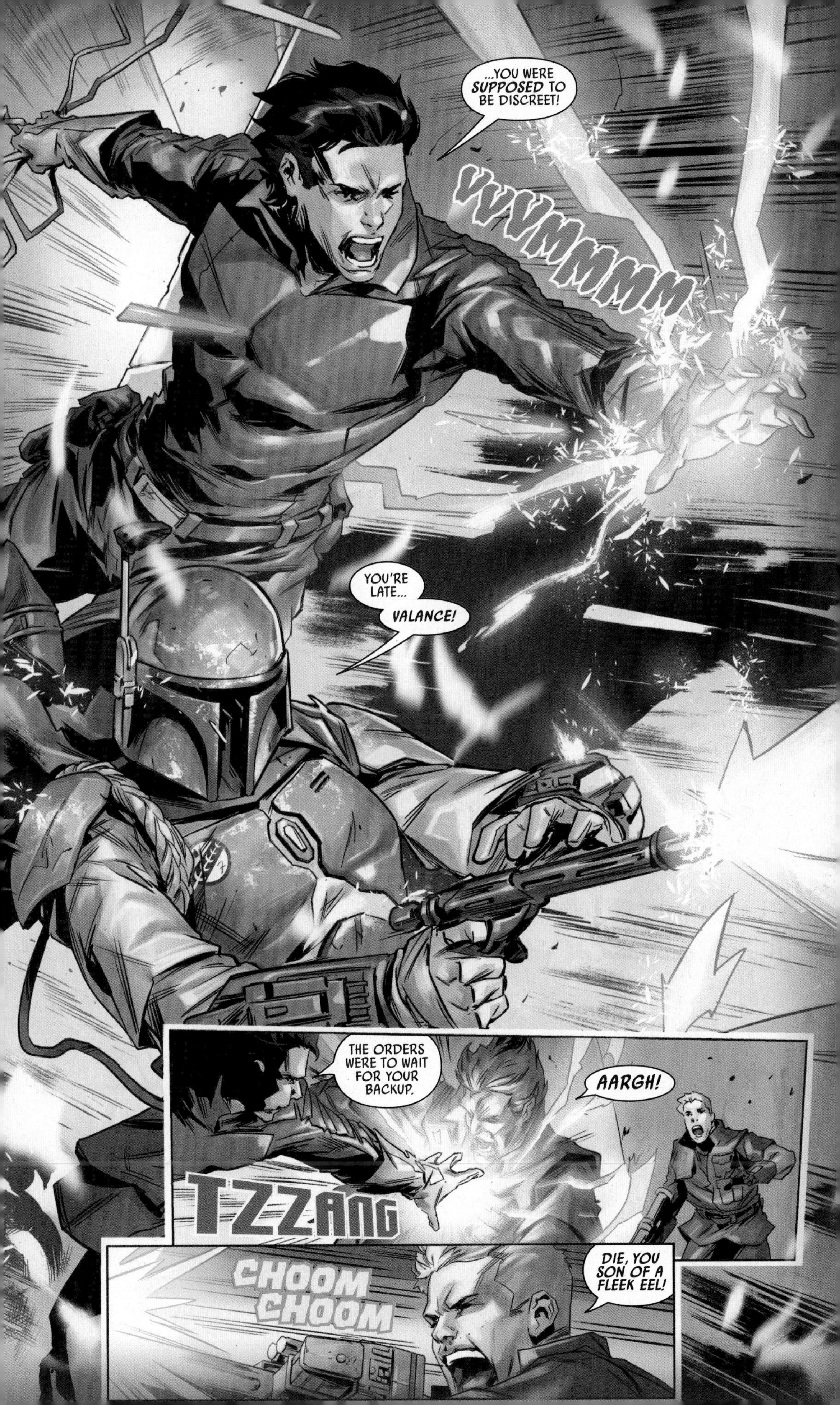
...YOU WERE SUPPOSED TO BE DISCREET!
VVVMMMMM
YOU'RE LATE... VALANCE!
THE ORDERS WERE TO WAIT FOR YOUR BACKUP.
AARGH!
TZZANG
CHOOM CHOOM
DIE, YOU SON OF A FLEEK EEL!

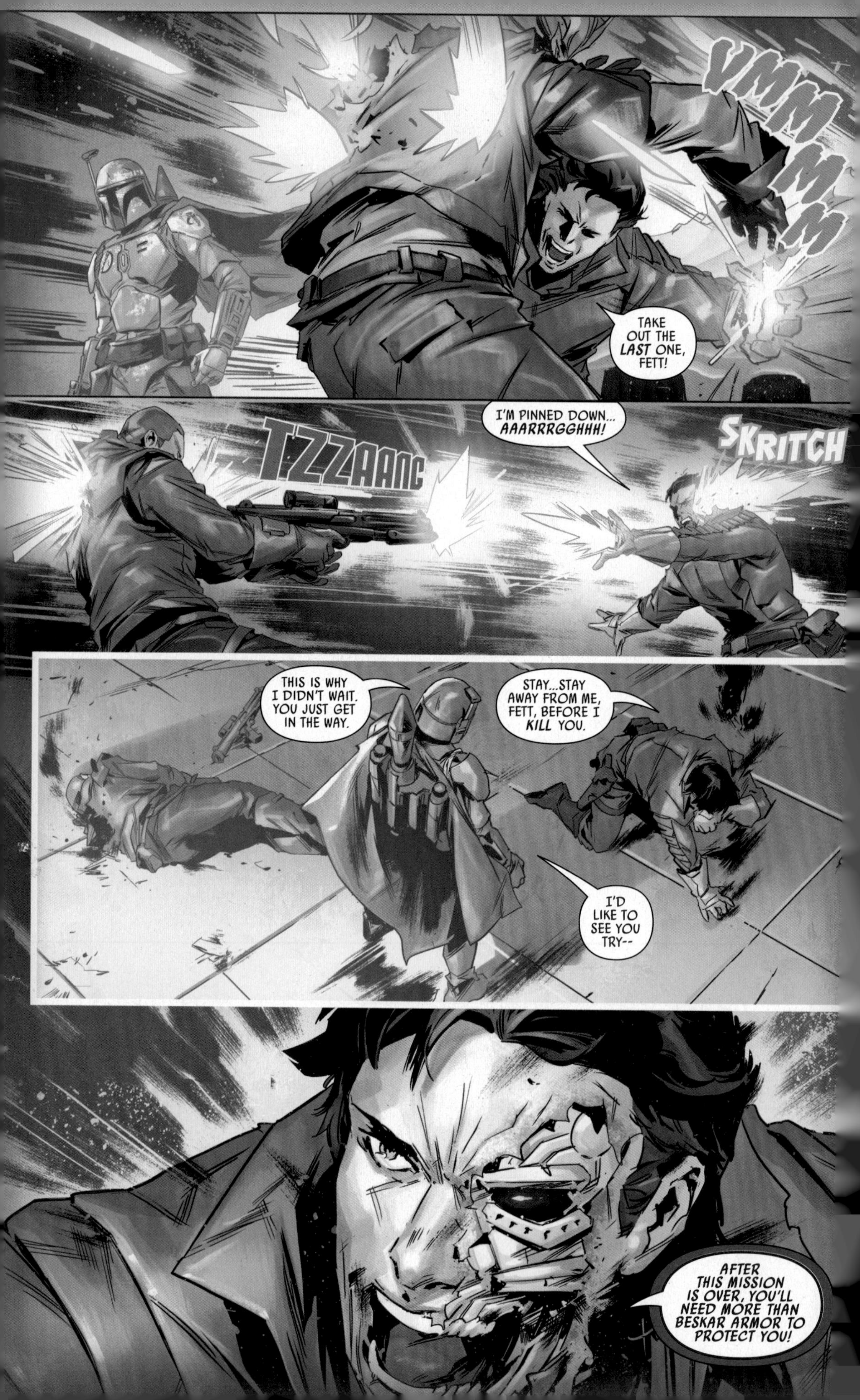

VMMMMMM
TAKE OUT THE LAST ONE, FETT!
I'M PINNED DOWN... AAARRRGGHHH!
TZZAAANC
SKRITCH
THIS IS WHY I DIDN'T WAIT. YOU JUST GET IN THE WAY.
STAY...STAY AWAY FROM ME, FETT, BEFORE I KILL YOU.
I'D LIKE TO SEE YOU TRY--
AFTER THIS MISSION IS OVER, YOU'LL NEED MORE THAN BESKAR ARMOR TO PROTECT YOU!

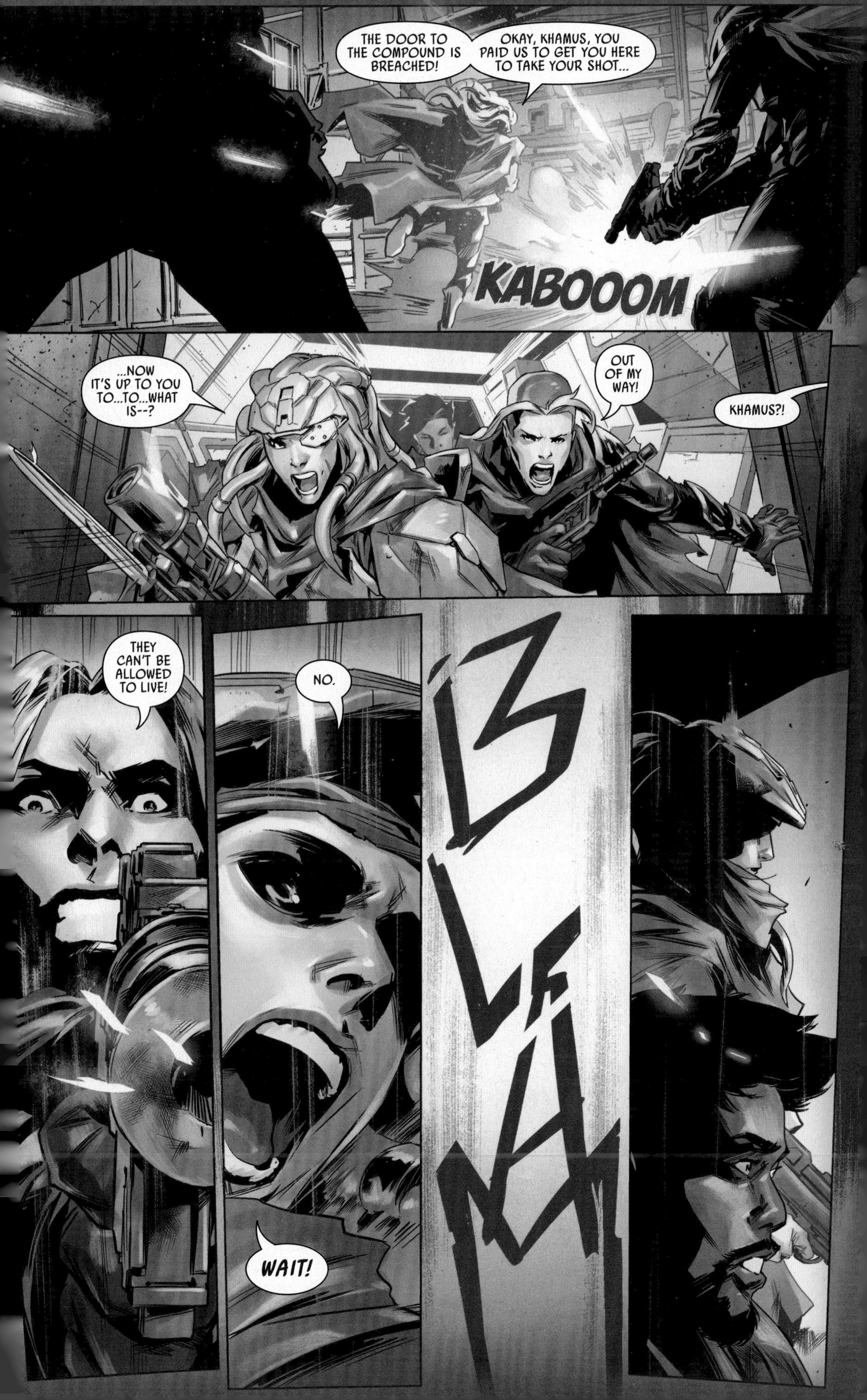
THE DOOR TO THE COMPOUND IS BREACHED!
OKAY, KHAMUS, YOU PAID US TO GET YOU HERE TO TAKE YOUR SHOT...
KABOOOM
...NOW IT'S UP TO YOU TO...TO...WHAT IS--?
OUT OF MY WAY!
KHAMUS?!
THEY CAN'T BE ALLOWED TO LIVE!
NO.
WAIT!

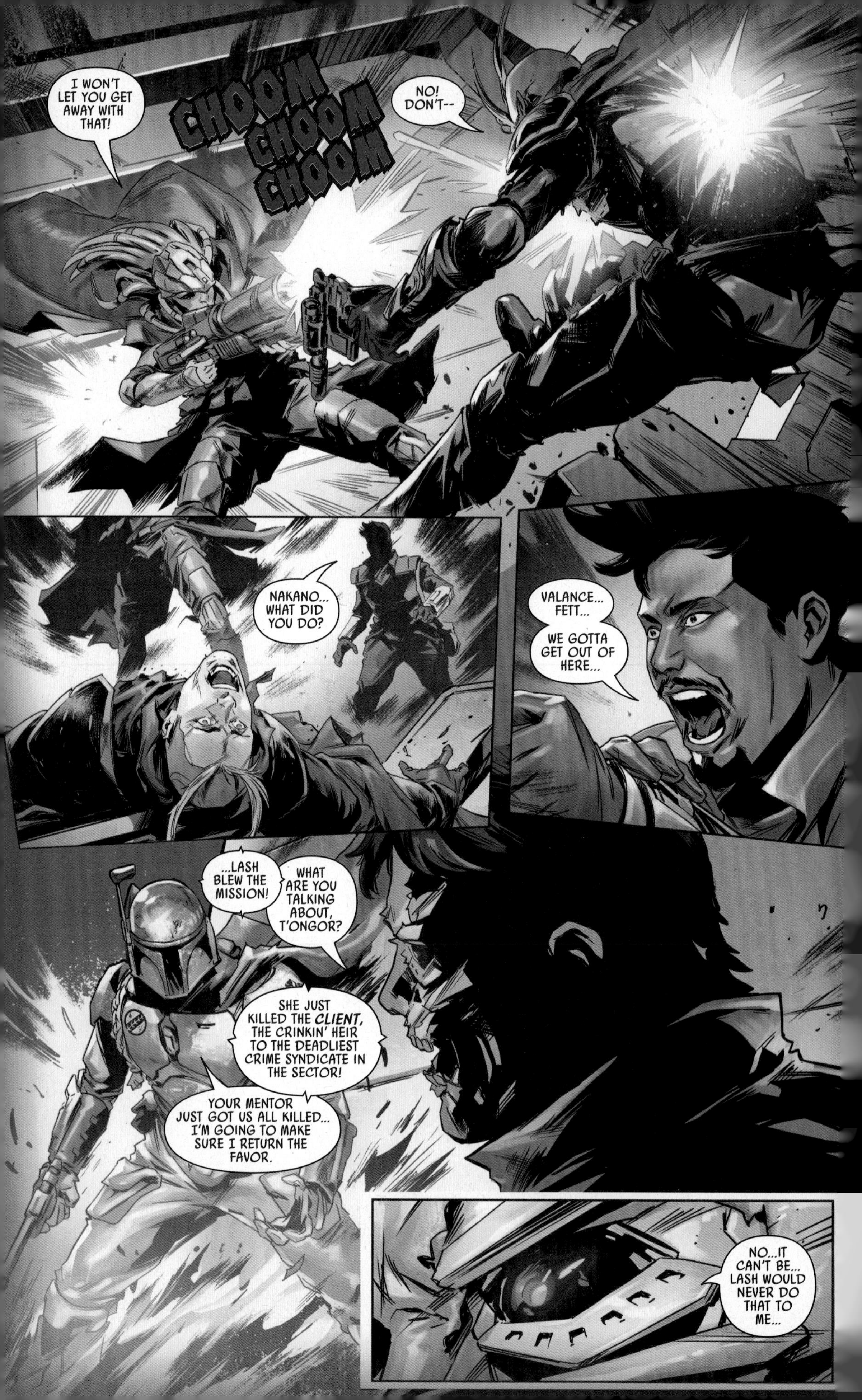
I WON'T LET YOU GET AWAY WITH THAT!
CHOOM CHOOM CHOOM
NO! DON'T--
NAKANO... WHAT DID YOU DO?
VALANCE... FETT...
WE GOTTA GET OUT OF HERE...
...LASH BLEW THE MISSION!
WHAT ARE YOU TALKING ABOUT, T'ONGOR?
SHE JUST KILLED THE *CLIENT*, THE CRINKIN' HEIR TO THE DEADLIEST CRIME SYNDICATE IN THE SECTOR!
YOUR MENTOR JUST GOT US ALL KILLED... I'M GOING TO MAKE SURE I RETURN THE FAVOR.
NO...IT CAN'T BE... LASH WOULD NEVER DO THAT TO ME...

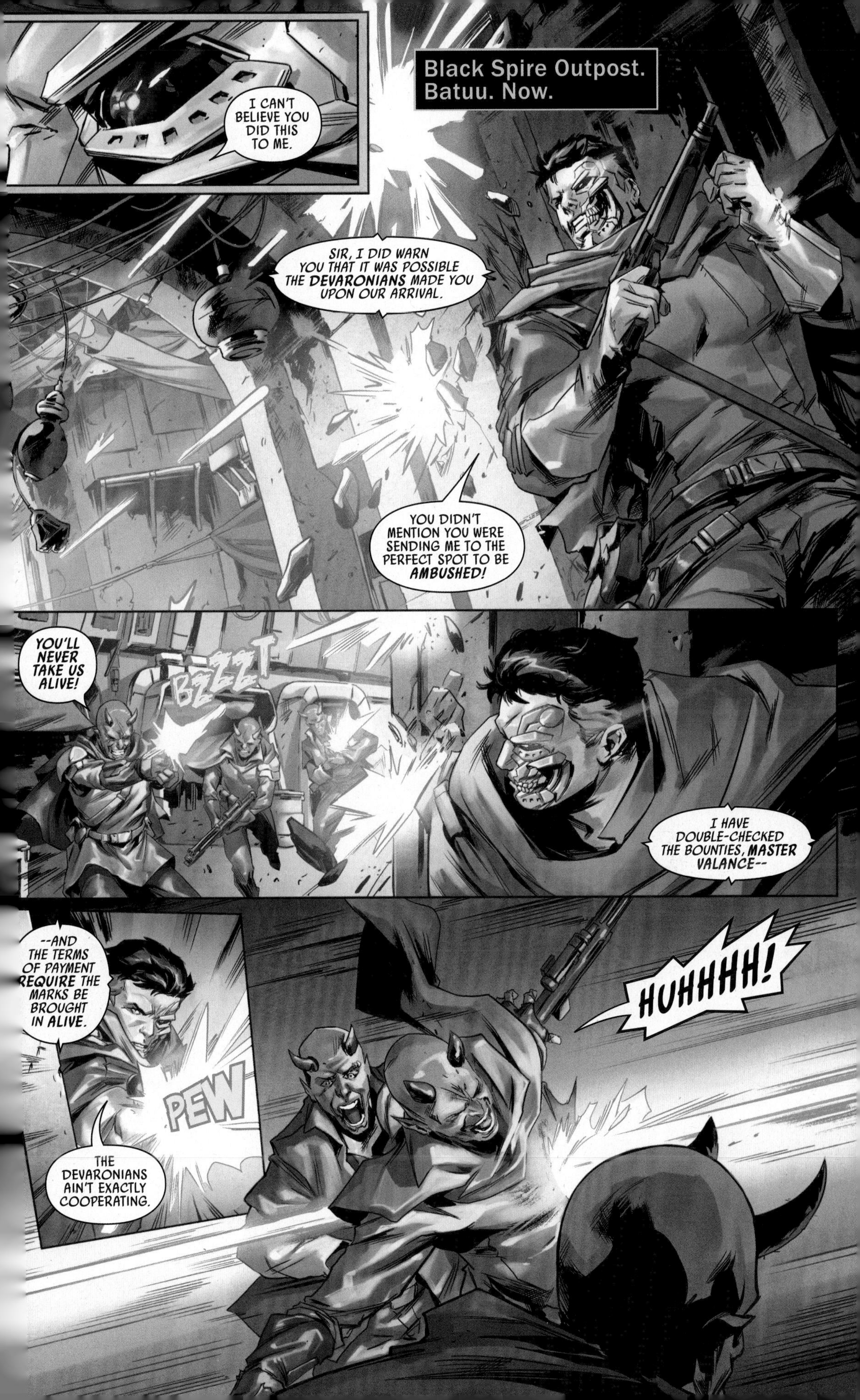
I CAN'T BELIEVE YOU DID THIS TO ME.
Black Spire Outpost. Batuu. Now.
SIR, I DID WARN YOU THAT IT WAS POSSIBLE THE DEVARONIANS MADE YOU UPON OUR ARRIVAL.
YOU DIDN'T MENTION YOU WERE SENDING ME TO THE PERFECT SPOT TO BE AMBUSHED!
YOU'LL NEVER TAKE US ALIVE!
BZZZT
I HAVE DOUBLE-CHECKED THE BOUNTIES, MASTER VALANCE--
--AND THE TERMS OF PAYMENT REQUIRE THE MARKS BE BROUGHT IN ALIVE.
HUHHHH!
PEW
THE DEVARONIANS AIN'T EXACTLY COOPERATING.

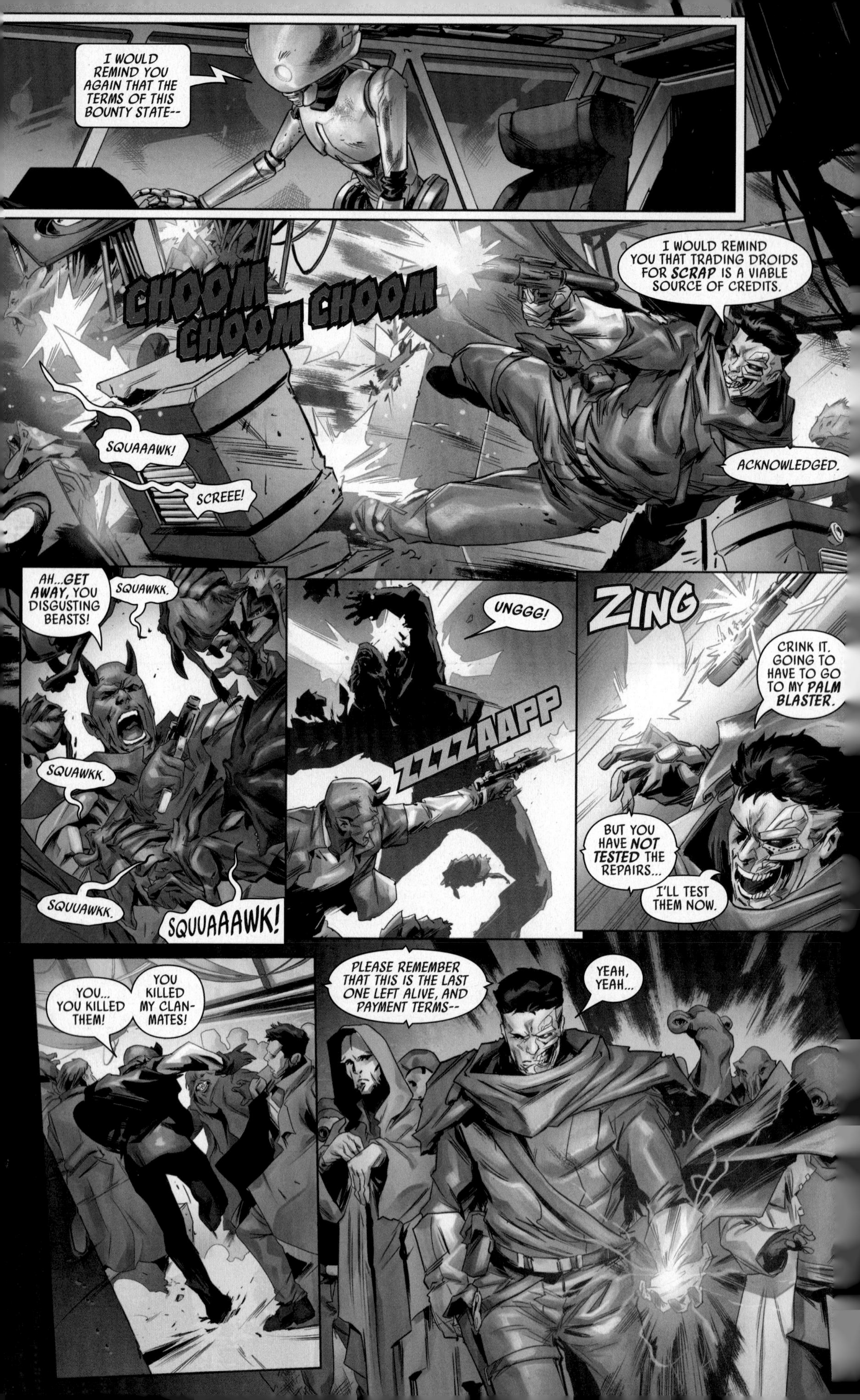
I WOULD REMIND YOU AGAIN THAT THE TERMS OF THIS BOUNTY STATE--
CHOOM CHOOM CHOOM
I WOULD REMIND YOU THAT TRADING DROIDS FOR SCRAP IS A VIABLE SOURCE OF CREDITS.
SQUAAAWK!
SCREEE!
ACKNOWLEDGED.
AH...GET AWAY, YOU DISGUSTING BEASTS!
SQUAWKK.
SQUAWKK.
SQUUAWKK.
SQUUAAAWK!
UNGGG!
ZZZZAAPP
ZING
CRINK IT. GOING TO HAVE TO GO TO MY PALM BLASTER.
BUT YOU HAVE NOT TESTED THE REPAIRS...
I'LL TEST THEM NOW.
YOU... YOU KILLED THEM!
YOU KILLED MY CLAN-MATES!
PLEASE REMEMBER THAT THIS IS THE LAST ONE LEFT ALIVE, AND PAYMENT TERMS--
YEAH, YEAH...

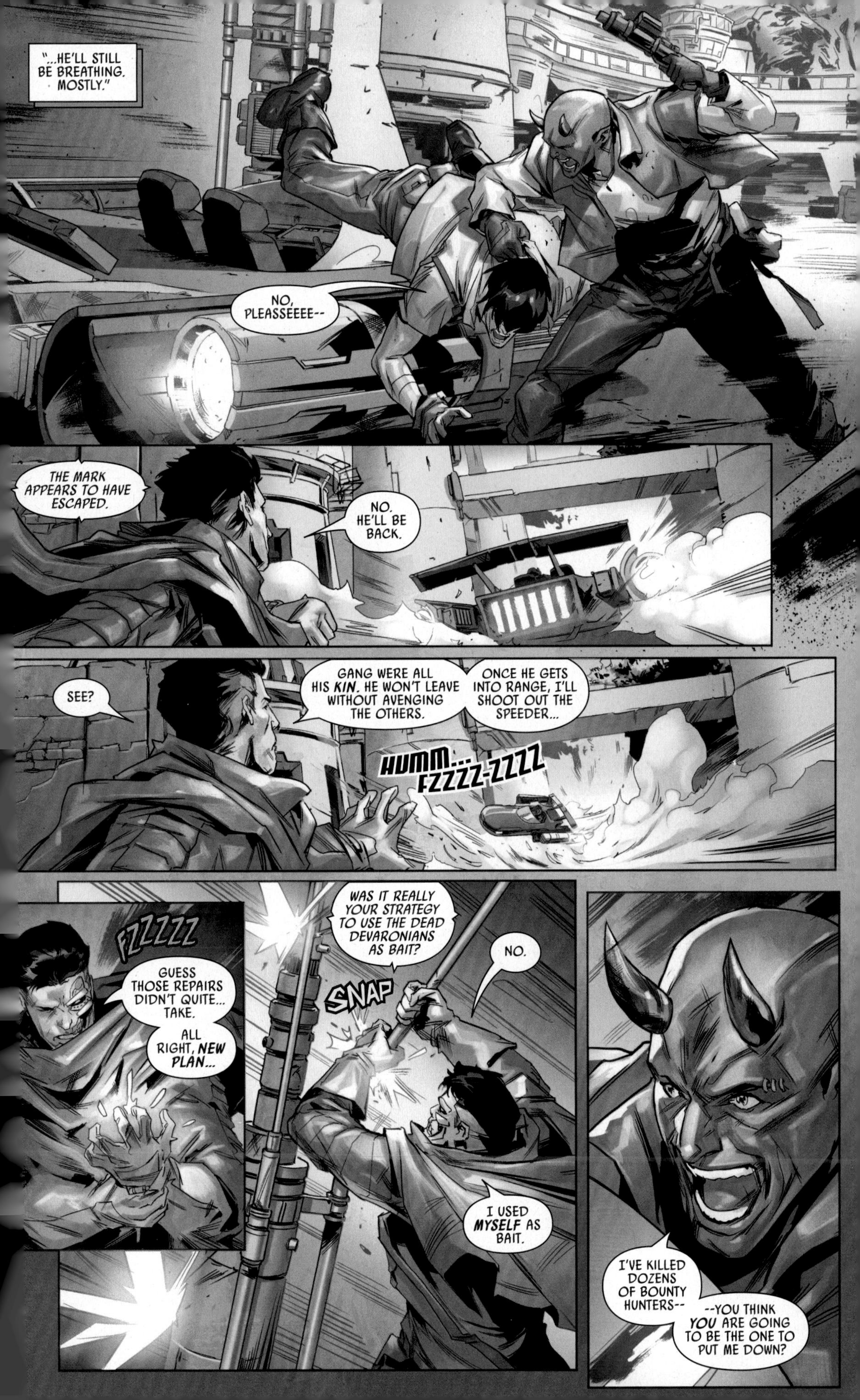
"...HE'LL STILL BE BREATHING. MOSTLY."
NO, PLEASSEEEE--
THE MARK APPEARS TO HAVE ESCAPED.
NO. HE'LL BE BACK.
SEE?
GANG WERE ALL HIS KIN. HE WON'T LEAVE WITHOUT AVENGING THE OTHERS.
ONCE HE GETS INTO RANGE, I'LL SHOOT OUT THE SPEEDER...
HUMM... FZZZZ-ZZZZ
FZZZZZ
GUESS THOSE REPAIRS DIDN'T QUITE... TAKE.
ALL RIGHT, NEW PLAN...
WAS IT REALLY YOUR STRATEGY TO USE THE DEAD DEVARONIANS AS BAIT?
NO.
SNAP
I USED MYSELF AS BAIT.
I'VE KILLED DOZENS OF BOUNTY HUNTERS--
--YOU THINK YOU ARE GOING TO BE THE ONE TO PUT ME DOWN?

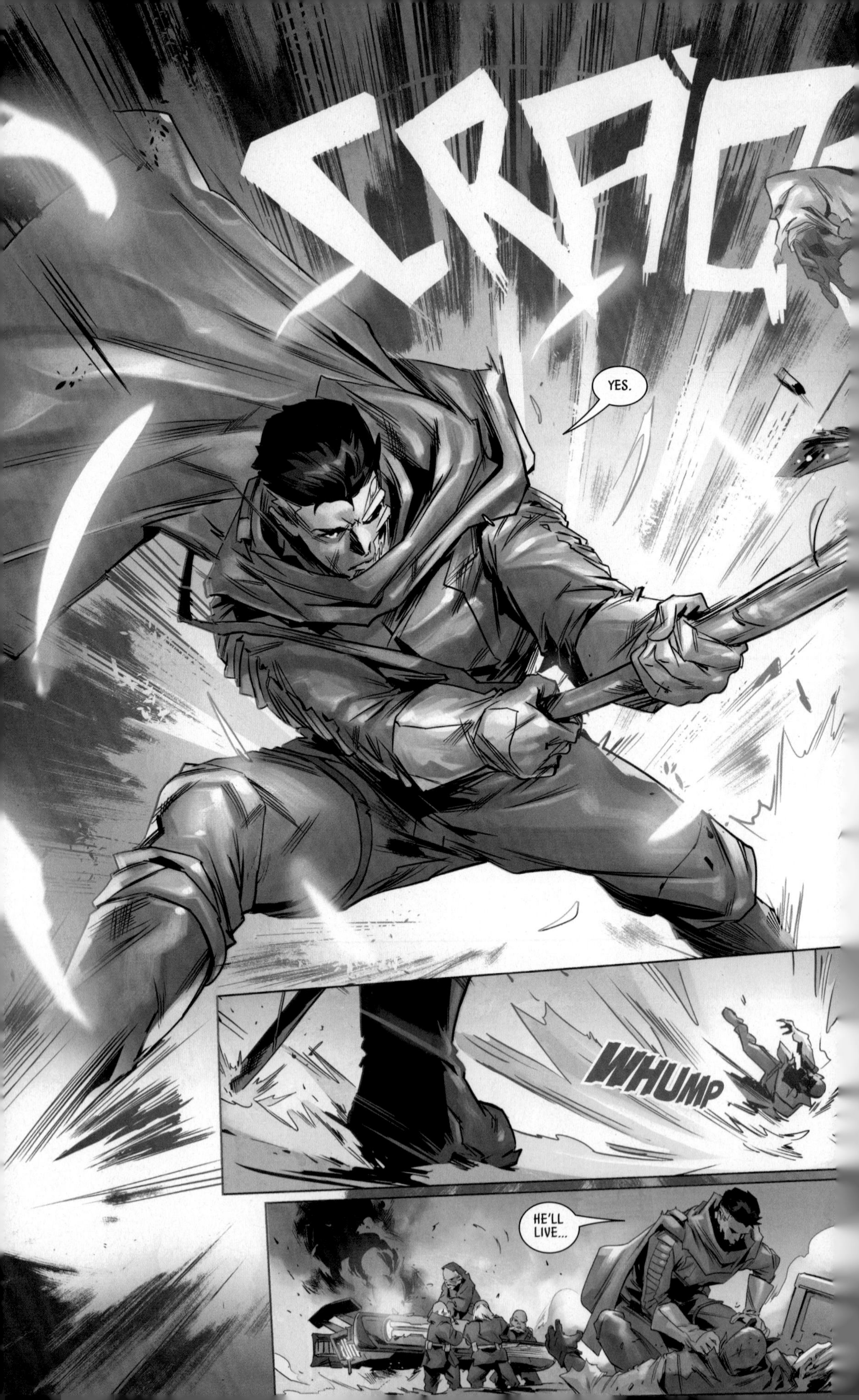
YES.
WHUMP
HE'LL LIVE...

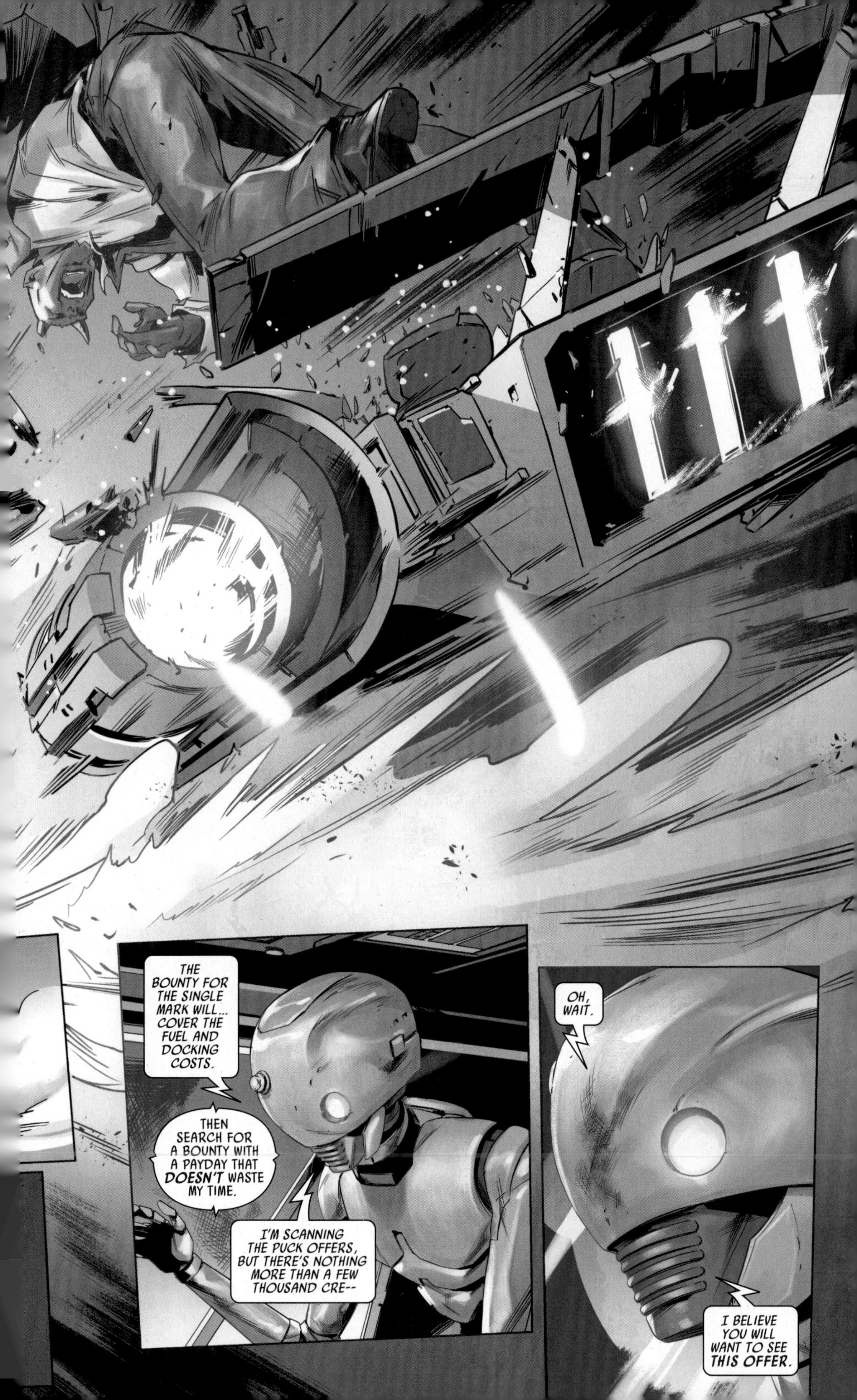
THE BOUNTY FOR THE SINGLE MARK WILL... COVER THE FUEL AND DOCKING COSTS.
THEN SEARCH FOR A BOUNTY WITH A PAYDAY THAT DOESN'T WASTE MY TIME.
I'M SCANNING THE PUCK OFFERS, BUT THERE'S NOTHING MORE THAN A FEW THOUSAND CRE--
OH, WAIT.
I BELIEVE YOU WILL WANT TO SEE THIS OFFER.

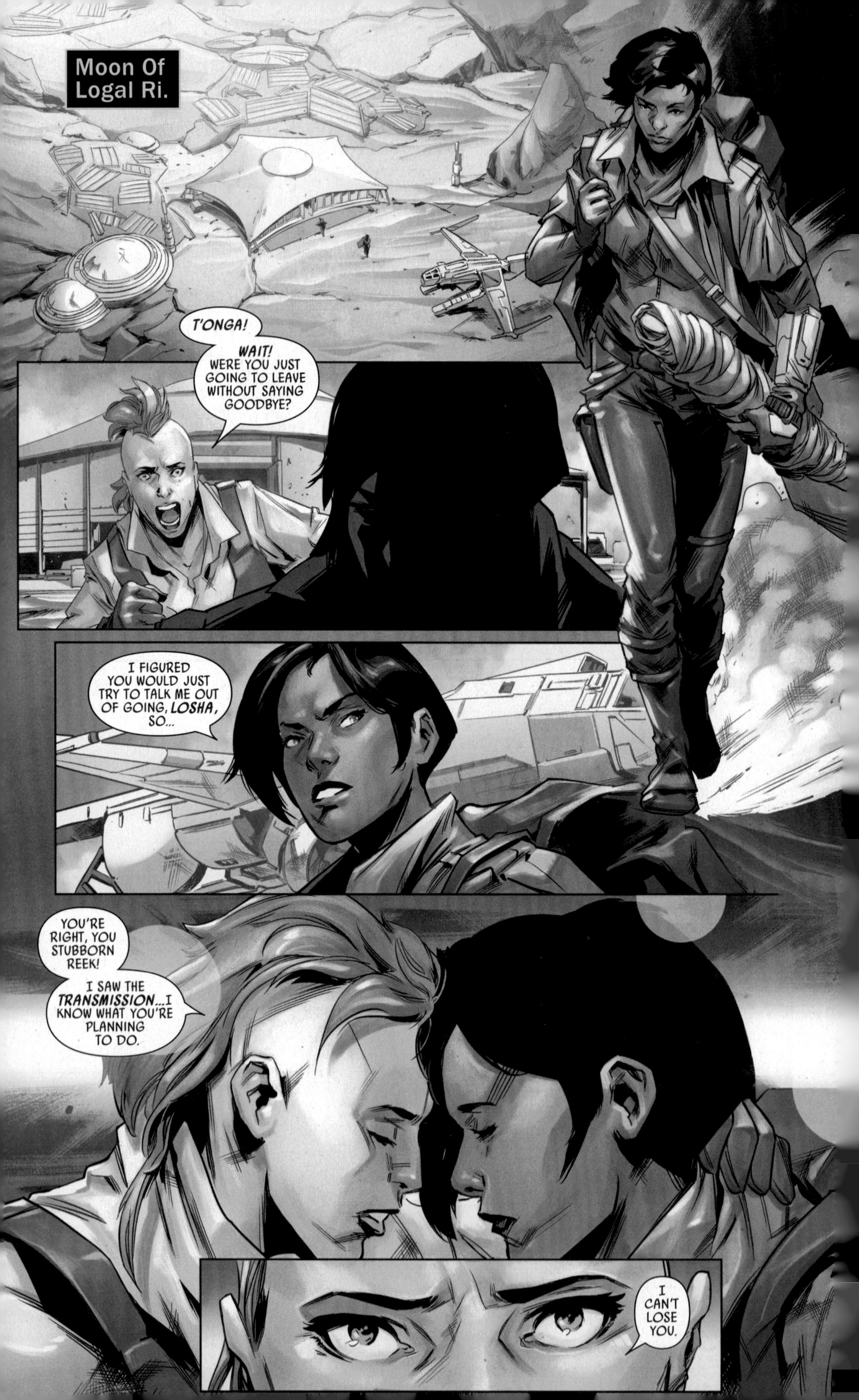

Moon Of Logal Ri.
T'ONGA!
WAIT! WERE YOU JUST GOING TO LEAVE WITHOUT SAYING GOODBYE?
I FIGURED YOU WOULD JUST TRY TO TALK ME OUT OF GOING, LOSHA, SO...
YOU'RE RIGHT, YOU STUBBORN REEK!
I SAW THE TRANSMISSION...I KNOW WHAT YOU'RE PLANNING TO DO.
I CAN'T LOSE YOU.

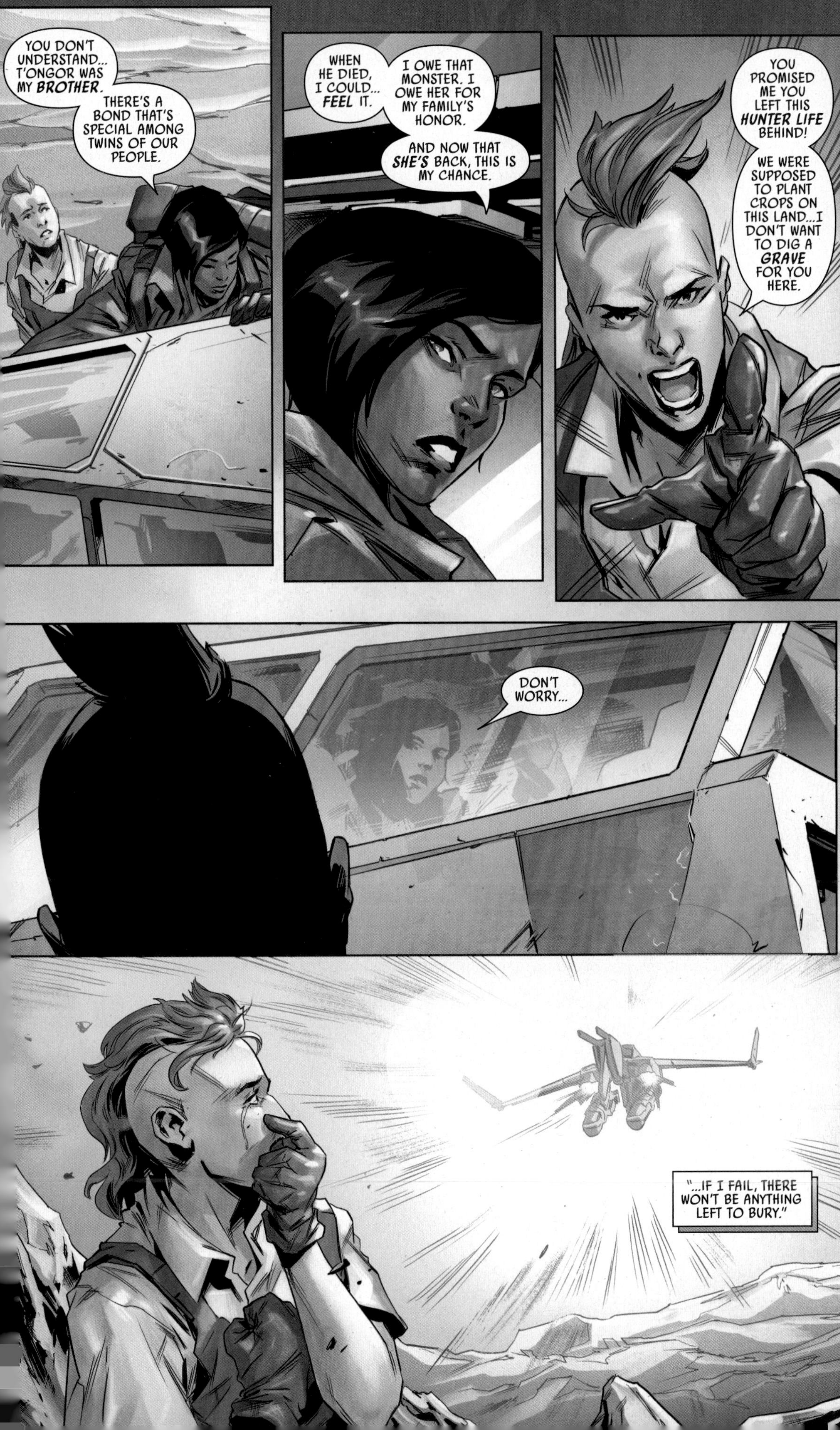
YOU DON'T UNDERSTAND... T'ONGOR WAS MY BROTHER.
THERE'S A BOND THAT'S SPECIAL AMONG TWINS OF OUR PEOPLE.
WHEN HE DIED, I COULD... FEEL IT.
I OWE THAT MONSTER. I OWE HER FOR MY FAMILY'S HONOR.
AND NOW THAT SHE'S BACK, THIS IS MY CHANCE.
YOU PROMISED ME YOU LEFT THIS HUNTER LIFE BEHIND!
WE WERE SUPPOSED TO PLANT CROPS ON THIS LAND...I DON'T WANT TO DIG A GRAVE FOR YOU HERE.
DON'T WORRY...
"...IF I FAIL, THERE WON'T BE ANYTHING LEFT TO BURY."

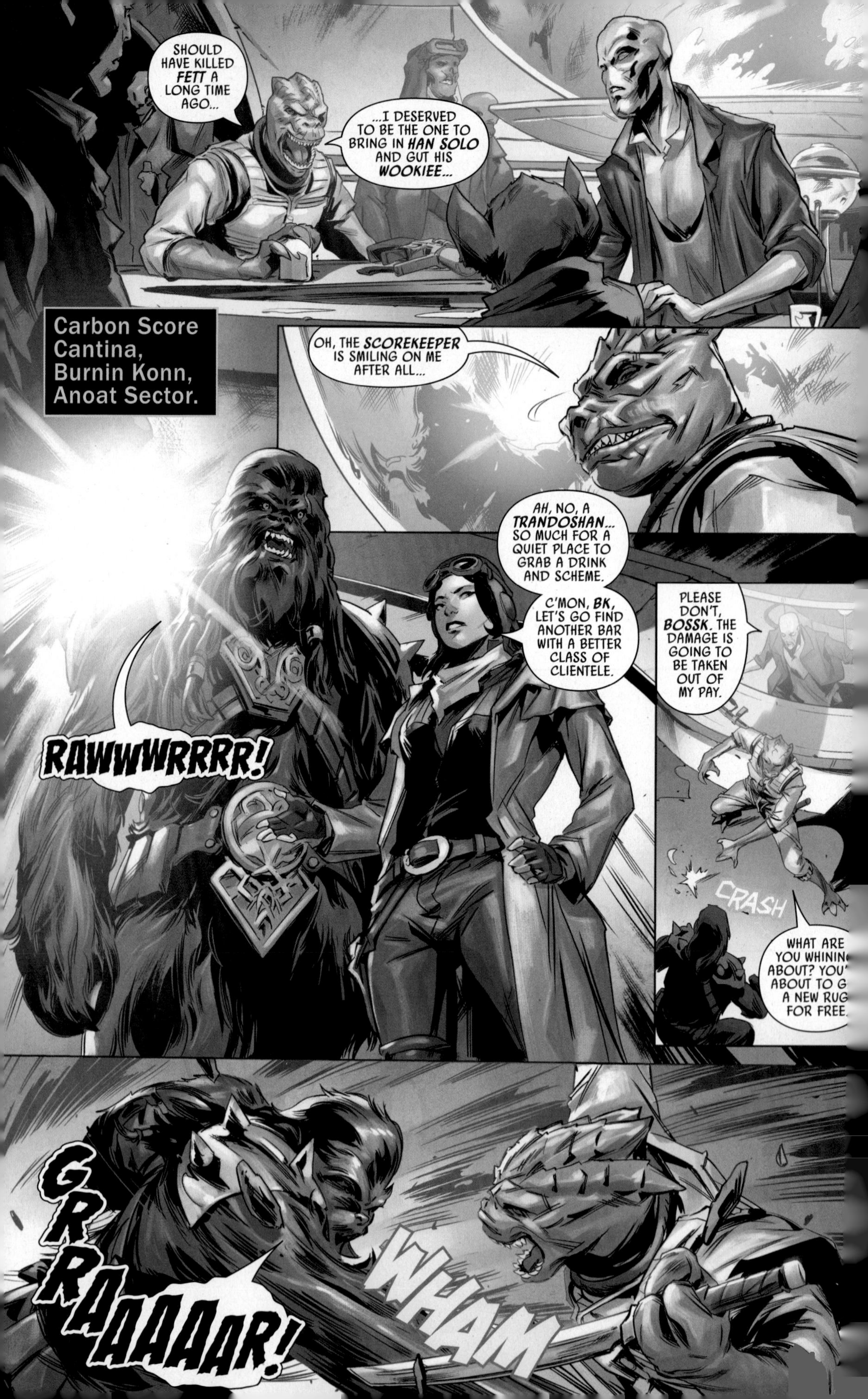
SHOULD HAVE KILLED FETT A LONG TIME AGO...
...I DESERVED TO BE THE ONE TO BRING IN HAN SOLO AND GUT HIS WOOKIEE...
Carbon Score Cantina, Burnin Konn, Anoat Sector.
OH, THE SCOREKEEPER IS SMILING ON ME AFTER ALL...
AH, NO, A TRANDOSHAN... SO MUCH FOR A QUIET PLACE TO GRAB A DRINK AND SCHEME.
C'MON, BK, LET'S GO FIND ANOTHER BAR WITH A BETTER CLASS OF CLIENTELE.
RAWWWRRRR!
PLEASE DON'T, BOSSK. THE DAMAGE IS GOING TO BE TAKEN OUT OF MY PAY.
CRASH
WHAT ARE YOU WHINING ABOUT? YOU' ABOUT TO G A NEW RUG FOR FREE.
GRRAAAAAR!
WHAM

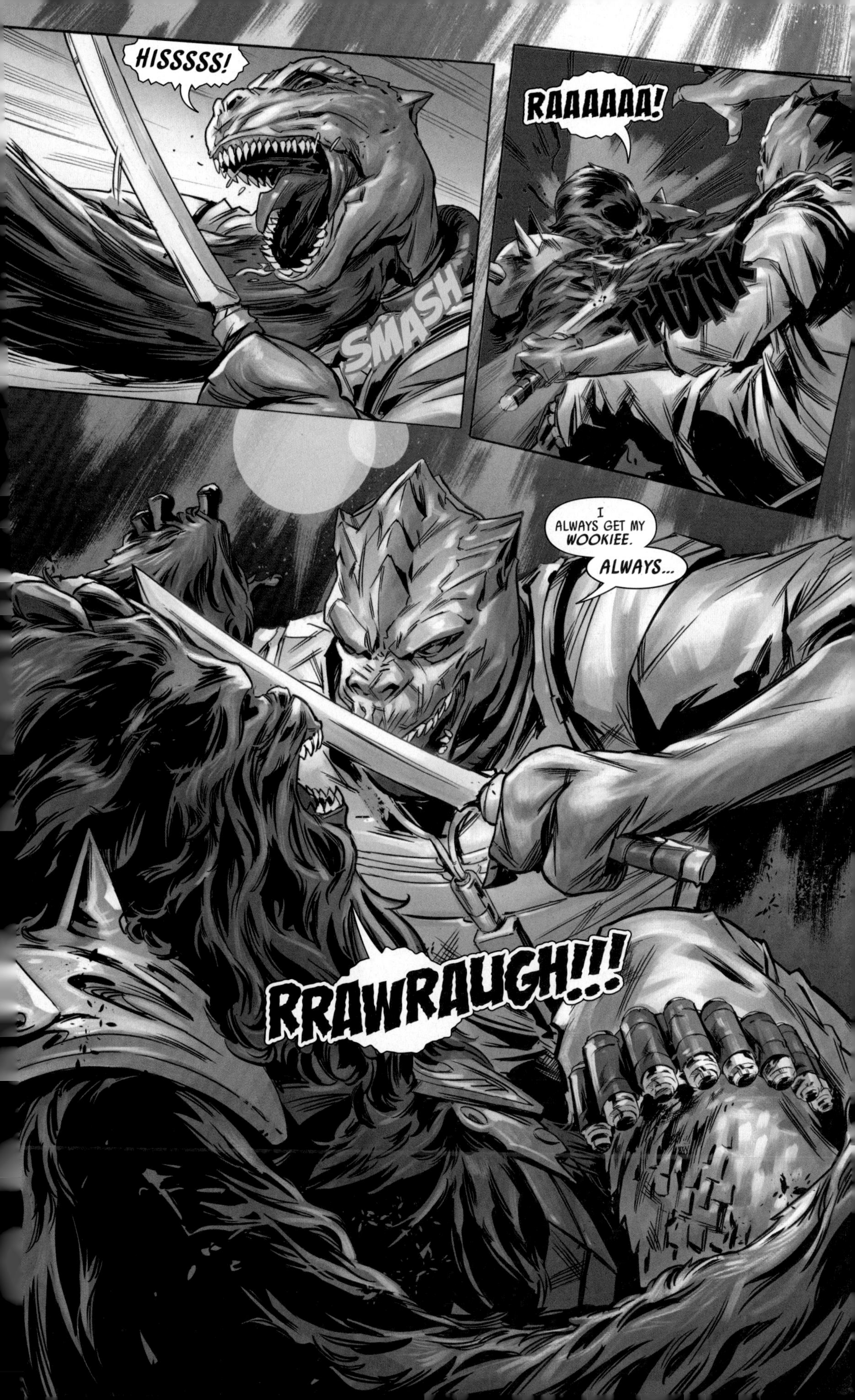
HISSSSS!
SMASH
RAAAAAA!
THUNK
I ALWAYS GET MY WOOKIEE.
ALWAYS...
RRAWRAUGH!!!

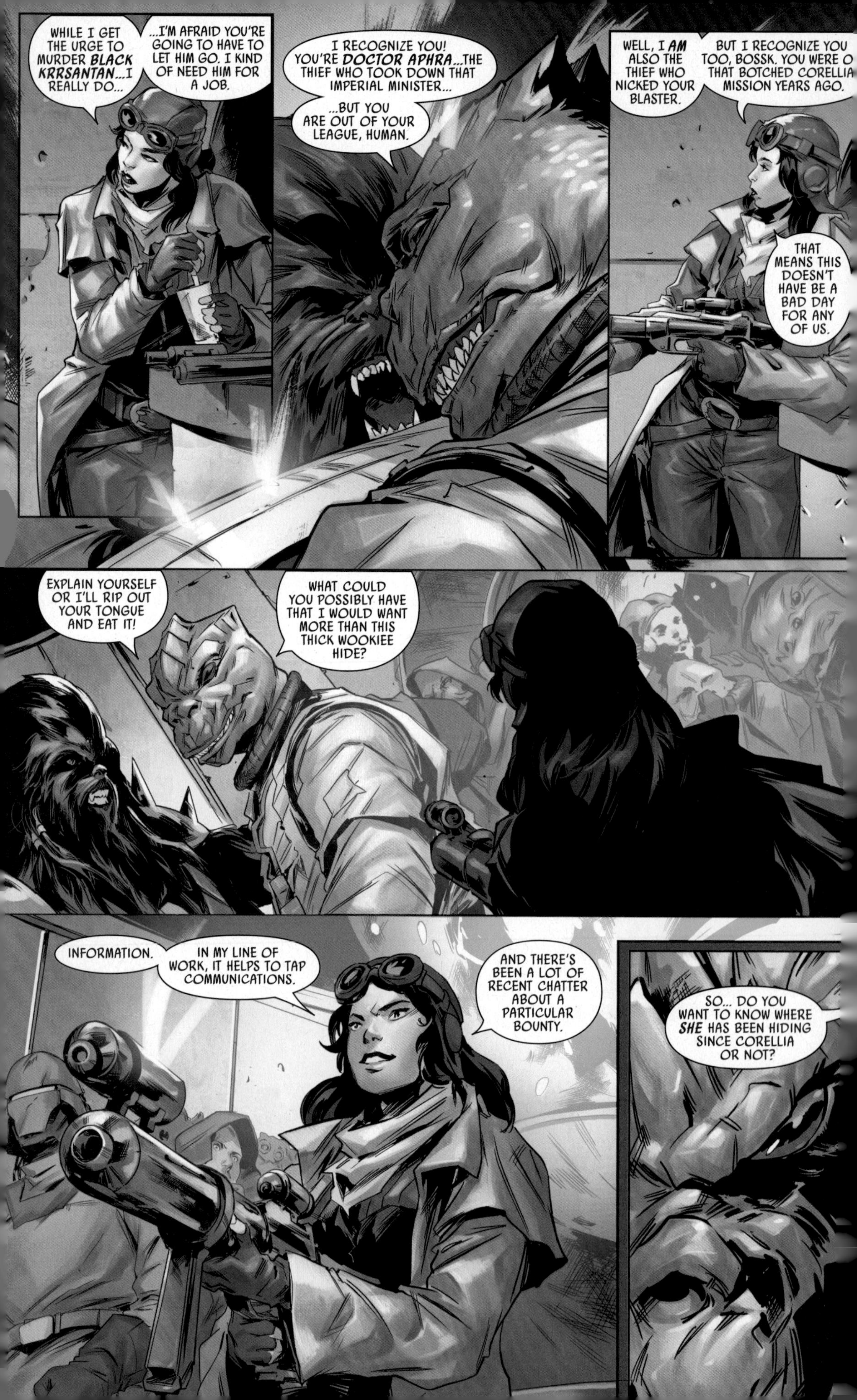
WHILE I GET THE URGE TO MURDER BLACK KRRSANTAN...I REALLY DO...
...I'M AFRAID YOU'RE GOING TO HAVE TO LET HIM GO. I KIND OF NEED HIM FOR A JOB.
I RECOGNIZE YOU! YOU'RE DOCTOR APHRA...THE THIEF WHO TOOK DOWN THAT IMPERIAL MINISTER...
...BUT YOU ARE OUT OF YOUR LEAGUE, HUMAN.
WELL, I AM ALSO THE THIEF WHO NICKED YOUR BLASTER.
BUT I RECOGNIZE YOU TOO, BOSSK. YOU WERE O THAT BOTCHED CORELLIA MISSION YEARS AGO.
THAT MEANS THIS DOESN'T HAVE BE A BAD DAY FOR ANY OF US.
EXPLAIN YOURSELF OR I'LL RIP OUT YOUR TONGUE AND EAT IT!
WHAT COULD YOU POSSIBLY HAVE THAT I WOULD WANT MORE THAN THIS THICK WOOKIEE HIDE?
INFORMATION.
IN MY LINE OF WORK, IT HELPS TO TAP COMMUNICATIONS.
AND THERE'S BEEN A LOT OF RECENT CHATTER ABOUT A PARTICULAR BOUNTY.
SO... DO YOU WANT TO KNOW WHERE SHE HAS BEEN HIDING SINCE CORELLIA OR NOT?

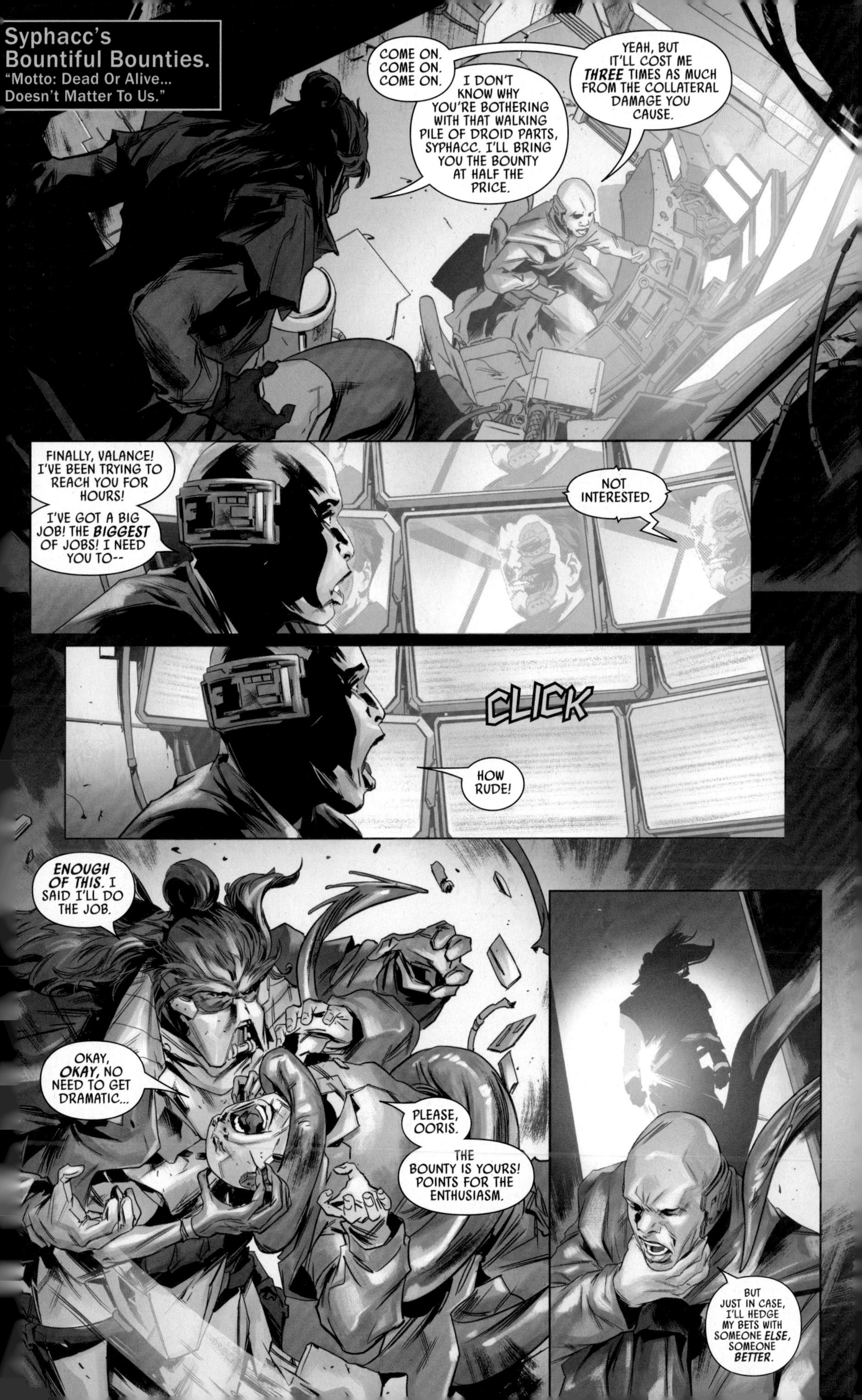
Syphacc's Bountiful Bounties.
"Motto: Dead Or Alive... Doesn't Matter To Us."
COME ON. COME ON. COME ON.
YEAH, BUT IT'LL COST ME THREE TIMES AS MUCH FROM THE COLLATERAL DAMAGE YOU CAUSE.
I DON'T KNOW WHY YOU'RE BOTHERING WITH THAT WALKING PILE OF DROID PARTS, SYPHACC. I'LL BRING YOU THE BOUNTY AT HALF THE PRICE.
FINALLY, VALANCE! I'VE BEEN TRYING TO REACH YOU FOR HOURS!
I'VE GOT A BIG JOB! THE BIGGEST OF JOBS! I NEED YOU TO--
NOT INTERESTED.
CLICK
HOW RUDE!
ENOUGH OF THIS. I SAID I'LL DO THE JOB.
OKAY, OKAY, NO NEED TO GET DRAMATIC...
PLEASE, OORIS.
THE BOUNTY IS YOURS! POINTS FOR THE ENTHUSIASM.
BUT JUST IN CASE, I'LL HEDGE MY BETS WITH SOMEONE ELSE, SOMEONE BETTER.

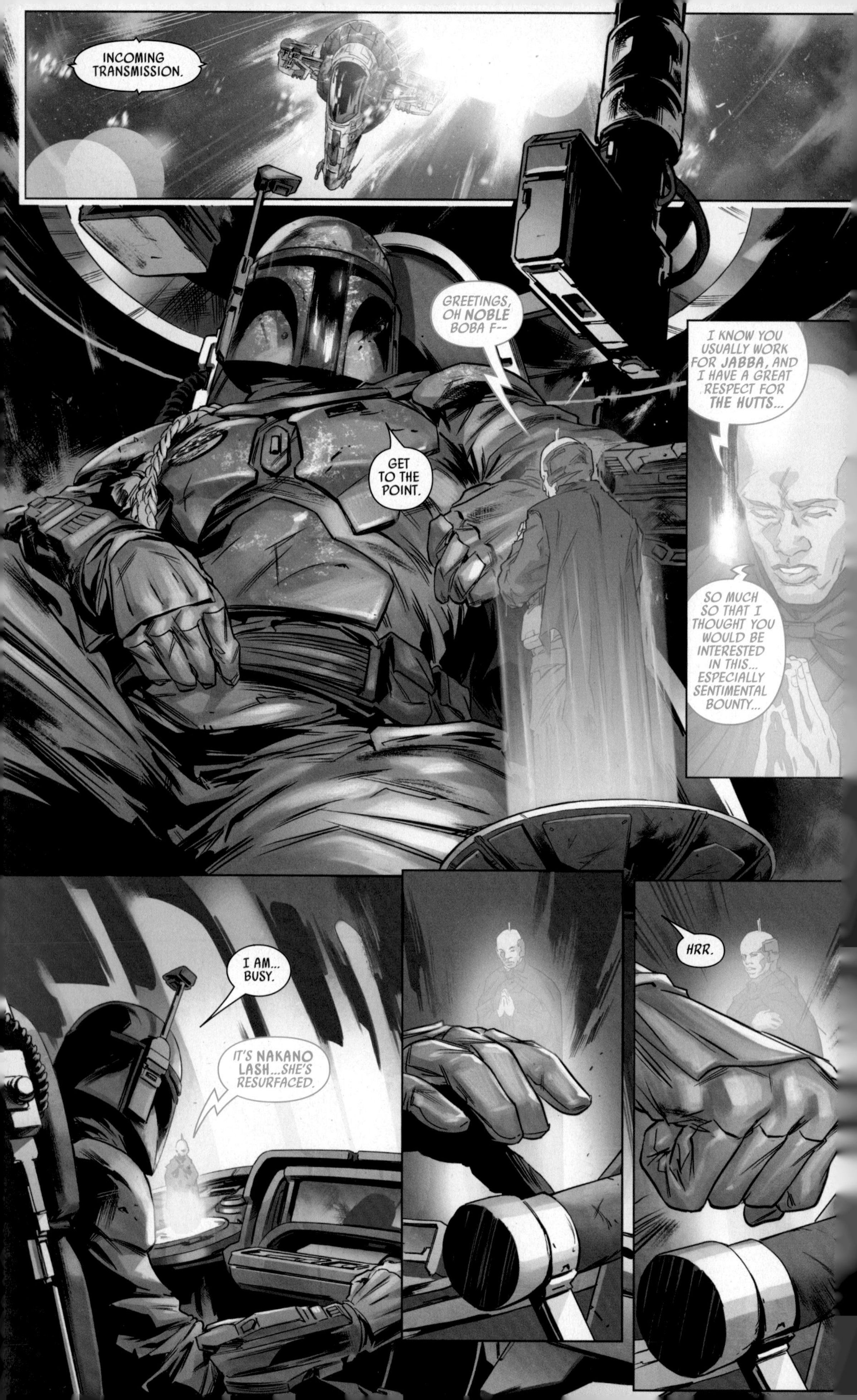
INCOMING TRANSMISSION.
GREETINGS, OH NOBLE BOBA F--
GET TO THE POINT.
I KNOW YOU USUALLY WORK FOR JABBA, AND I HAVE A GREAT RESPECT FOR THE HUTTS...
SO MUCH SO THAT I THOUGHT YOU WOULD BE INTERESTED IN THIS... ESPECIALLY SENTIMENTAL BOUNTY...
I AM... BUSY.
IT'S NAKANO LASH...SHE'S RESURFACED.
HRR.

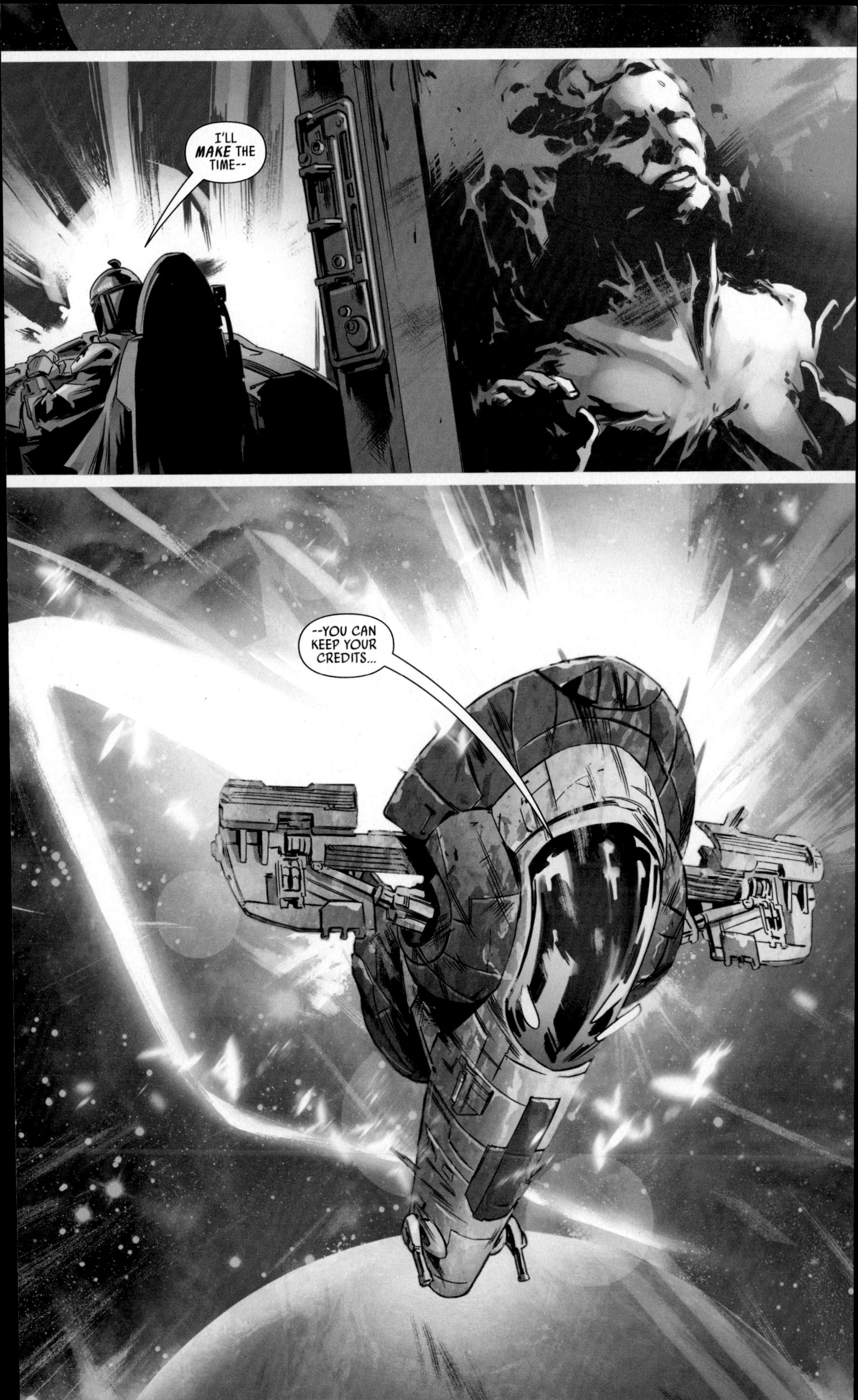
I'LL MAKE THE TIME--
--YOU CAN KEEP YOUR CREDITS...

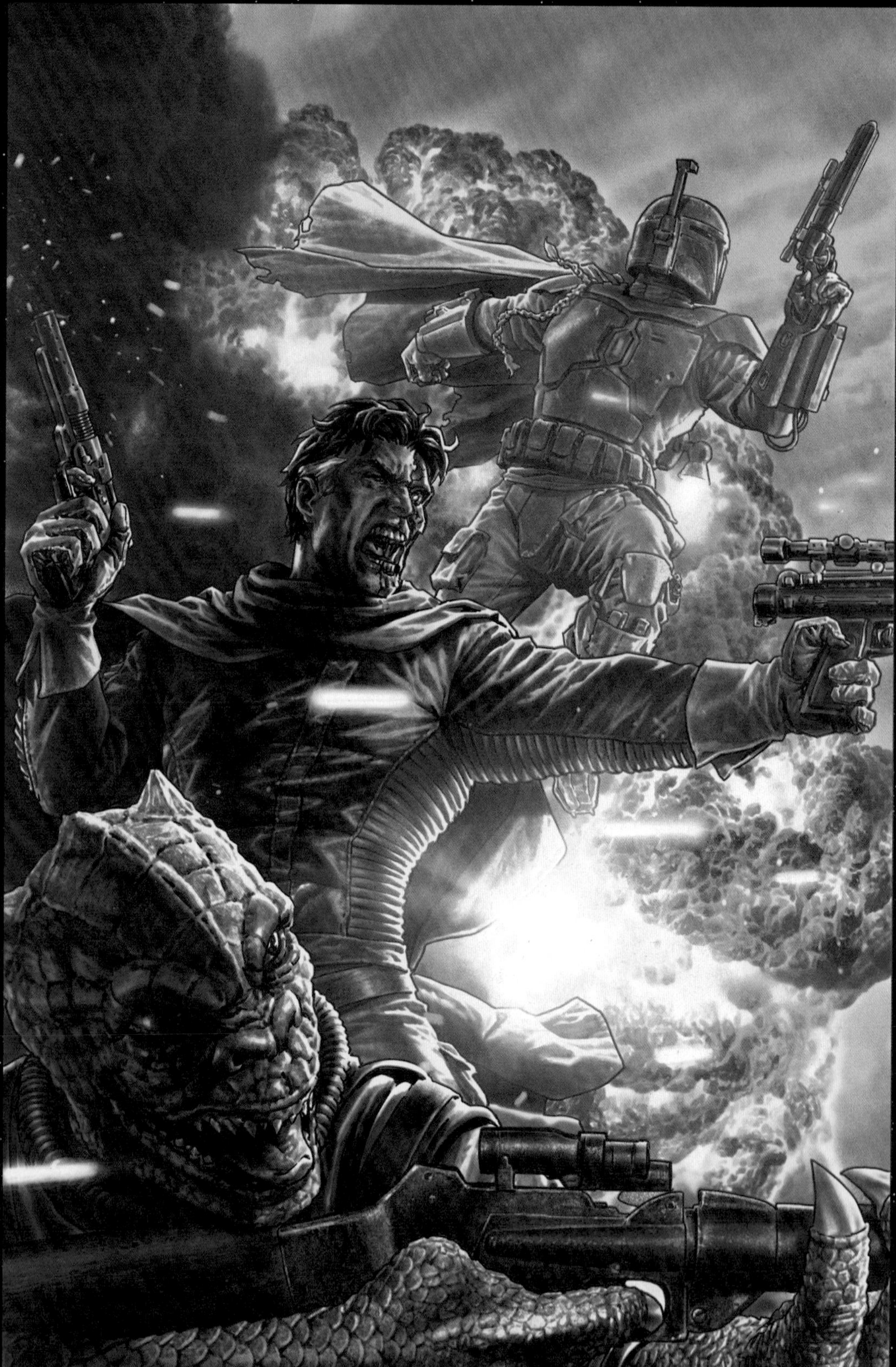

2

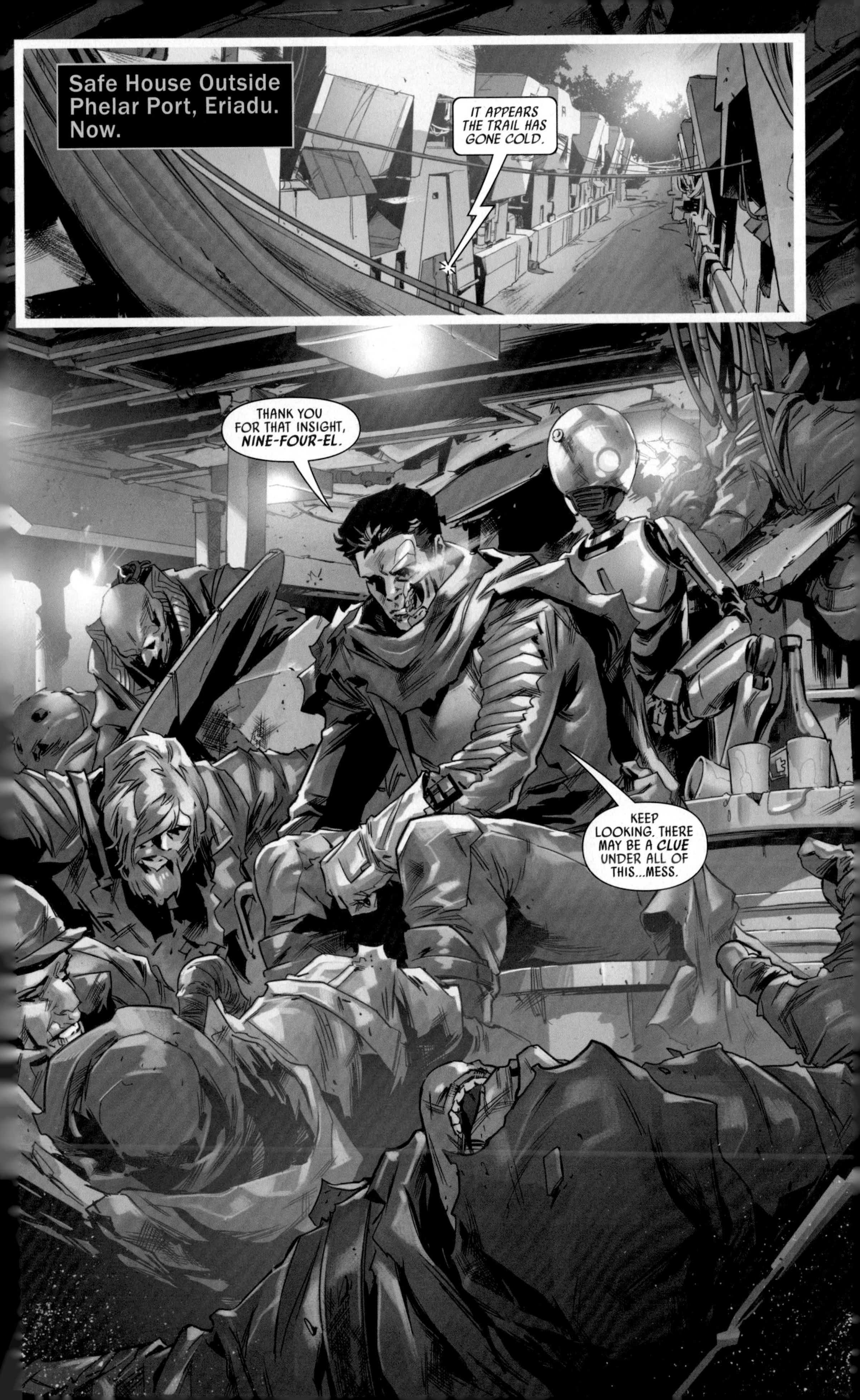

Safe House Outside Phelar Port, Eriadu. Now.
IT APPEARS THE TRAIL HAS GONE COLD.
THANK YOU FOR THAT INSIGHT, NINE-FOUR-EL.
KEEP LOOKING. THERE MAY BE A CLUE UNDER ALL OF THIS...MESS.

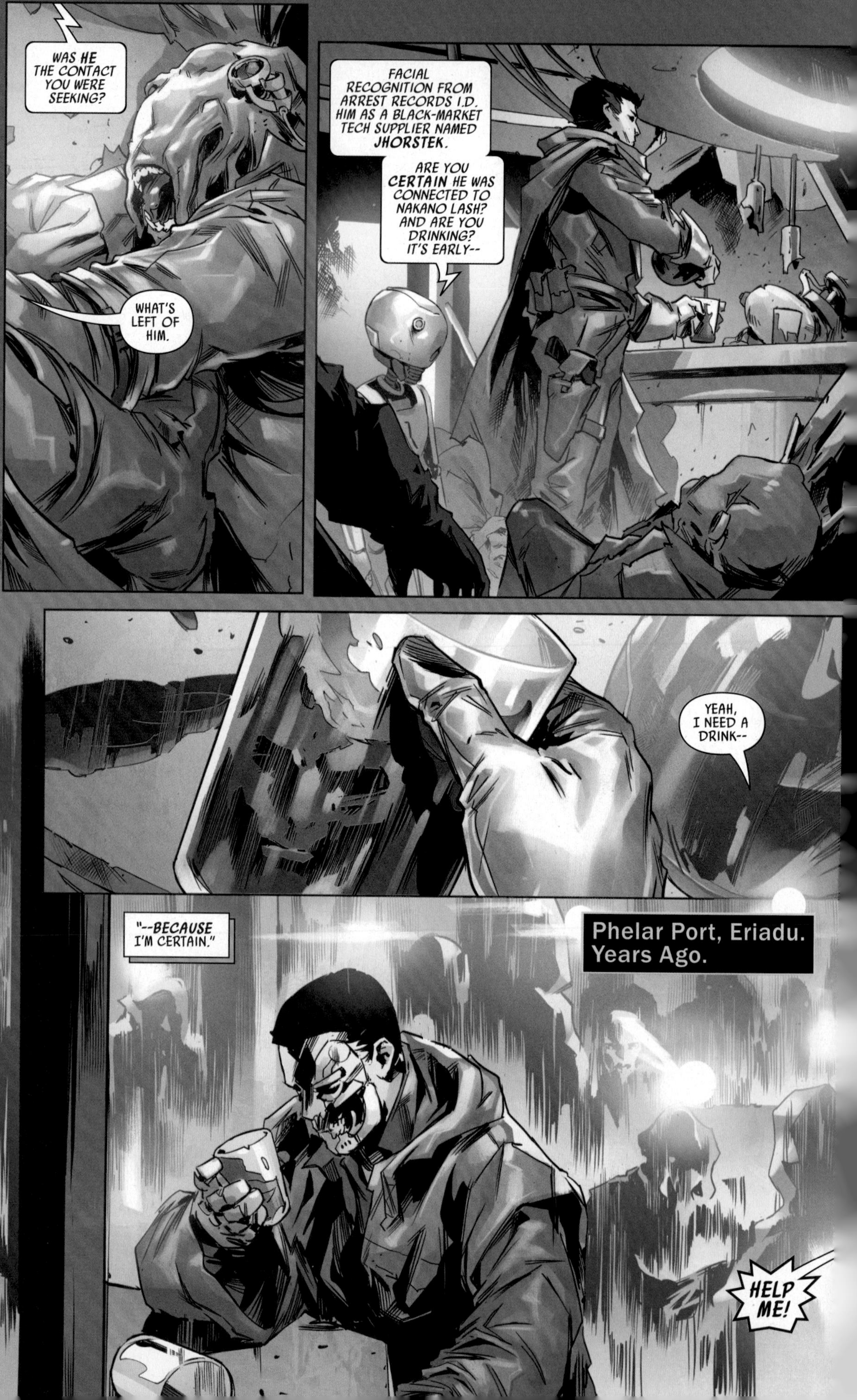
WAS HE THE CONTACT YOU WERE SEEKING?
WHAT'S LEFT OF HIM.
FACIAL RECOGNITION FROM ARREST RECORDS I.D. HIM AS A BLACK-MARKET TECH SUPPLIER NAMED JHORSTEK.
ARE YOU CERTAIN HE WAS CONNECTED TO NAKANO LASH? AND ARE YOU DRINKING? IT'S EARLY--
YEAH, I NEED A DRINK--
"--BECAUSE I'M CERTAIN."
Phelar Port, Eriadu. Years Ago.
HELP ME!

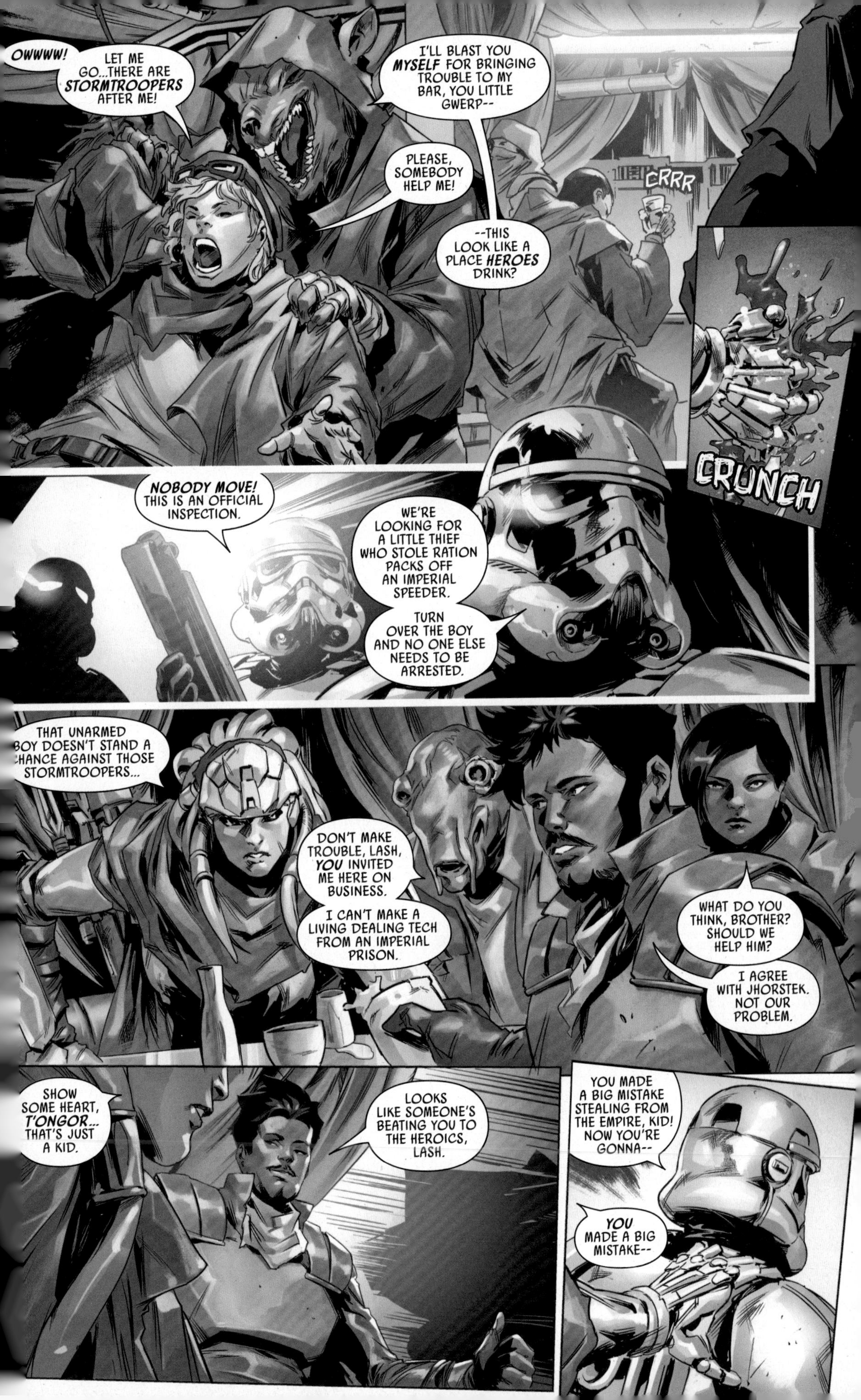
OWWWW!
LET ME GO...THERE ARE STORMTROOPERS AFTER ME!
I'LL BLAST YOU MYSELF FOR BRINGING TROUBLE TO MY BAR, YOU LITTLE GWERP--
PLEASE, SOMEBODY HELP ME!
--THIS LOOK LIKE A PLACE HEROES DRINK?
CRRR
CRUNCH
NOBODY MOVE! THIS IS AN OFFICIAL INSPECTION.
WE'RE LOOKING FOR A LITTLE THIEF WHO STOLE RATION PACKS OFF AN IMPERIAL SPEEDER.
TURN OVER THE BOY AND NO ONE ELSE NEEDS TO BE ARRESTED.
THAT UNARMED BOY DOESN'T STAND A CHANCE AGAINST THOSE STORMTROOPERS...
DON'T MAKE TROUBLE, LASH, YOU INVITED ME HERE ON BUSINESS.
I CAN'T MAKE A LIVING DEALING TECH FROM AN IMPERIAL PRISON.
WHAT DO YOU THINK, BROTHER? SHOULD WE HELP HIM?
I AGREE WITH JHORSTEK. NOT OUR PROBLEM.
SHOW SOME HEART, T'ONGOR... THAT'S JUST A KID.
LOOKS LIKE SOMEONE'S BEATING YOU TO THE HEROICS, LASH.
YOU MADE A BIG MISTAKE STEALING FROM THE EMPIRE, KID! NOW YOU'RE GONNA--
YOU MADE A BIG MISTAKE--

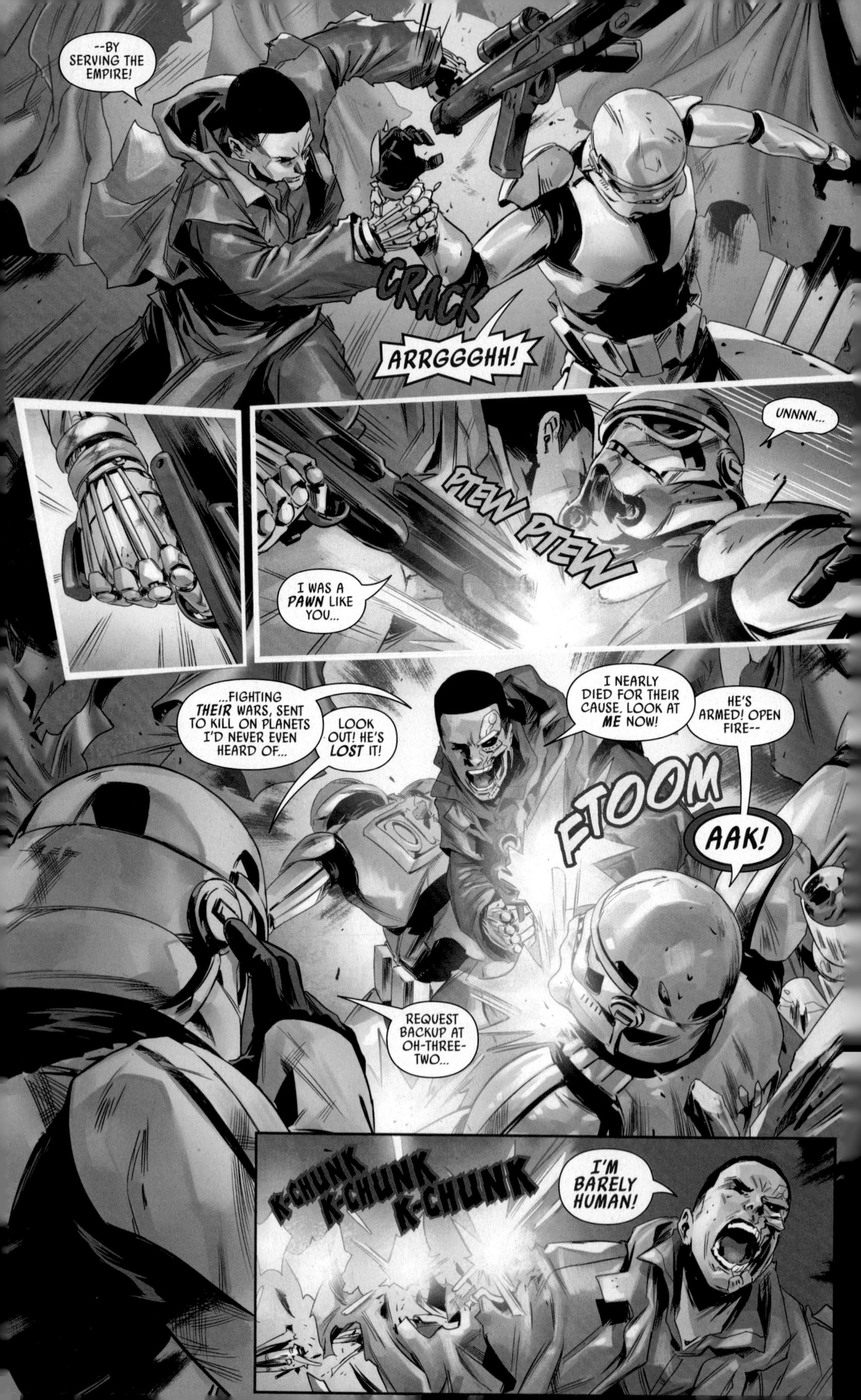

--BY SERVING THE EMPIRE!
CRACK
ARRGGGHH!
UNNNN...
PTEW PTEW
I WAS A PAWN LIKE YOU...
...FIGHTING THEIR WARS, SENT TO KILL ON PLANETS I'D NEVER EVEN HEARD OF...
LOOK OUT! HE'S LOST IT!
I NEARLY DIED FOR THEIR CAUSE. LOOK AT ME NOW!
HE'S ARMED! OPEN FIRE--
FTOOM
AAK!
REQUEST BACKUP AT OH-THREE-TWO...
K-CHUNK K-CHUNK K-CHUNK
I'M BARELY HUMAN!

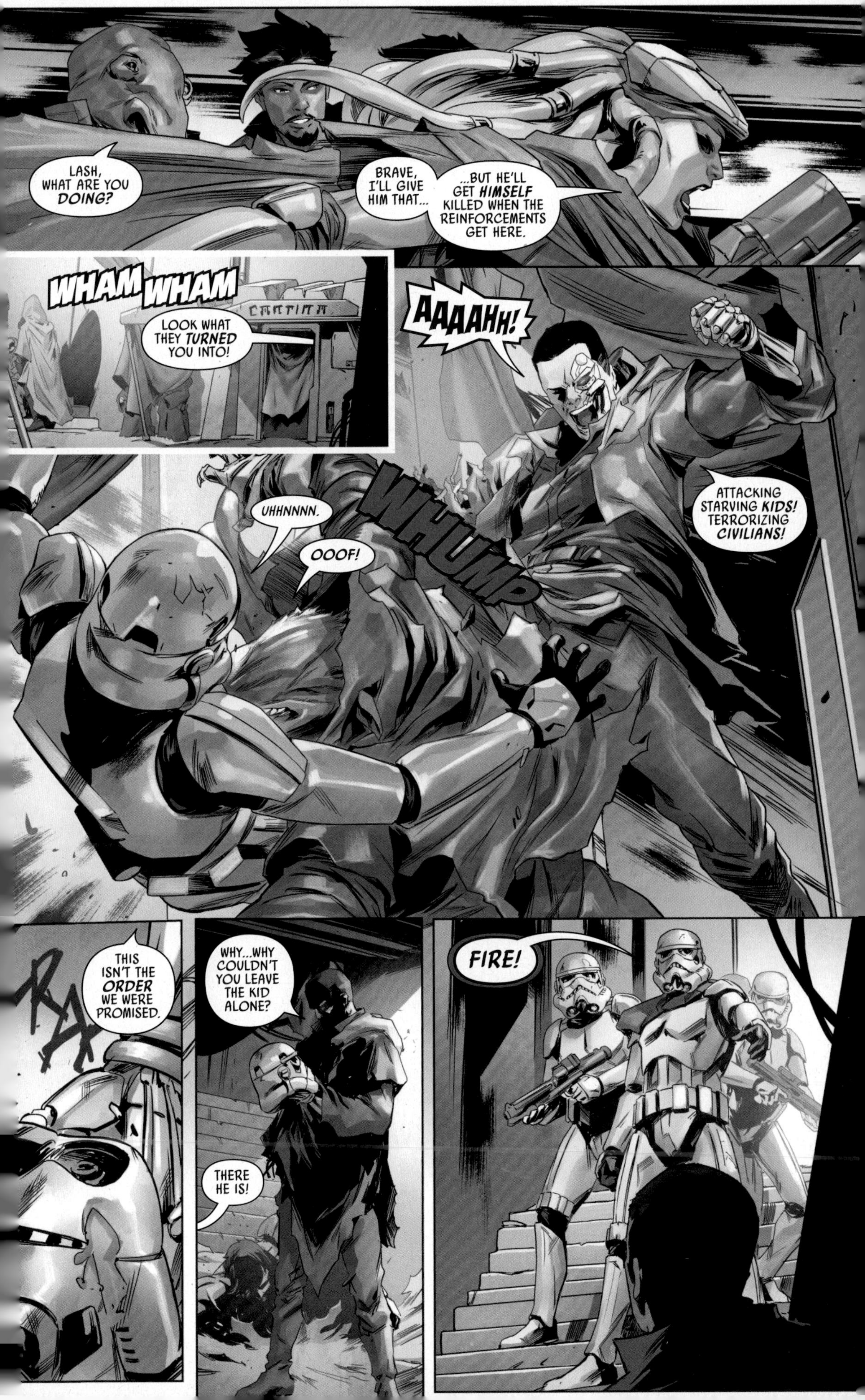
LASH, WHAT ARE YOU DOING?
BRAVE, I'LL GIVE HIM THAT...
...BUT HE'LL GET HIMSELF KILLED WHEN THE REINFORCEMENTS GET HERE.
WHAM WHAM
LOOK WHAT THEY TURNED YOU INTO!
AAAAHH!
ATTACKING STARVING KIDS! TERRORIZING CIVILIANS!
UHHNNNN.
OOOF!
WHUMP
THIS ISN'T THE ORDER WE WERE PROMISED.
WHY...WHY COULDN'T YOU LEAVE THE KID ALONE?
THERE HE IS!
FIRE!

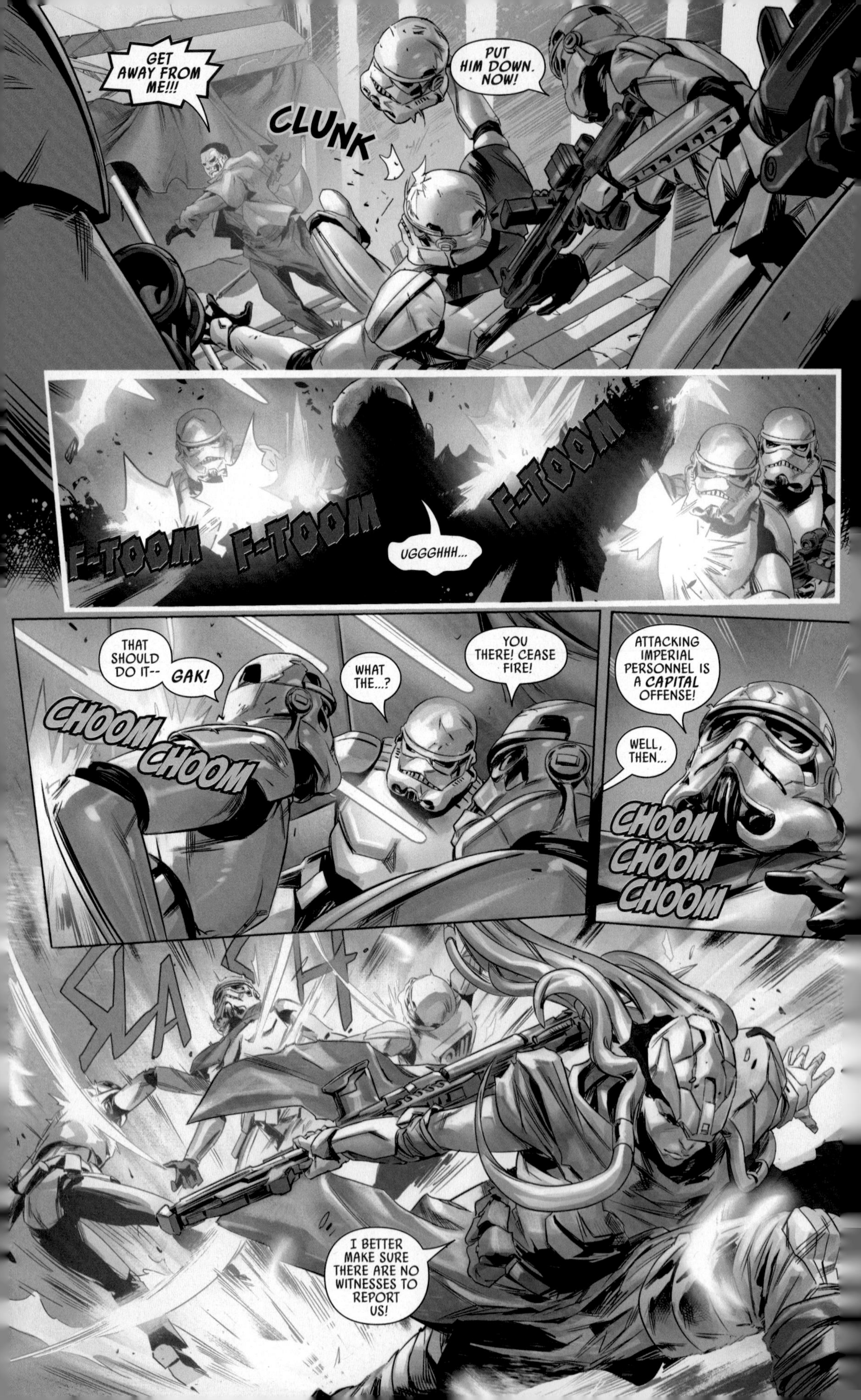
GET AWAY FROM ME!!!
PUT HIM DOWN. NOW!
CLUNK
F-TOOM
F-TOOM
F-TOOM
UGGGHHH...
THAT SHOULD DO IT--
GAK!
CHOOM CHOOM
WHAT THE...?
YOU THERE! CEASE FIRE!
ATTACKING IMPERIAL PERSONNEL IS A CAPITAL OFFENSE!
WELL, THEN...
CHOOM CHOOM CHOOM
SKA
I BETTER MAKE SURE THERE ARE NO WITNESSES TO REPORT US!

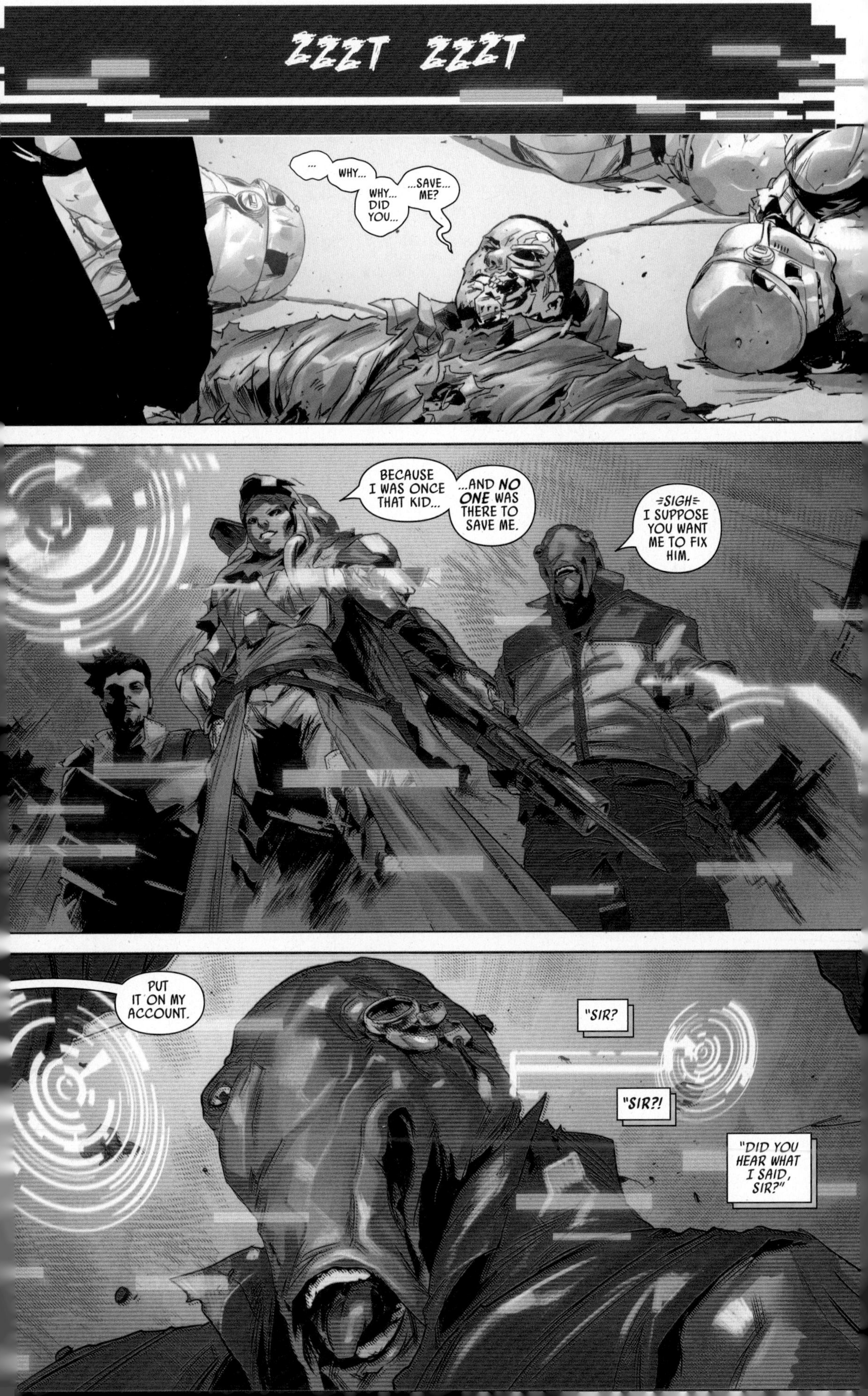
ZZZT ZZZT
...
WHY...
WHY... DID YOU...
...SAVE... ME?
BECAUSE I WAS ONCE THAT KID...
...AND NO ONE WAS THERE TO SAVE ME.
≡SIGH≡ I SUPPOSE YOU WANT ME TO FIX HIM.
PUT IT ON MY ACCOUNT.
"SIR?
"SIR?!
"DID YOU HEAR WHAT I SAID, SIR?"

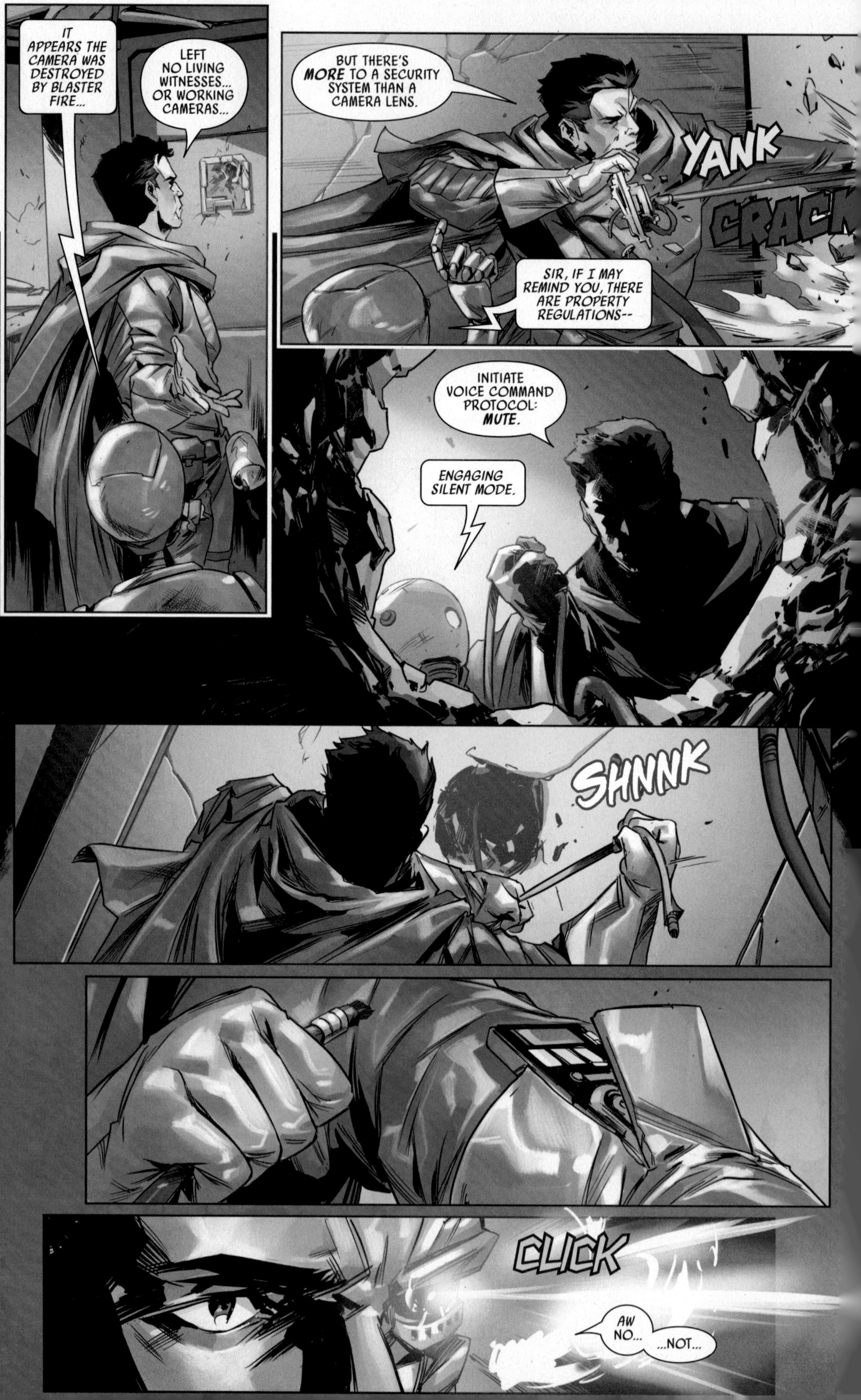
IT APPEARS THE CAMERA WAS DESTROYED BY BLASTER FIRE...
LEFT NO LIVING WITNESSES... OR WORKING CAMERAS...
BUT THERE'S MORE TO A SECURITY SYSTEM THAN A CAMERA LENS.
YANK
CRACK
SIR, IF I MAY REMIND YOU, THERE ARE PROPERTY REGULATIONS--
INITIATE VOICE COMMAND PROTOCOL: MUTE.
ENGAGING SILENT MODE.
SHNNK
CLICK
AW NO...
...NOT...

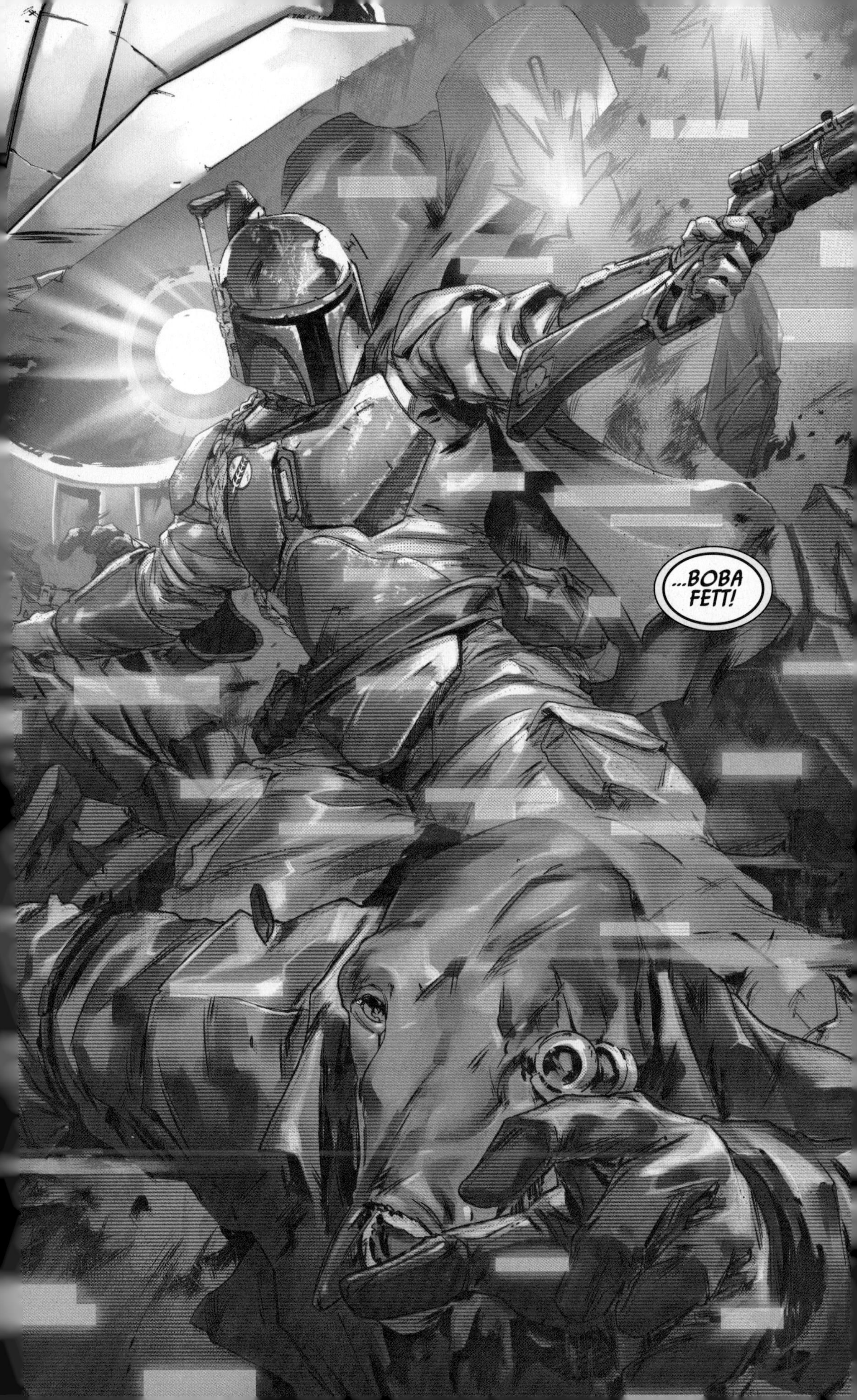
...BOBA FETT!

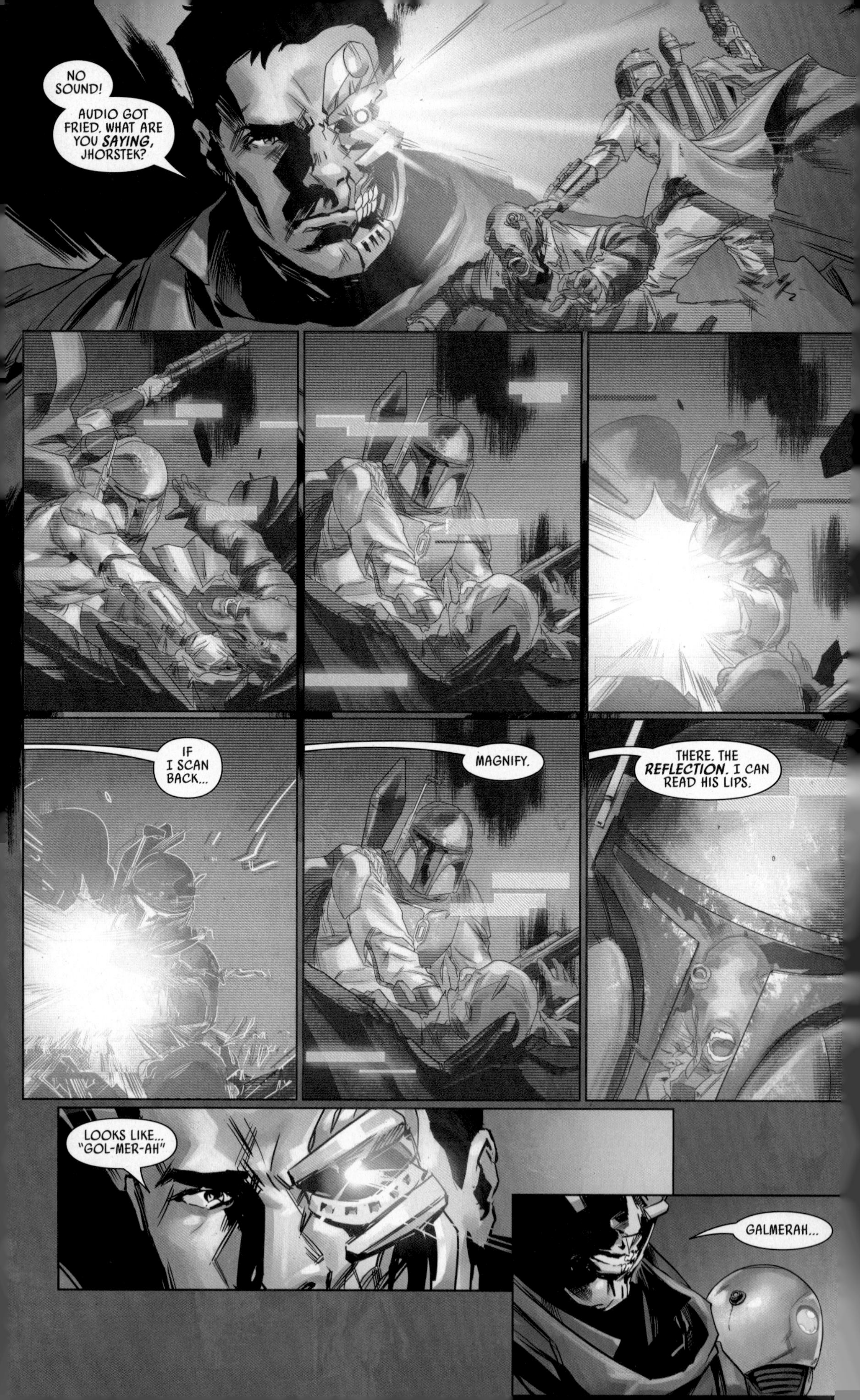
NO SOUND!
AUDIO GOT FRIED. WHAT ARE YOU SAYING, JHORSTEK?
IF I SCAN BACK...
MAGNIFY.
THERE. THE REFLECTION. I CAN READ HIS LIPS.
LOOKS LIKE... "GOL-MER-AH"
GALMERAH...

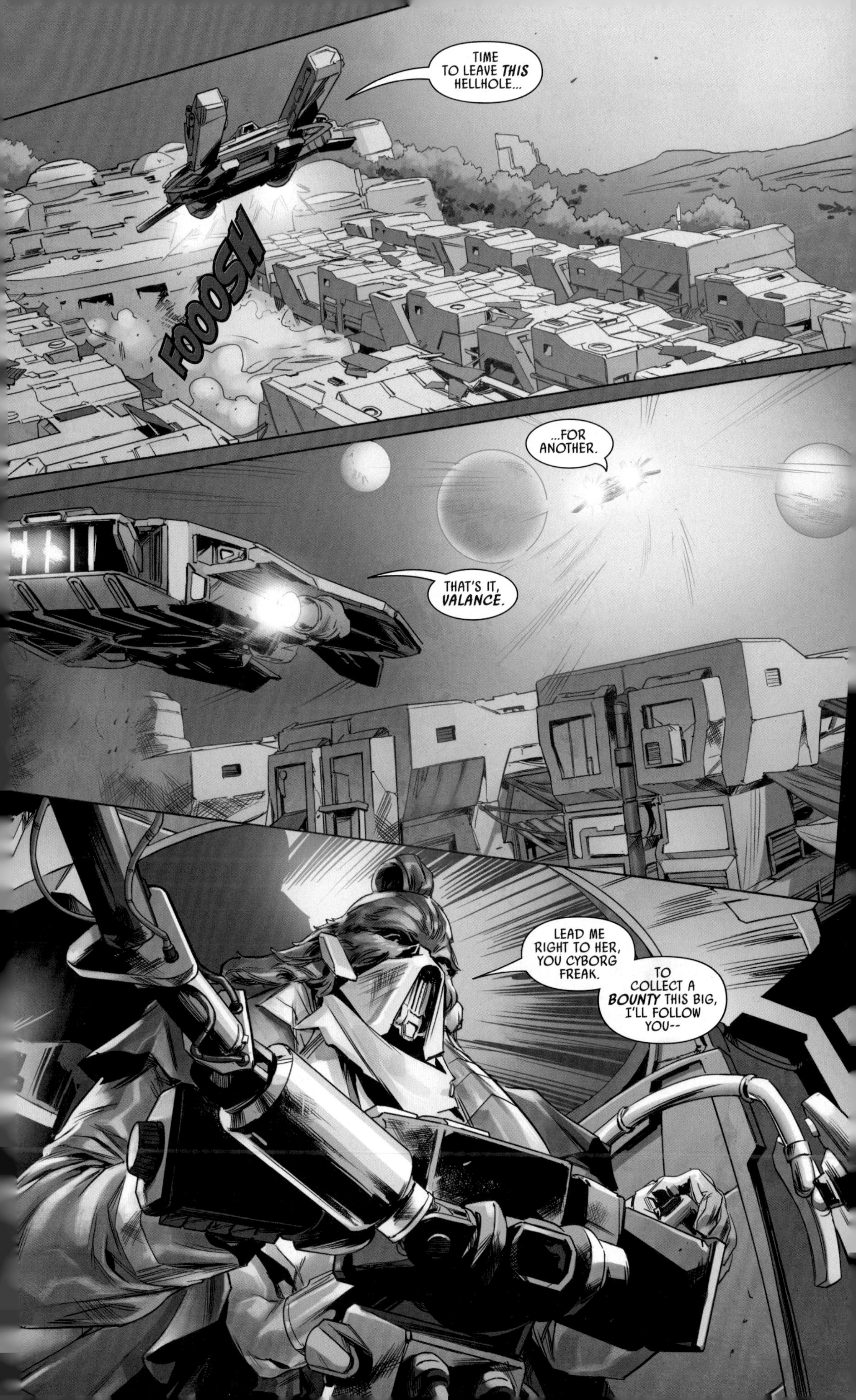
TIME TO LEAVE THIS HELLHOLE...
FOOOSH
...FOR ANOTHER.
THAT'S IT, VALANCE.
LEAD ME RIGHT TO HER, YOU CYBORG FREAK.
TO COLLECT A BOUNTY THIS BIG, I'LL FOLLOW YOU--

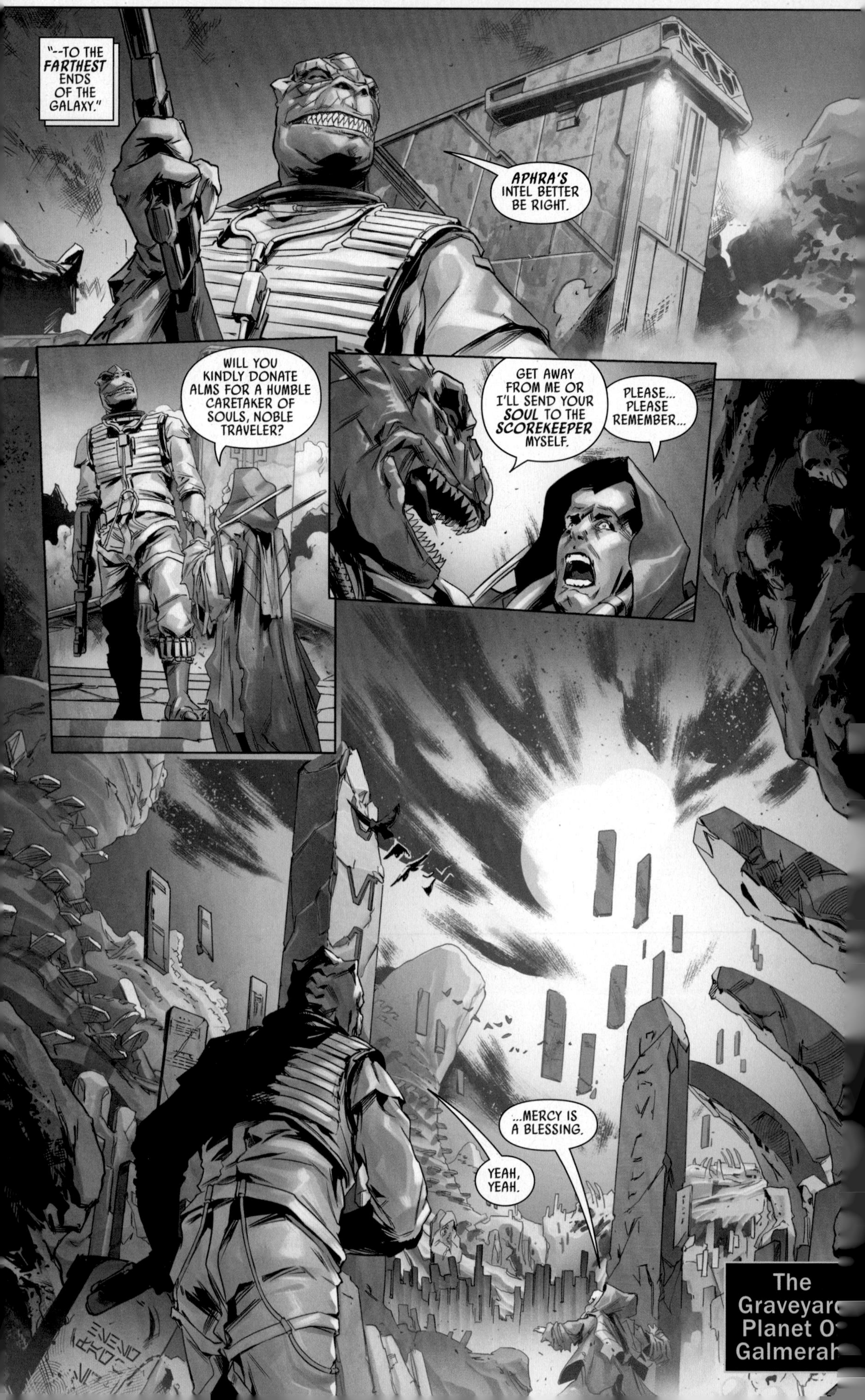
"--TO THE FARTHEST ENDS OF THE GALAXY."
APHRA'S INTEL BETTER BE RIGHT.
WILL YOU KINDLY DONATE ALMS FOR A HUMBLE CARETAKER OF SOULS, NOBLE TRAVELER?
GET AWAY FROM ME OR I'LL SEND YOUR SOUL TO THE SCOREKEEPER MYSELF.
PLEASE... PLEASE REMEMBER...
...MERCY IS A BLESSING.
YEAH, YEAH.
The Graveyar
Planet O
Galmerah

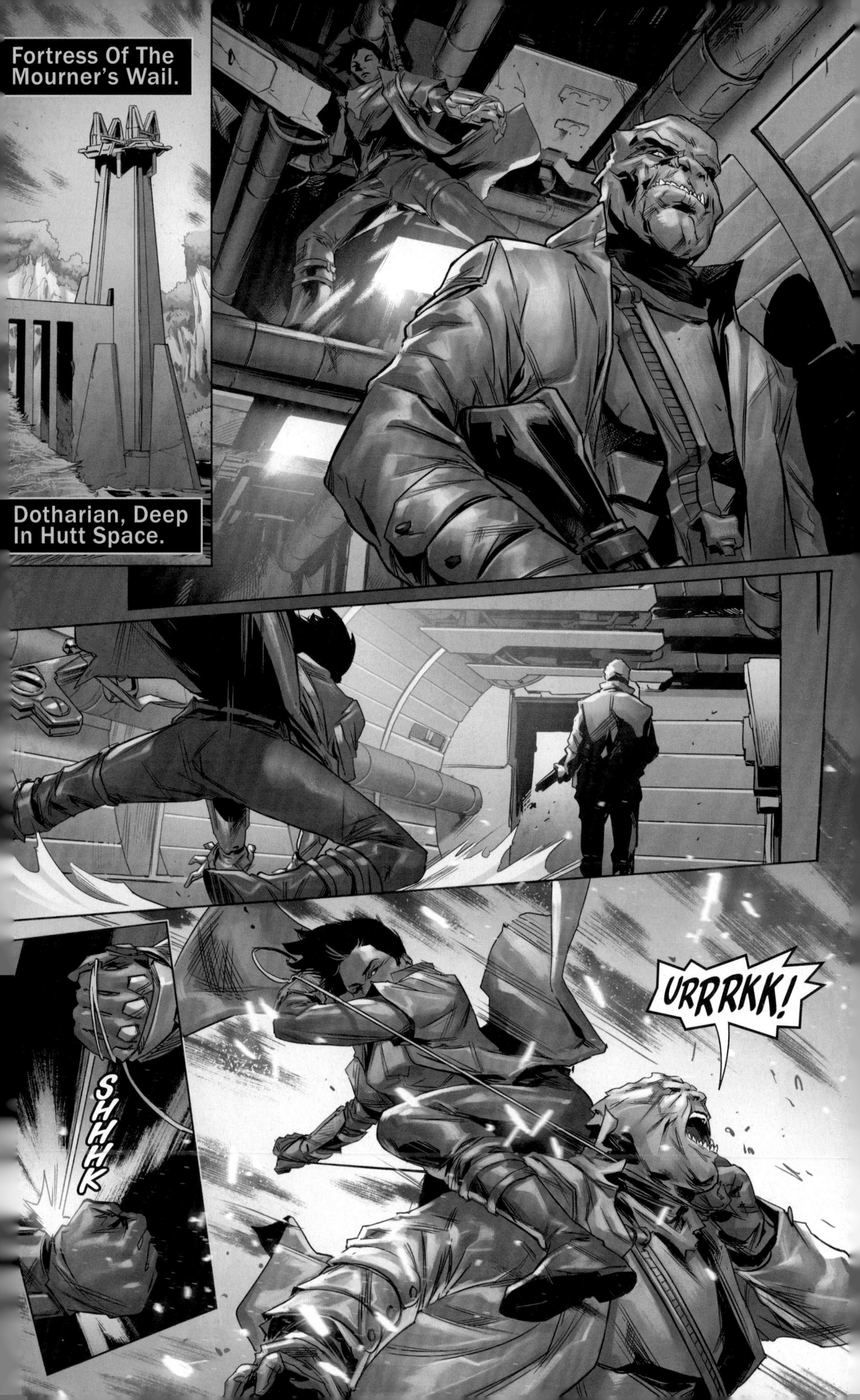
Fortress Of The Mourner's Wail.
Dotharian, Deep In Hutt Space.
SHHHK
URRRKK!

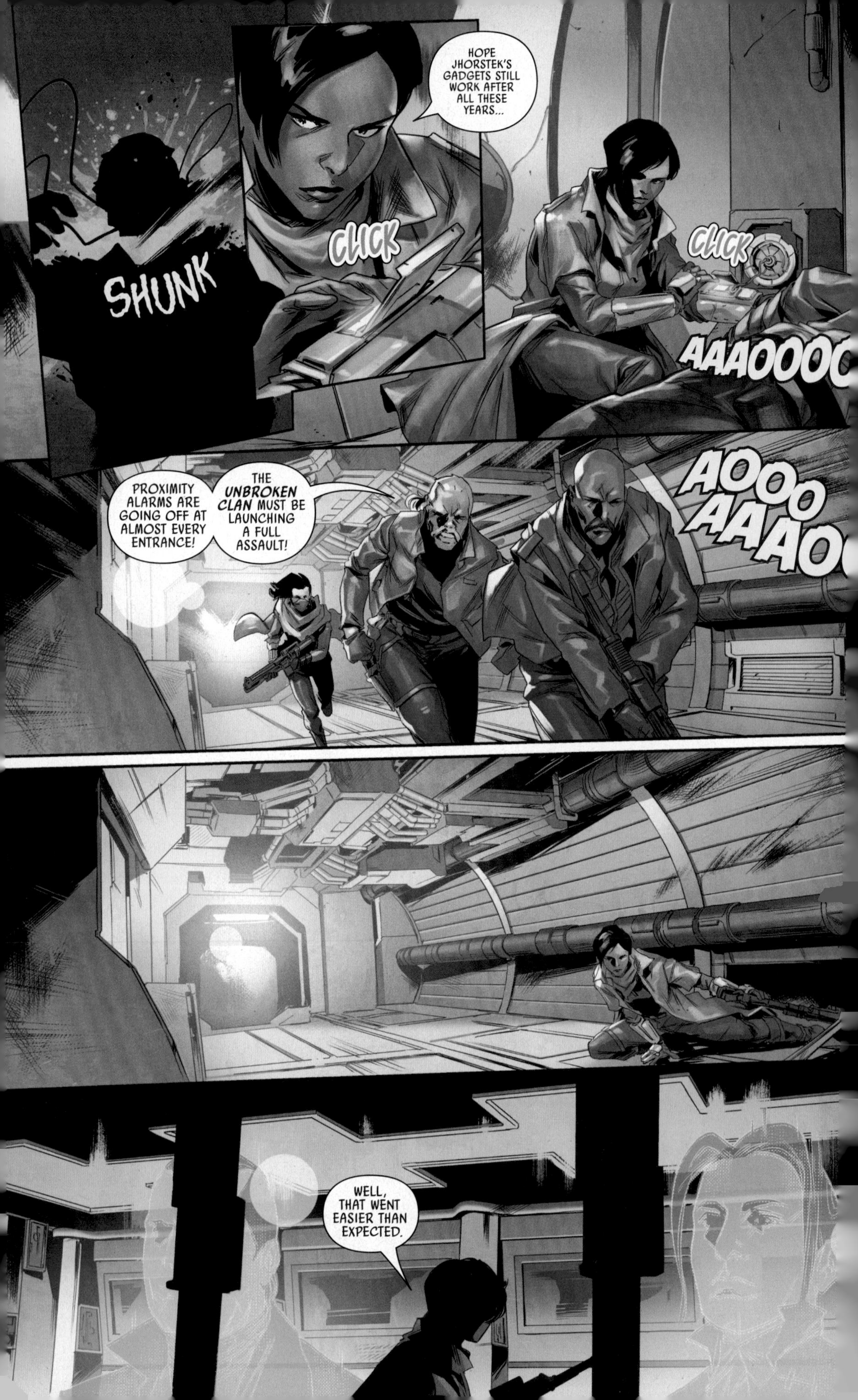
SHUNK
HOPE JHORSTEK'S GADGETS STILL WORK AFTER ALL THESE YEARS...
CLICK
CLICK
AAAOOOO
PROXIMITY ALARMS ARE GOING OFF AT ALMOST EVERY ENTRANCE!
THE UNBROKEN CLAN MUST BE LAUNCHING A FULL ASSAULT!
AOOO AAAAOO
WELL, THAT WENT EASIER THAN EXPECTED.

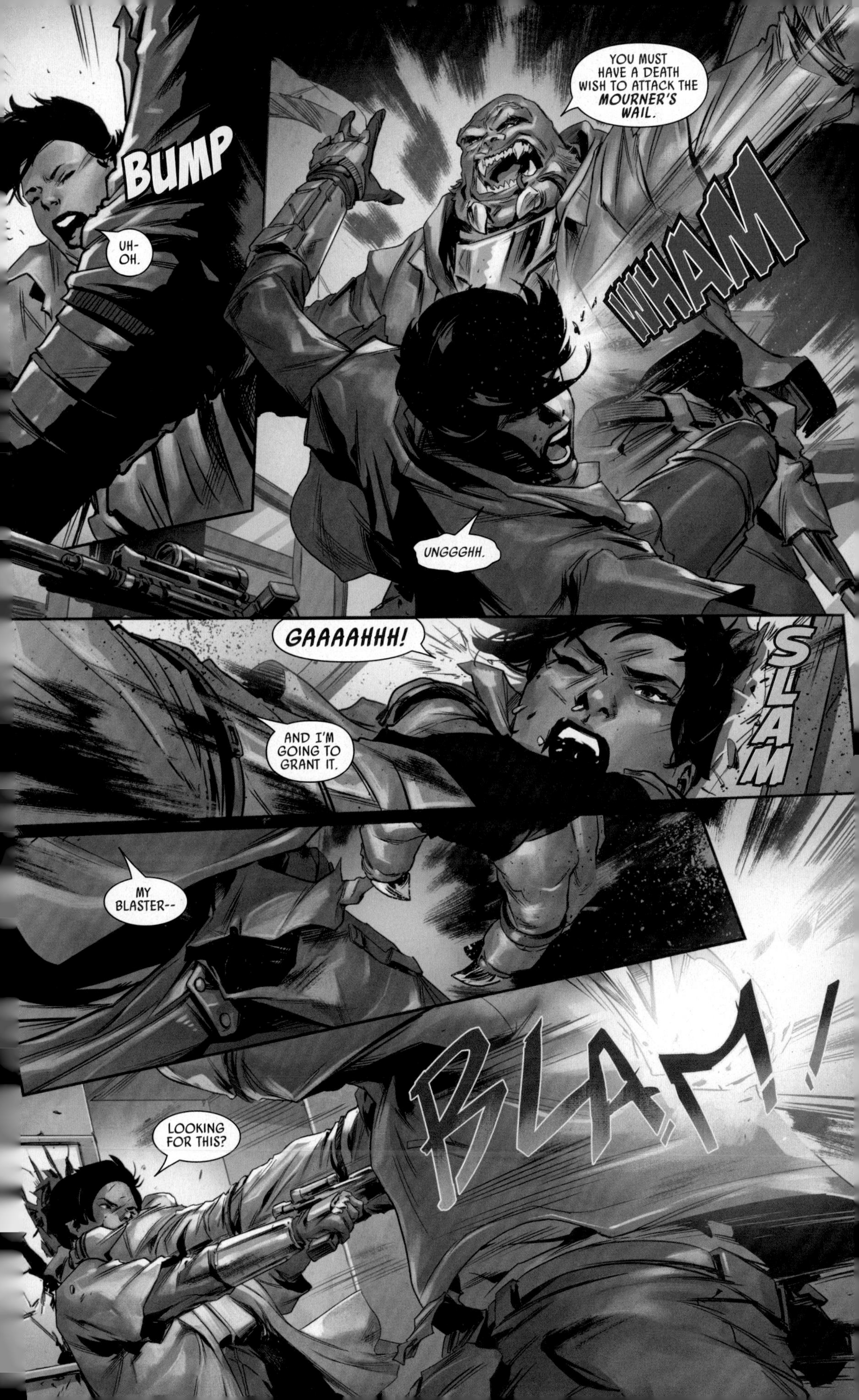
BUMP
UH-OH.
YOU MUST HAVE A DEATH WISH TO ATTACK THE MOURNER'S WAIL.
WHAM
UNGGGHH.
GAAAAHHH!
AND I'M GOING TO GRANT IT.
SLAM
MY BLASTER--
LOOKING FOR THIS?
BLAM!

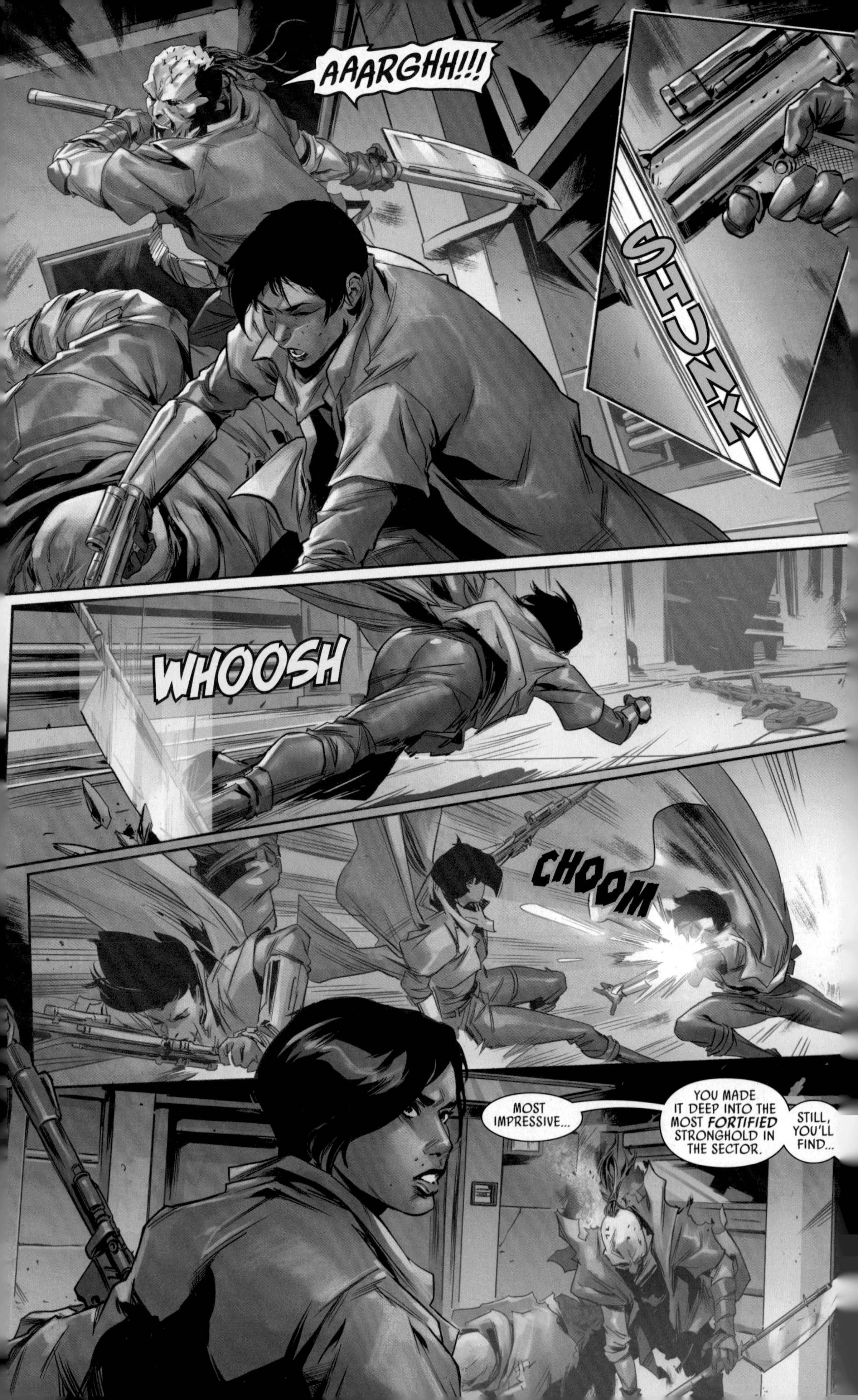
AAARGHH!!!
SHUNK
WHOOSH
CHOOM
MOST IMPRESSIVE...
YOU MADE IT DEEP INTO THE MOST FORTIFIED STRONGHOLD IN THE SECTOR.
STILL, YOU'LL FIND...

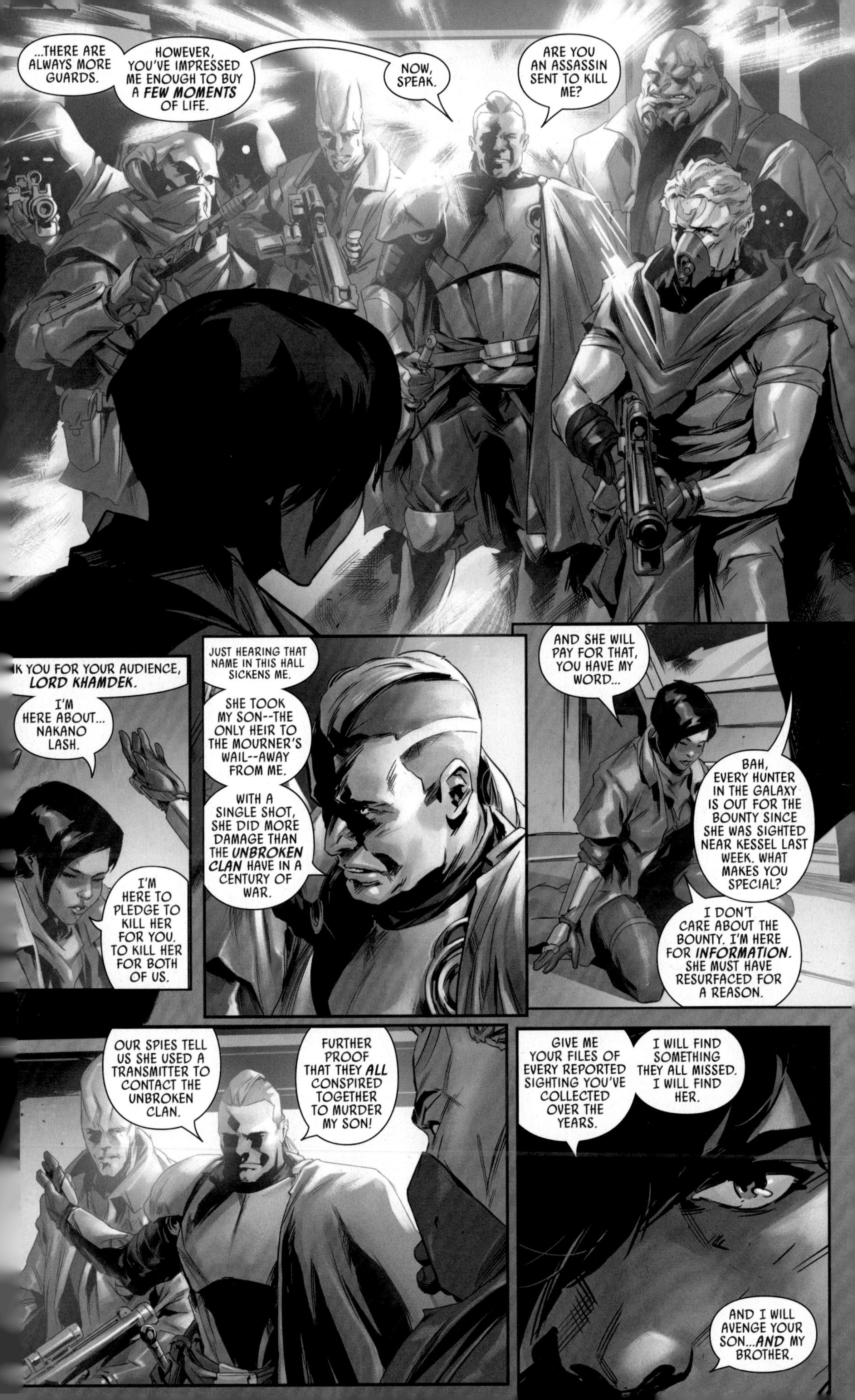
...THERE ARE ALWAYS MORE GUARDS.
HOWEVER, YOU'VE IMPRESSED ME ENOUGH TO BUY A **FEW MOMENTS** OF LIFE.
NOW, SPEAK.
ARE YOU AN ASSASSIN SENT TO KILL ME?
K YOU FOR YOUR AUDIENCE, **LORD KHAMDEK.**
I'M HERE ABOUT... NAKANO LASH.
I'M HERE TO PLEDGE TO KILL HER FOR YOU. TO KILL HER FOR BOTH OF US.
JUST HEARING THAT NAME IN THIS HALL SICKENS ME.
SHE TOOK MY SON--THE ONLY HEIR TO THE MOURNER'S WAIL--AWAY FROM ME.
WITH A SINGLE SHOT, SHE DID MORE DAMAGE THAN THE **UNBROKEN CLAN** HAVE IN A CENTURY OF WAR.
AND SHE WILL PAY FOR THAT, YOU HAVE MY WORD...
BAH, EVERY HUNTER IN THE GALAXY IS OUT FOR THE BOUNTY SINCE SHE WAS SIGHTED NEAR KESSEL LAST WEEK. WHAT MAKES YOU SPECIAL?
I DON'T CARE ABOUT THE BOUNTY. I'M HERE FOR **INFORMATION.** SHE MUST HAVE RESURFACED FOR A REASON.
OUR SPIES TELL US SHE USED A TRANSMITTER TO CONTACT THE UNBROKEN CLAN.
FURTHER PROOF THAT THEY **ALL** CONSPIRED TOGETHER TO MURDER MY SON!
GIVE ME YOUR FILES OF EVERY REPORTED SIGHTING YOU'VE COLLECTED OVER THE YEARS.
I WILL FIND SOMETHING THEY ALL MISSED. I WILL FIND HER.
AND I WILL AVENGE YOUR SON...**AND** MY BROTHER.

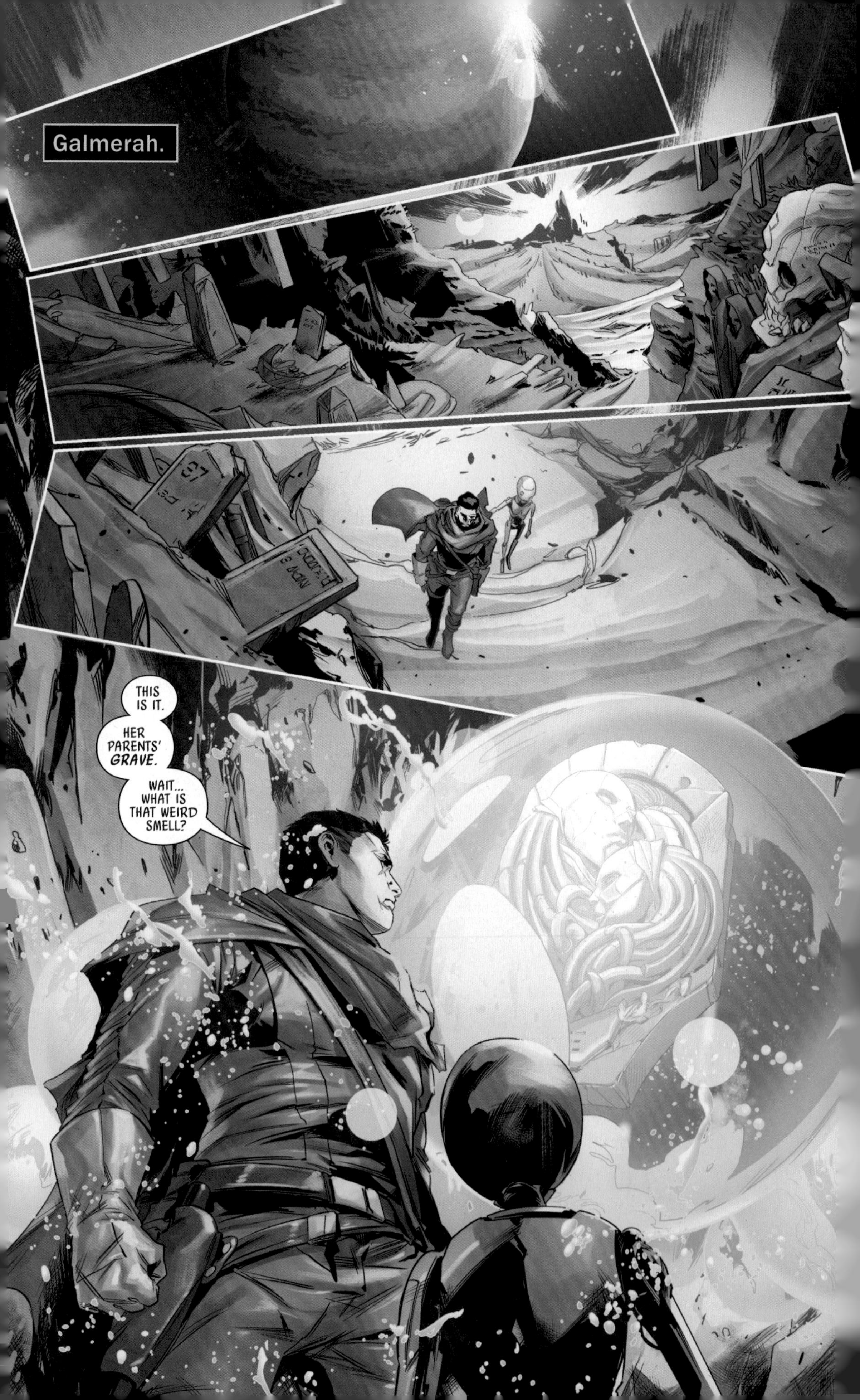
Galmerah.
THIS IS IT.
HER PARENTS' GRAVE.
WAIT... WHAT IS THAT WEIRD SMELL?

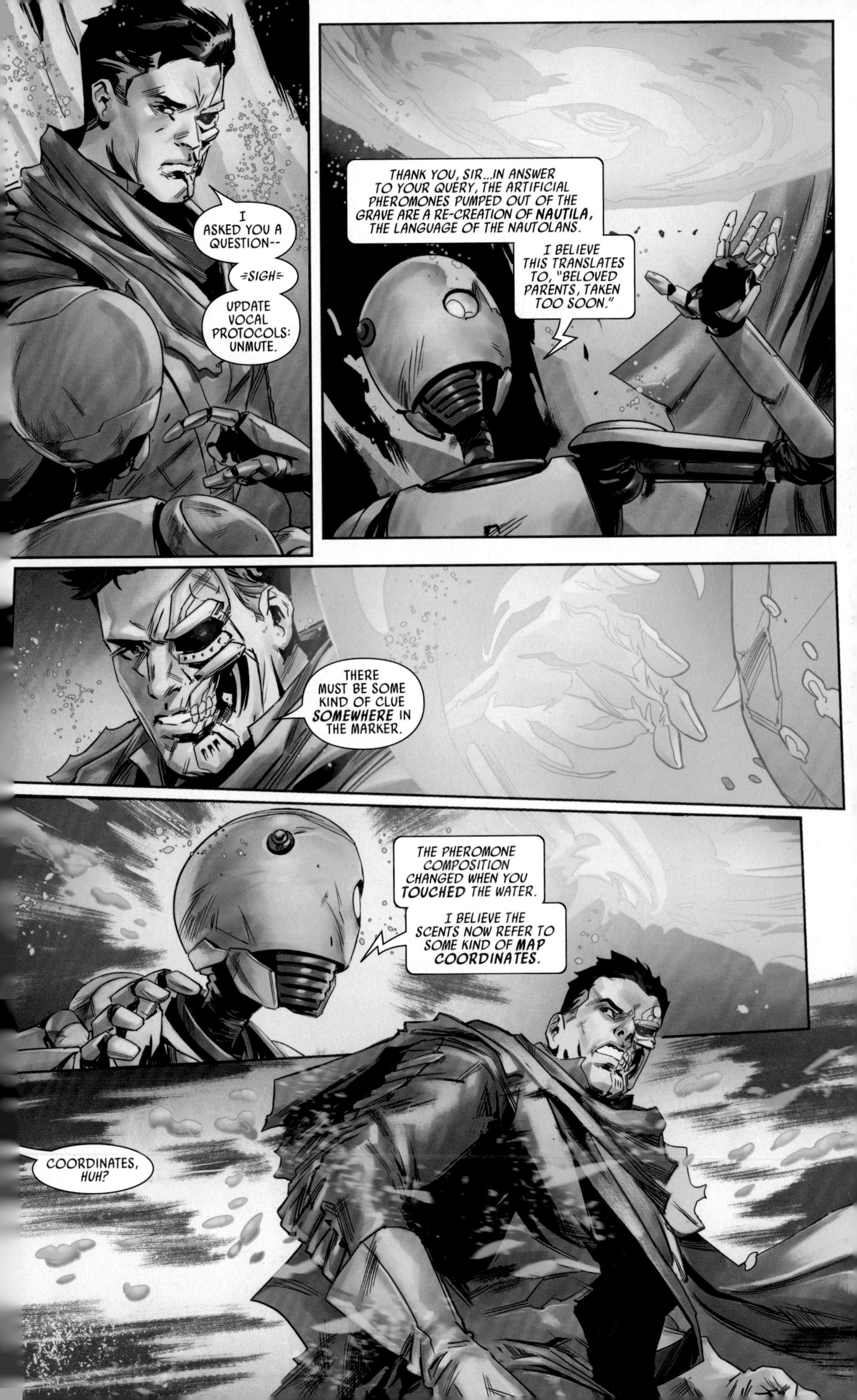
I ASKED YOU A QUESTION--
=SIGH=
UPDATE VOCAL PROTOCOLS: UNMUTE.
THANK YOU, SIR...IN ANSWER TO YOUR QUERY, THE ARTIFICIAL PHEROMONES PUMPED OUT OF THE GRAVE ARE A RE-CREATION OF NAUTILA, THE LANGUAGE OF THE NAUTOLANS.
I BELIEVE THIS TRANSLATES TO, "BELOVED PARENTS, TAKEN TOO SOON."
THERE MUST BE SOME KIND OF CLUE SOMEWHERE IN THE MARKER.
THE PHEROMONE COMPOSITION CHANGED WHEN YOU TOUCHED THE WATER.
I BELIEVE THE SCENTS NOW REFER TO SOME KIND OF MAP COORDINATES.
COORDINATES, HUH?

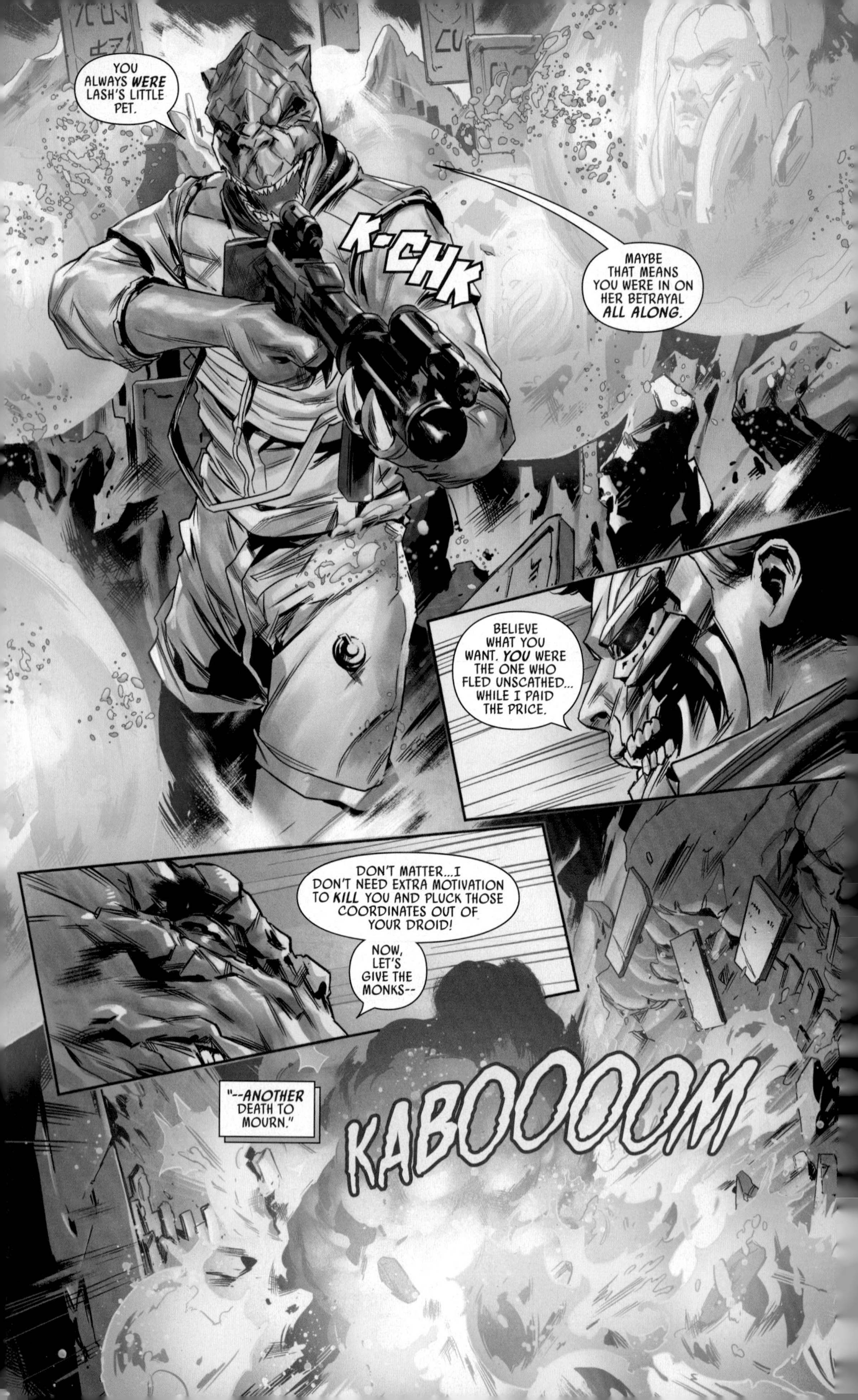
YOU ALWAYS WERE LASH'S LITTLE PET.
K-CHK
MAYBE THAT MEANS YOU WERE IN ON HER BETRAYAL ALL ALONG.
BELIEVE WHAT YOU WANT. YOU WERE THE ONE WHO FLED UNSCATHED... WHILE I PAID THE PRICE.
DON'T MATTER...I DON'T NEED EXTRA MOTIVATION TO KILL YOU AND PLUCK THOSE COORDINATES OUT OF YOUR DROID!
NOW, LET'S GIVE THE MONKS--
"--ANOTHER DEATH TO MOURN."
KABOOOOOM

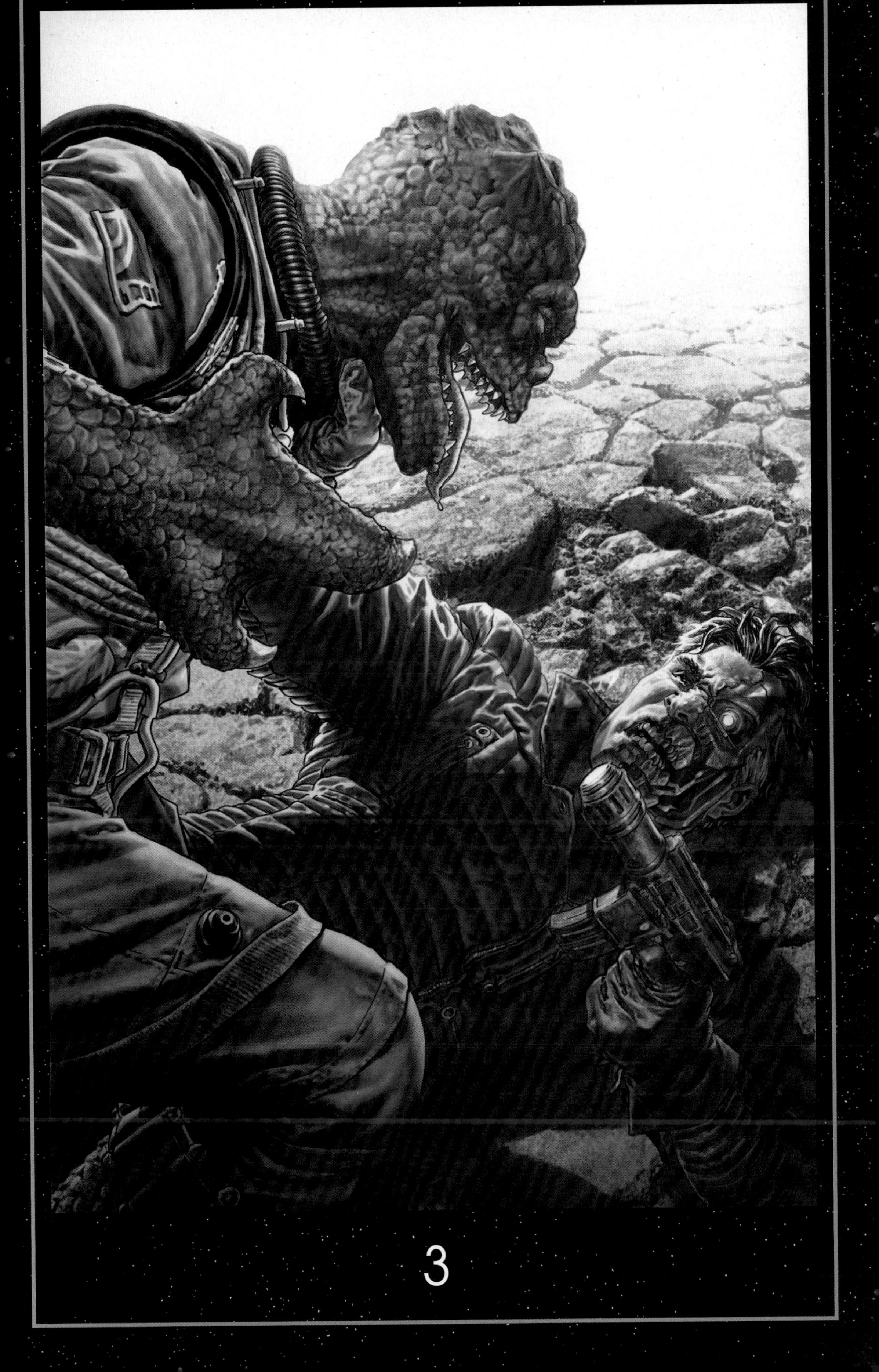

3

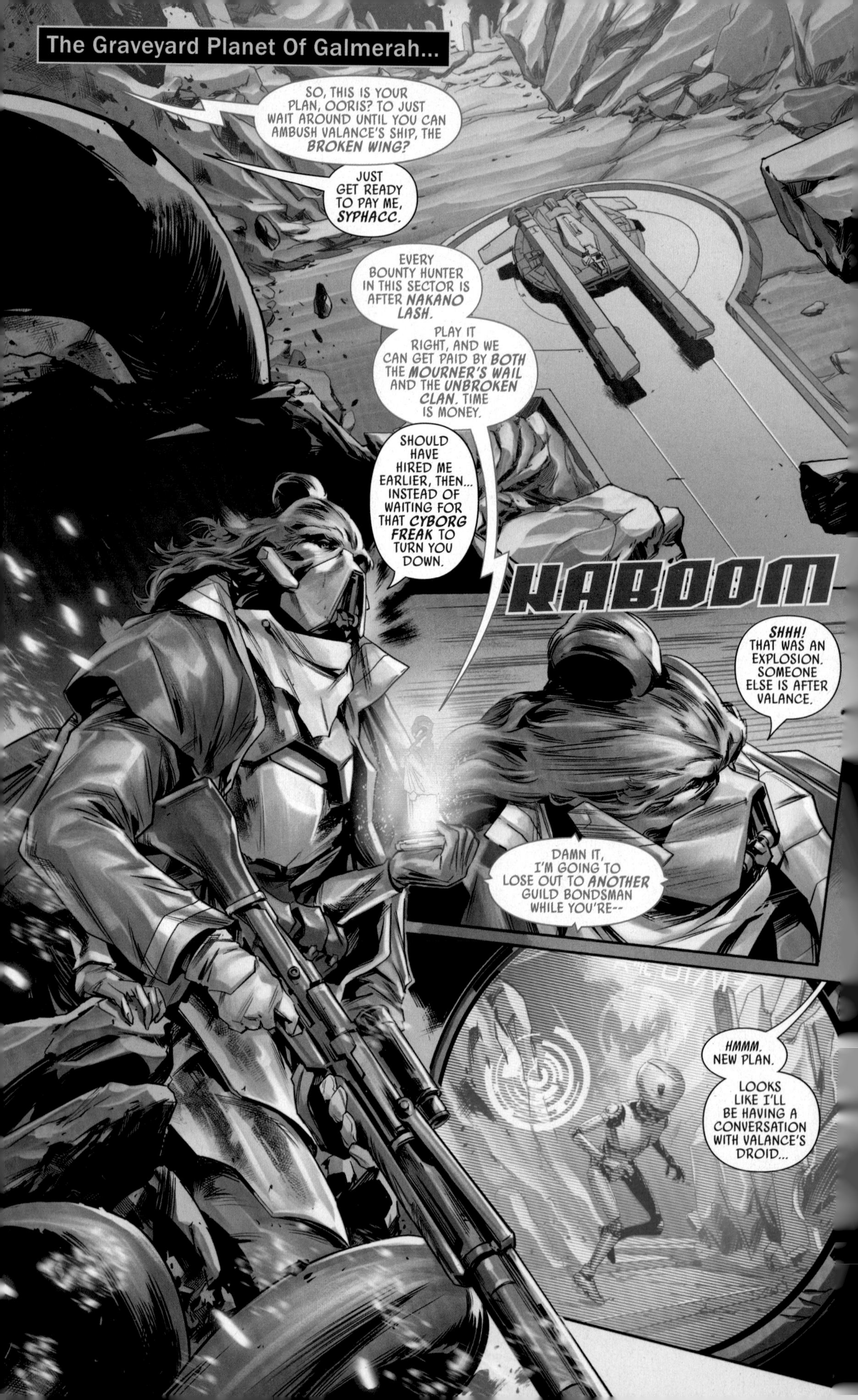
The Graveyard Planet Of Galmerah...
SO, THIS IS YOUR PLAN, OORIS? TO JUST WAIT AROUND UNTIL YOU CAN AMBUSH VALANCE'S SHIP, THE BROKEN WING?
JUST GET READY TO PAY ME, SYPHACC.
EVERY BOUNTY HUNTER IN THIS SECTOR IS AFTER NAKANO LASH.
PLAY IT RIGHT, AND WE CAN GET PAID BY BOTH THE MOURNER'S WAIL AND THE UNBROKEN CLAN. TIME IS MONEY.
SHOULD HAVE HIRED ME EARLIER, THEN... INSTEAD OF WAITING FOR THAT CYBORG FREAK TO TURN YOU DOWN.
KABOOM
SHHH! THAT WAS AN EXPLOSION. SOMEONE ELSE IS AFTER VALANCE.
DAMN IT, I'M GOING TO LOSE OUT TO ANOTHER GUILD BONDSMAN WHILE YOU'RE--
HMMM. NEW PLAN.
LOOKS LIKE I'LL BE HAVING A CONVERSATION WITH VALANCE'S DROID...

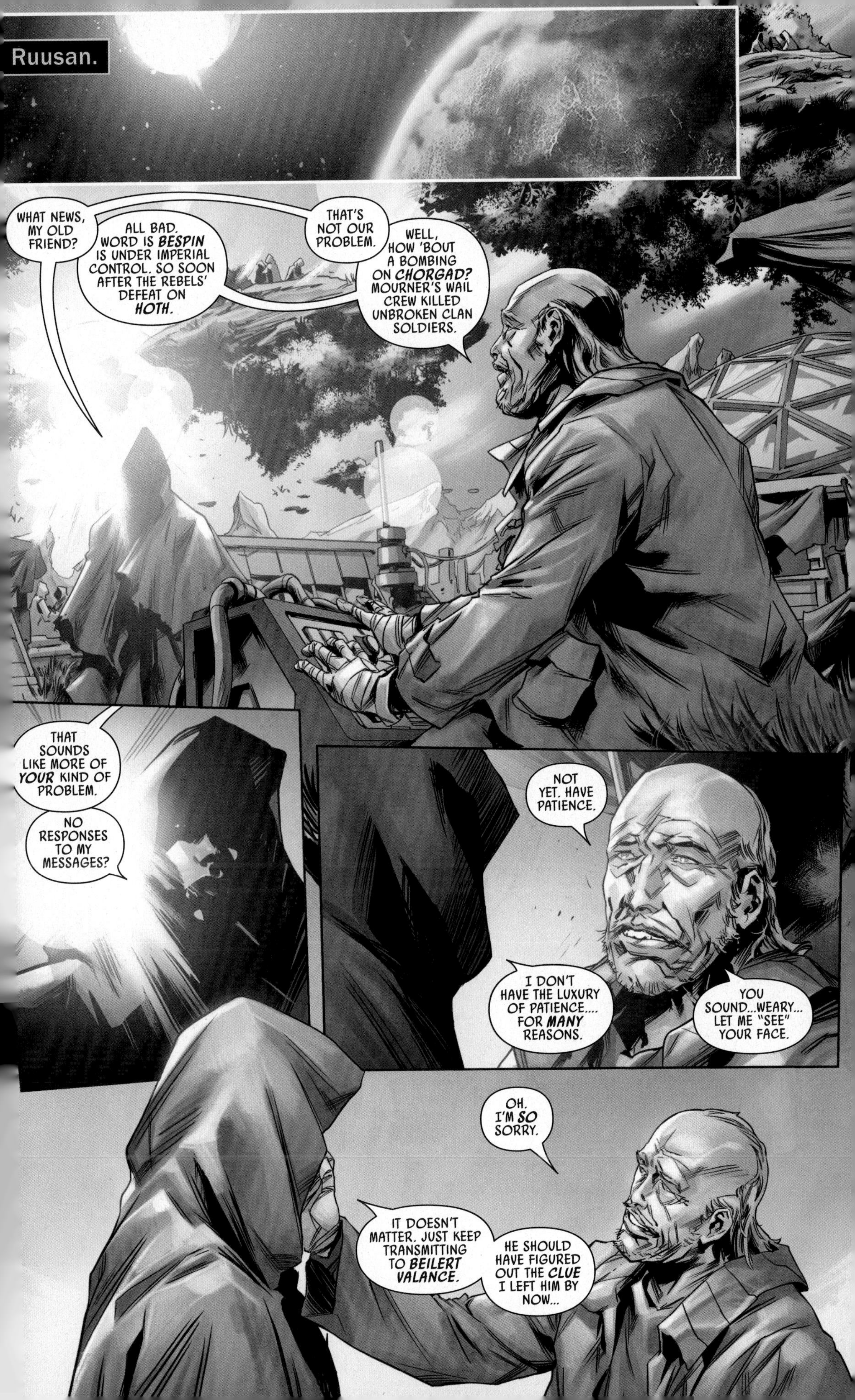
Ruusan.
WHAT NEWS, MY OLD FRIEND?
ALL BAD. WORD IS BESPIN IS UNDER IMPERIAL CONTROL. SO SOON AFTER THE REBELS' DEFEAT ON HOTH.
THAT'S NOT OUR PROBLEM.
WELL, HOW 'BOUT A BOMBING ON CHORGAD? MOURNER'S WAIL CREW KILLED UNBROKEN CLAN SOLDIERS.
THAT SOUNDS LIKE MORE OF YOUR KIND OF PROBLEM.
NO RESPONSES TO MY MESSAGES?
NOT YET. HAVE PATIENCE.
I DON'T HAVE THE LUXURY OF PATIENCE.... FOR MANY REASONS.
YOU SOUND...WEARY... LET ME "SEE" YOUR FACE.
OH. I'M SO SORRY.
IT DOESN'T MATTER. JUST KEEP TRANSMITTING TO BEILERT VALANCE.
HE SHOULD HAVE FIGURED OUT THE CLUE I LEFT HIM BY NOW...

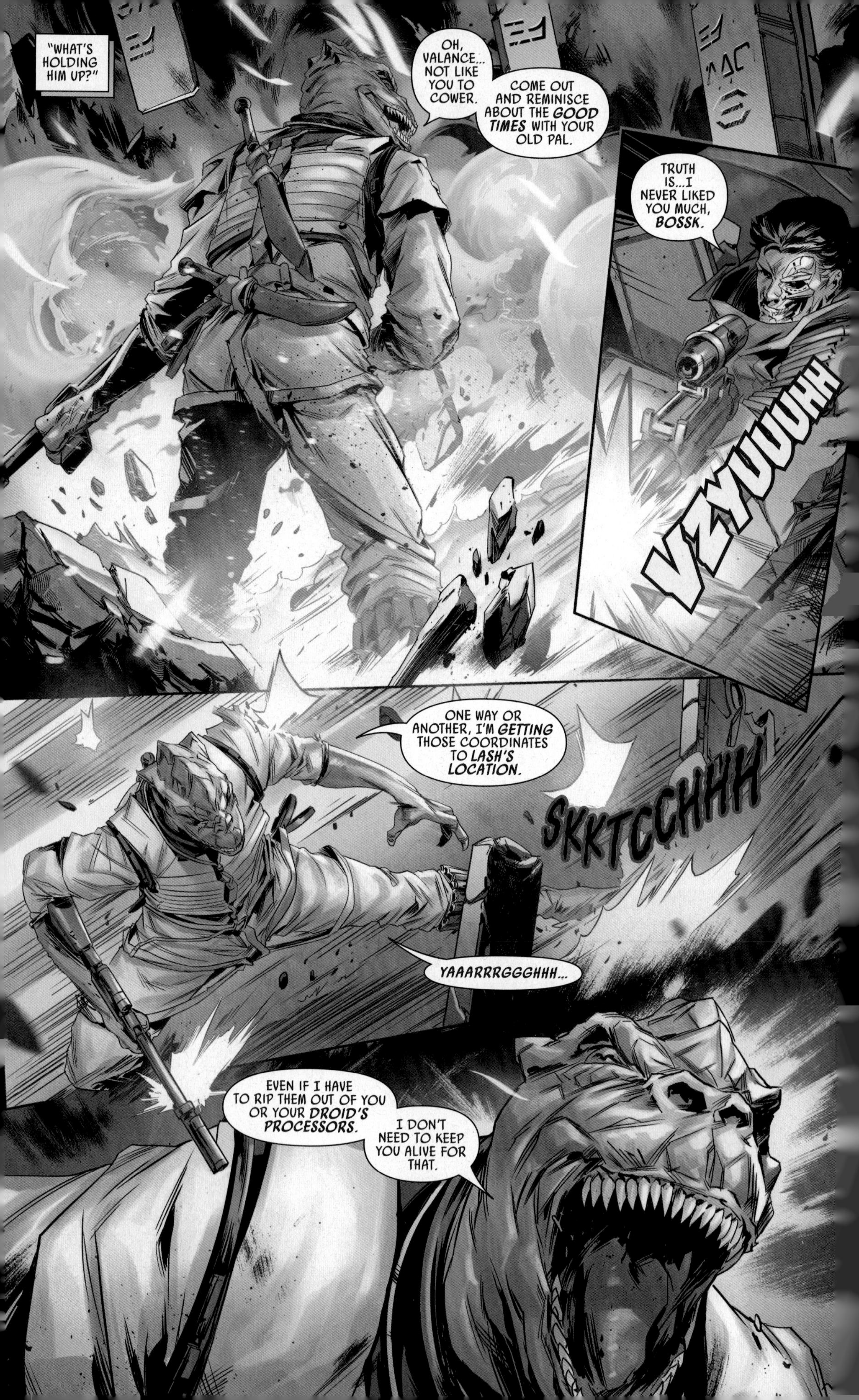
"WHAT'S HOLDING HIM UP?"
OH, VALANCE... NOT LIKE YOU TO COWER.
COME OUT AND REMINISCE ABOUT THE GOOD TIMES WITH YOUR OLD PAL.
TRUTH IS...I NEVER LIKED YOU MUCH, BOSSK.
VZYUUUHH
ONE WAY OR ANOTHER, I'M GETTING THOSE COORDINATES TO LASH'S LOCATION.
SKKTCCHHH
YAAARRRGGGHHH...
EVEN IF I HAVE TO RIP THEM OUT OF YOU OR YOUR DROID'S PROCESSORS.
I DON'T NEED TO KEEP YOU ALIVE FOR THAT.

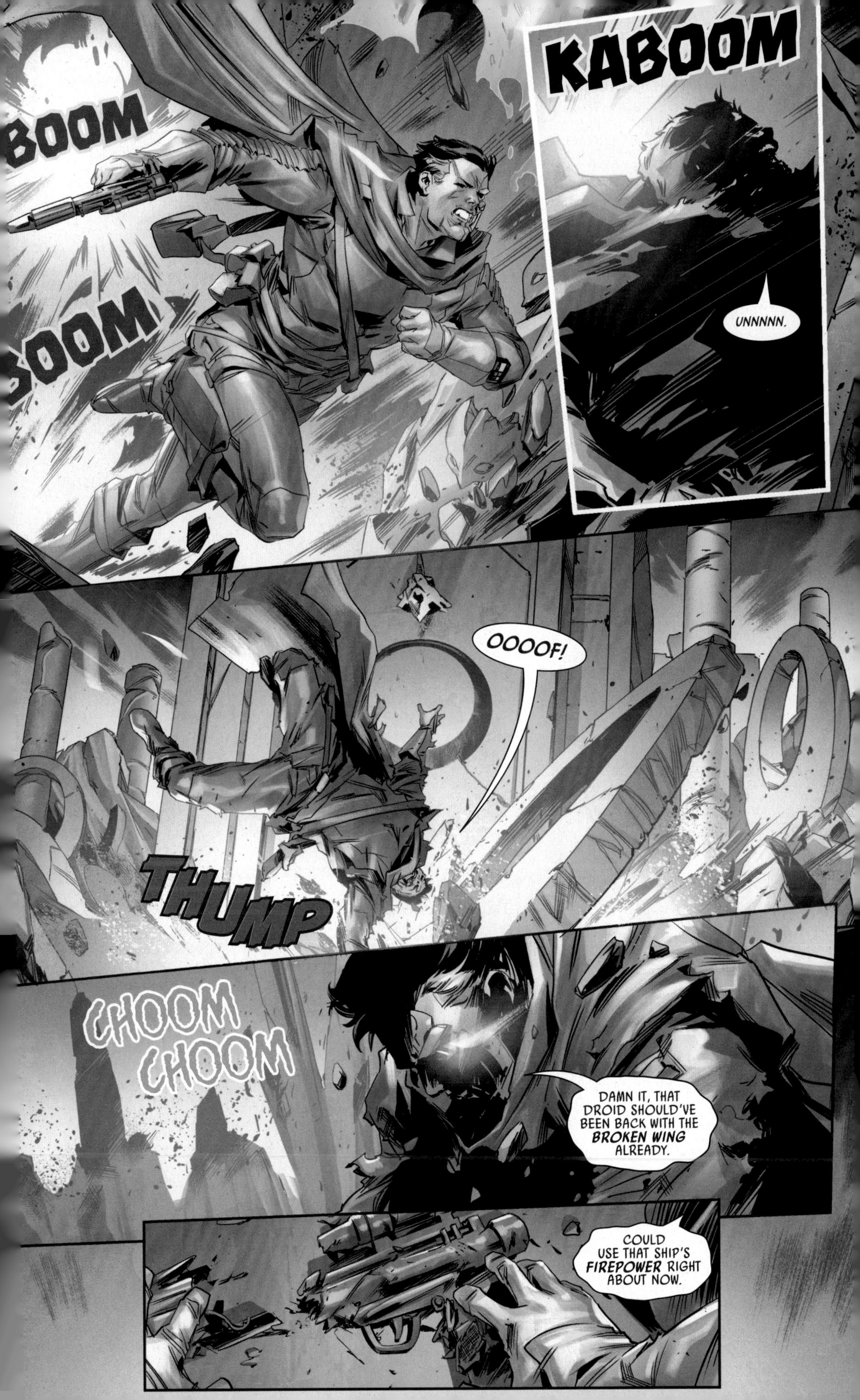
BOOM
BOOM
KABOOM
UNNNNN.
OOOOF!
THUMP
CHOOM
CHOOM
DAMN IT, THAT DROID SHOULD'VE BEEN BACK WITH THE BROKEN WING ALREADY.
COULD USE THAT SHIP'S FIREPOWER RIGHT ABOUT NOW.

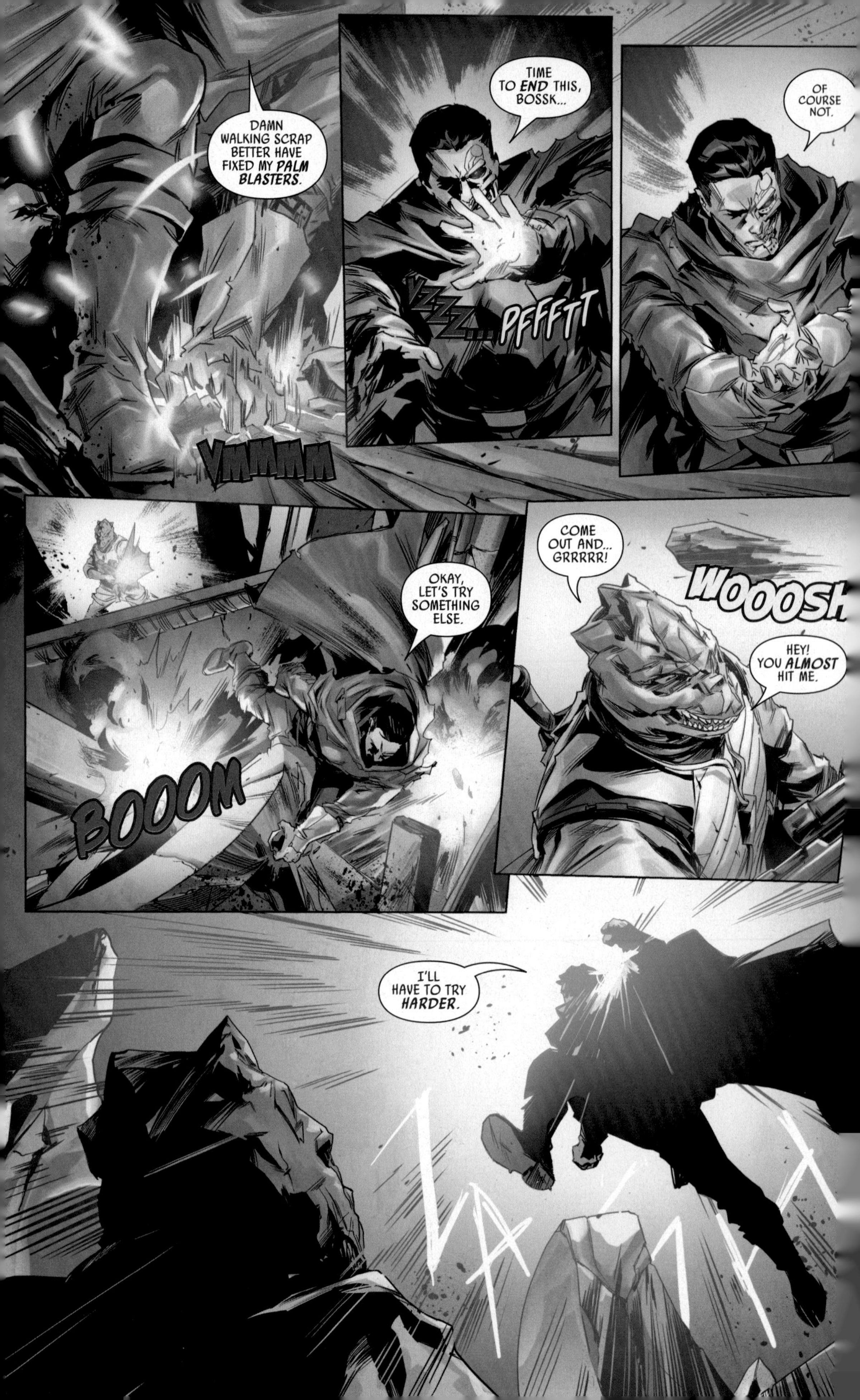
DAMN WALKING SCRAP BETTER HAVE FIXED MY PALM BLASTERS.
VMMMM
TIME TO END THIS, BOSSK...
VZZZ... PFFFTT
OF COURSE NOT.
OKAY, LET'S TRY SOMETHING ELSE.
BOOOM
COME OUT AND... GRRRRR!
WOOOSH
HEY! YOU ALMOST HIT ME.
I'LL HAVE TO TRY HARDER.

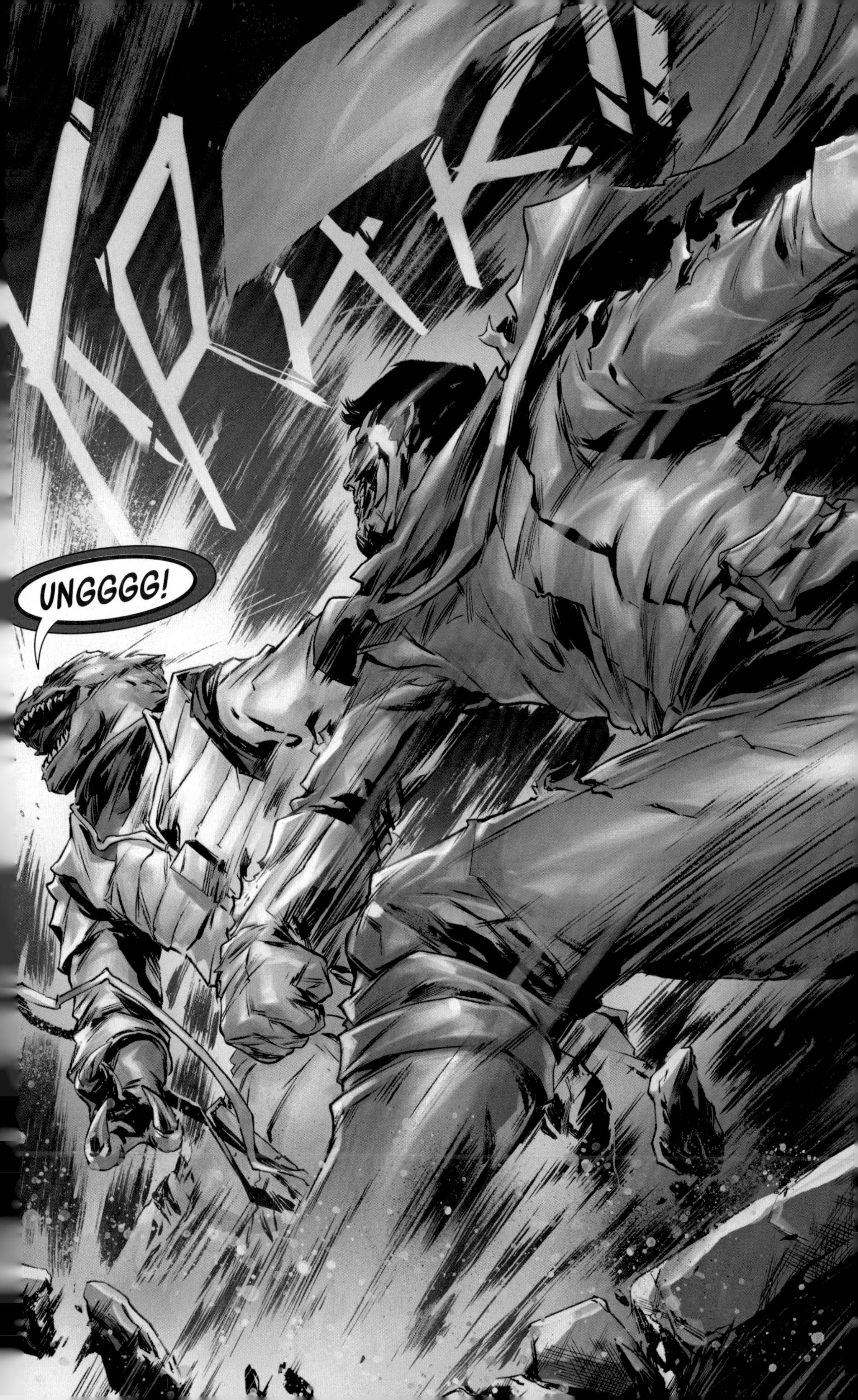
UNGGGG!

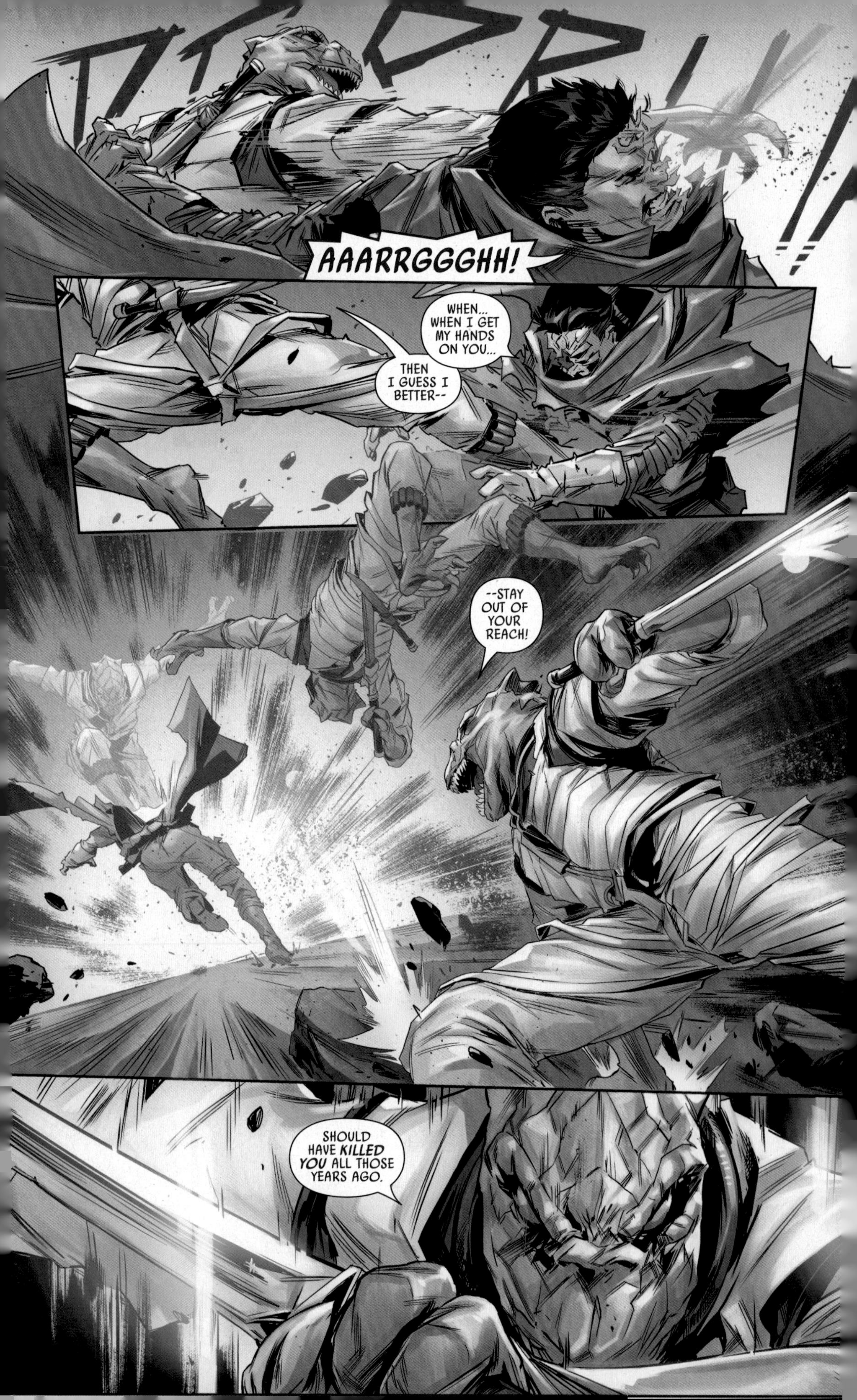
AAARRGGGHH!
WHEN... WHEN I GET MY HANDS ON YOU...
THEN I GUESS I BETTER--
--STAY OUT OF YOUR REACH!
SHOULD HAVE KILLED YOU ALL THOSE YEARS AGO.

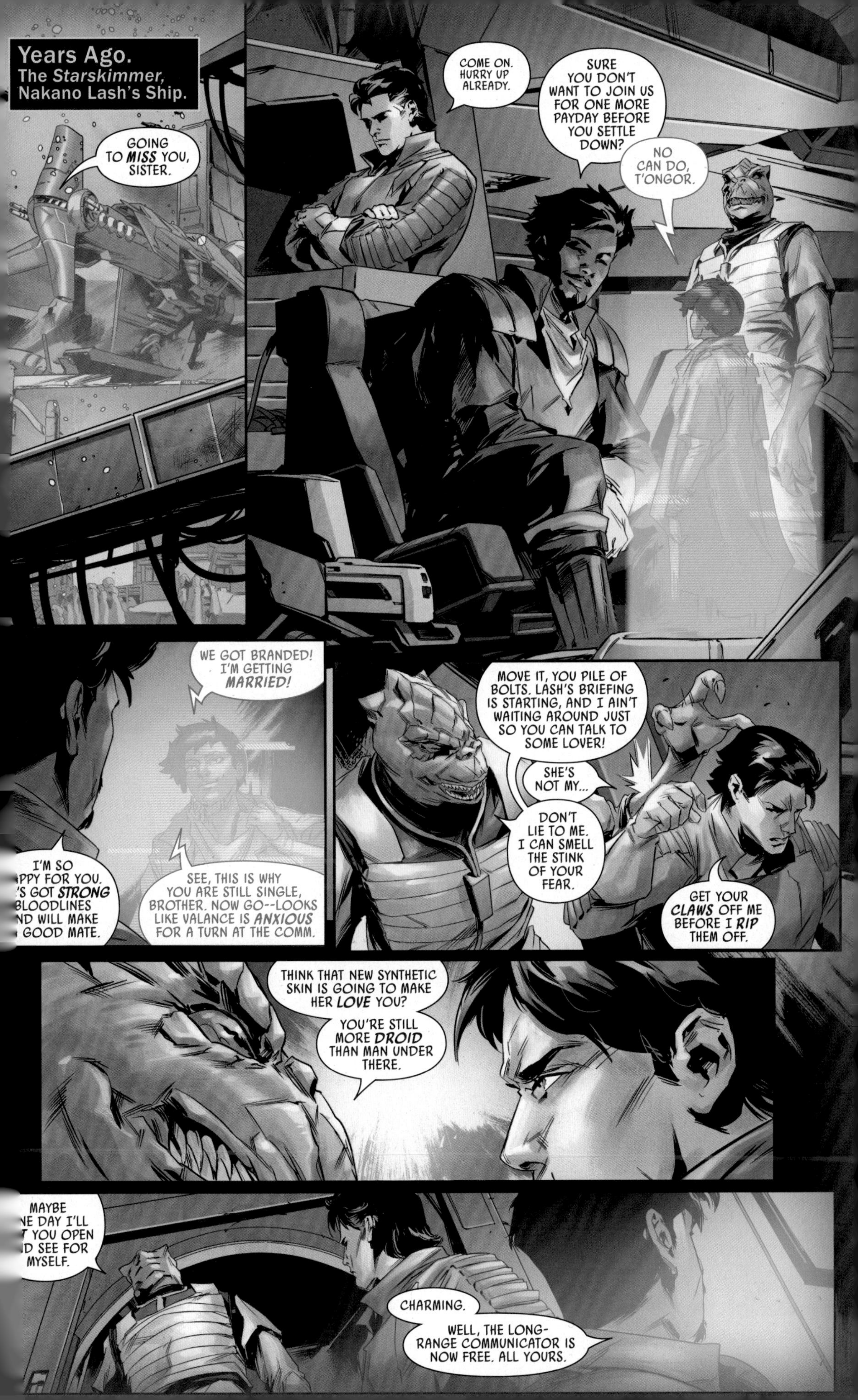

Years Ago.
The Starskimmer, Nakano Lash's Ship.
GOING TO MISS YOU, SISTER.
COME ON. HURRY UP ALREADY.
SURE YOU DON'T WANT TO JOIN US FOR ONE MORE PAYDAY BEFORE YOU SETTLE DOWN?
NO CAN DO, T'ONGOR.
WE GOT BRANDED! I'M GETTING MARRIED!
I'M SO PPY FOR YOU. 'S GOT STRONG BLOODLINES ND WILL MAKE GOOD MATE.
SEE, THIS IS WHY YOU ARE STILL SINGLE, BROTHER. NOW GO--LOOKS LIKE VALANCE IS ANXIOUS FOR A TURN AT THE COMM.
MOVE IT, YOU PILE OF BOLTS. LASH'S BRIEFING IS STARTING, AND I AIN'T WAITING AROUND JUST SO YOU CAN TALK TO SOME LOVER!
SHE'S NOT MY...
DON'T LIE TO ME. I CAN SMELL THE STINK OF YOUR FEAR.
GET YOUR CLAWS OFF ME BEFORE I RIP THEM OFF.
THINK THAT NEW SYNTHETIC SKIN IS GOING TO MAKE HER LOVE YOU?
YOU'RE STILL MORE DROID THAN MAN UNDER THERE.
MAYBE NE DAY I'LL T YOU OPEN D SEE FOR MYSELF.
CHARMING.
WELL, THE LONG-RANGE COMMUNICATOR IS NOW FREE. ALL YOURS.

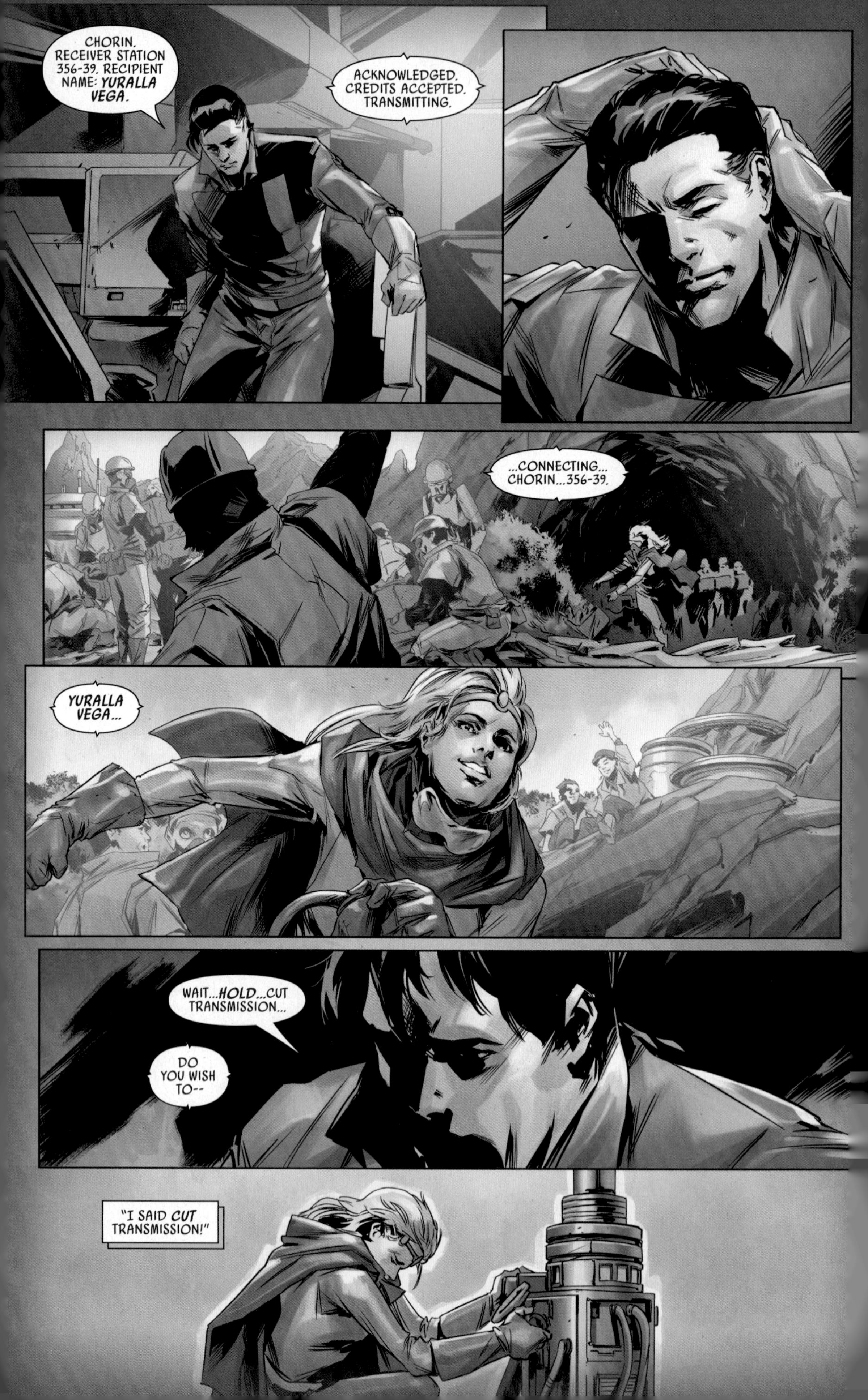
CHORIN. RECEIVER STATION 356-39. RECIPIENT NAME: YURALLA VEGA.
ACKNOWLEDGED. CREDITS ACCEPTED. TRANSMITTING.
...CONNECTING... CHORIN...356-39.
YURALLA VEGA...
WAIT...HOLD...CUT TRANSMISSION...
DO YOU WISH TO--
"I SAID CUT TRANSMISSION!"

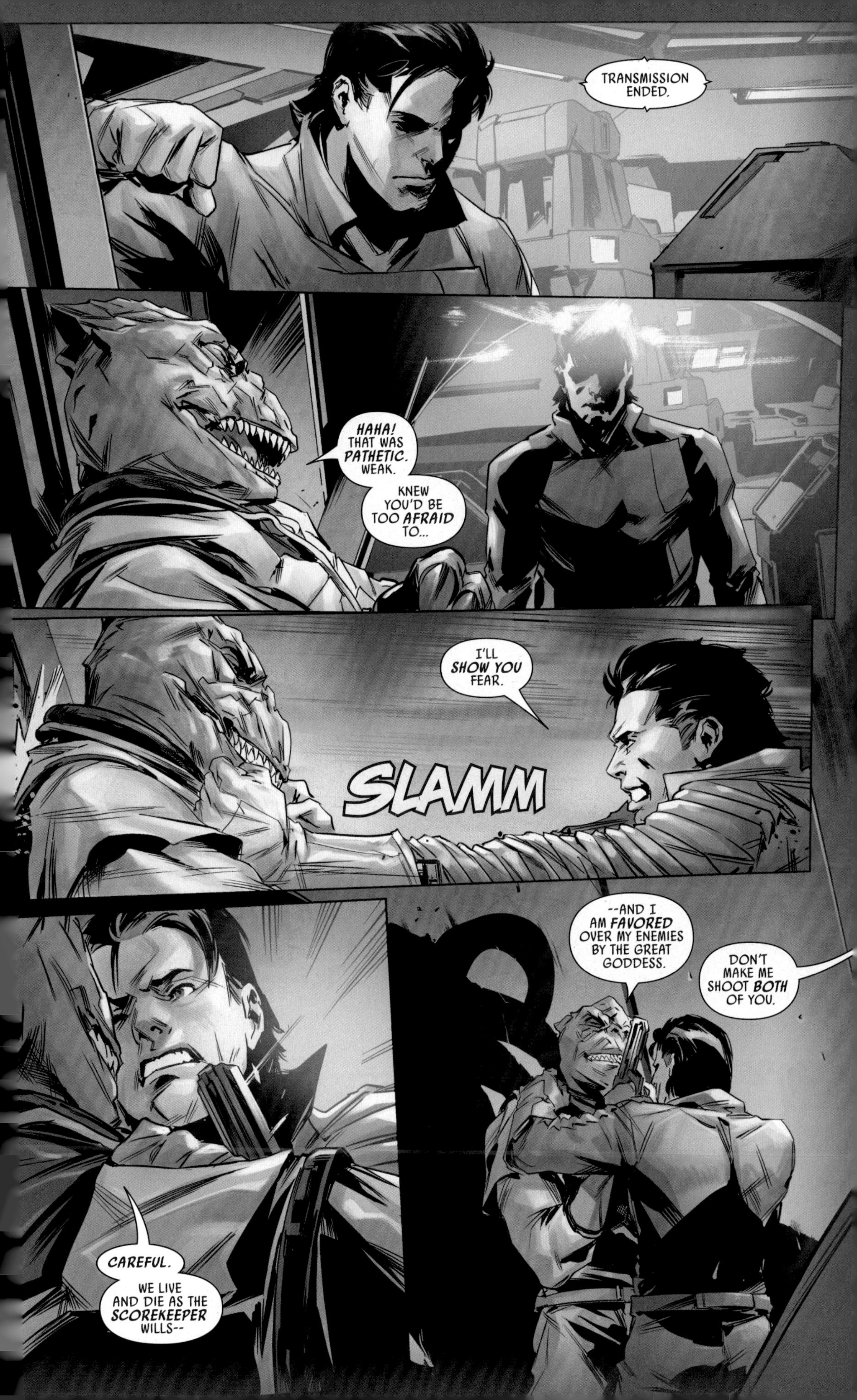
TRANSMISSION ENDED.
HAHA! THAT WAS PATHETIC. WEAK.
KNEW YOU'D BE TOO AFRAID TO...
I'LL SHOW YOU FEAR.
SLAMM
CAREFUL.
WE LIVE AND DIE AS THE SCOREKEEPER WILLS--
--AND I AM FAVORED OVER MY ENEMIES BY THE GREAT GODDESS.
DON'T MAKE ME SHOOT BOTH OF YOU.

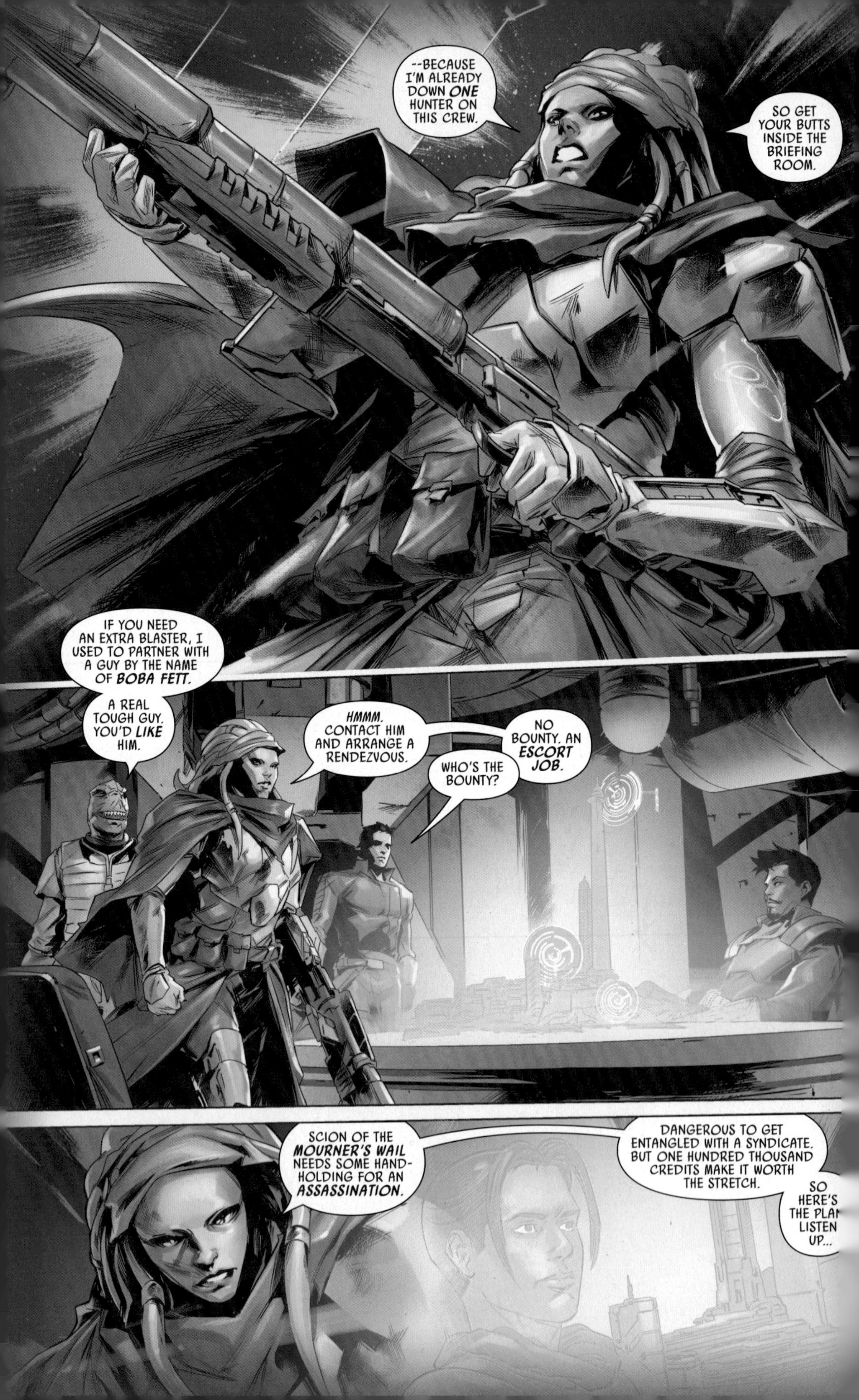
--BECAUSE I'M ALREADY DOWN ONE HUNTER ON THIS CREW.
SO GET YOUR BUTTS INSIDE THE BRIEFING ROOM.
IF YOU NEED AN EXTRA BLASTER, I USED TO PARTNER WITH A GUY BY THE NAME OF BOBA FETT.
A REAL TOUGH GUY. YOU'D LIKE HIM.
HMMM. CONTACT HIM AND ARRANGE A RENDEZVOUS.
WHO'S THE BOUNTY?
NO BOUNTY. AN ESCORT JOB.
SCION OF THE MOURNER'S WAIL NEEDS SOME HAND-HOLDING FOR AN ASSASSINATION.
DANGEROUS TO GET ENTANGLED WITH A SYNDICATE. BUT ONE HUNDRED THOUSAND CREDITS MAKE IT WORTH THE STRETCH.
SO HERE'S THE PLA LISTEN UP...

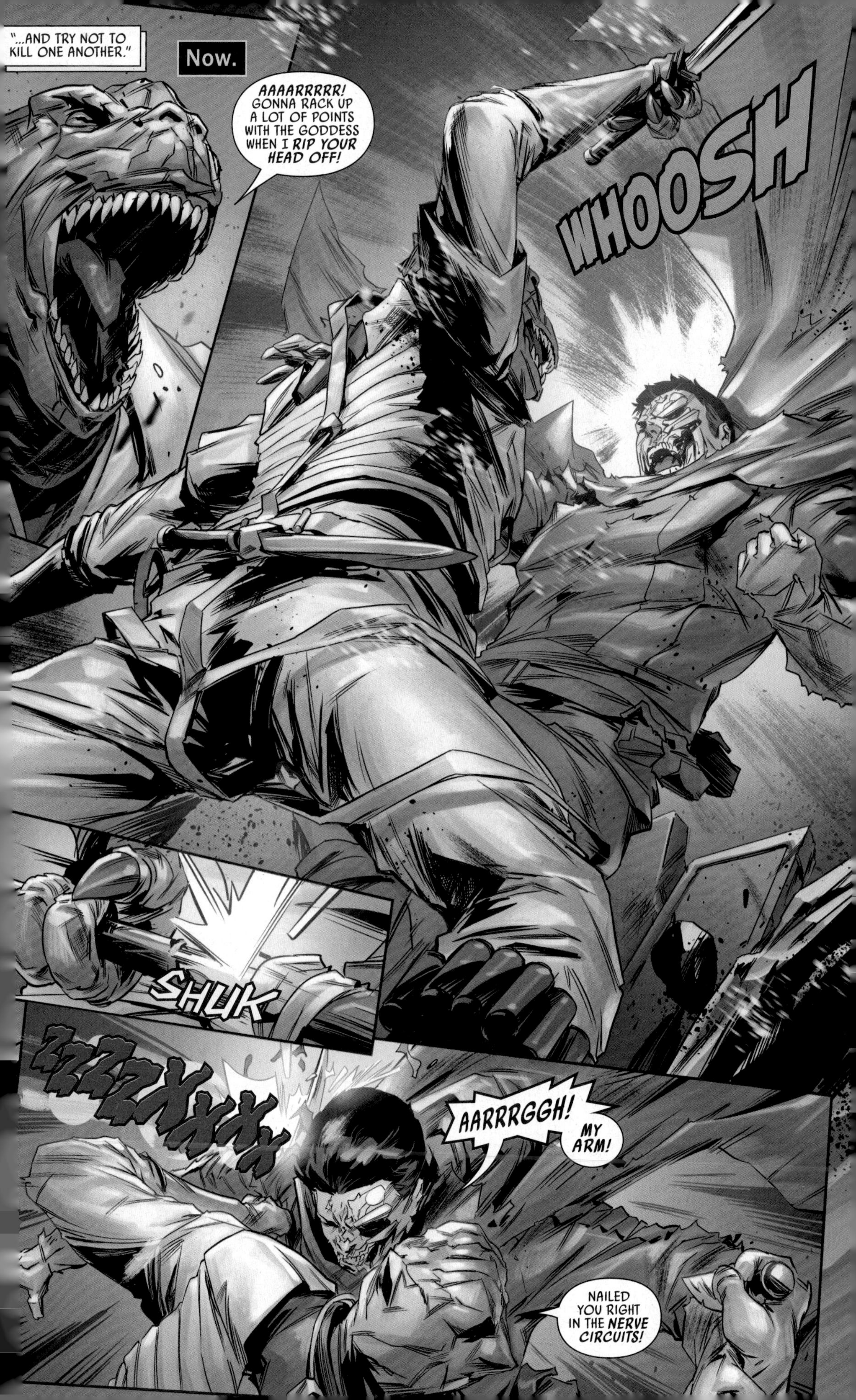
"...AND TRY NOT TO KILL ONE ANOTHER."
Now.
AAAARRRRR! GONNA RACK UP A LOT OF POINTS WITH THE GODDESS WHEN I RIP YOUR HEAD OFF!
WHOOSH
SHUK
ZZZZZXXXXX
AARRRGGH!
MY ARM!
NAILED YOU RIGHT IN THE NERVE CIRCUITS!

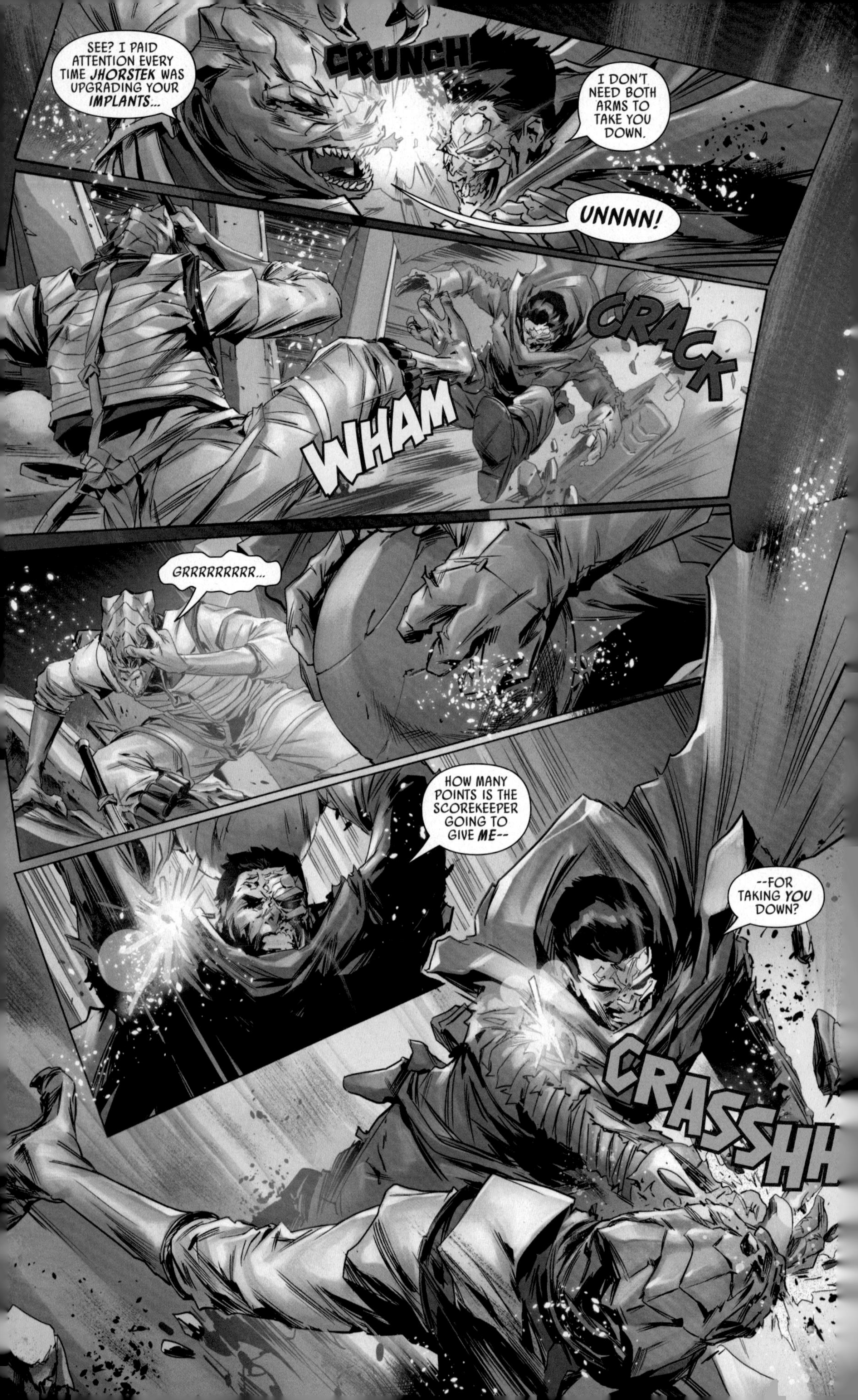
SEE? I PAID ATTENTION EVERY TIME JHORSTEK WAS UPGRADING YOUR IMPLANTS...
CRUNCH
I DON'T NEED BOTH ARMS TO TAKE YOU DOWN.
UNNNN!
CRACK
WHAM
GRRRRRRRRR...
HOW MANY POINTS IS THE SCOREKEEPER GOING TO GIVE ME--
--FOR TAKING YOU DOWN?
CRASSHH

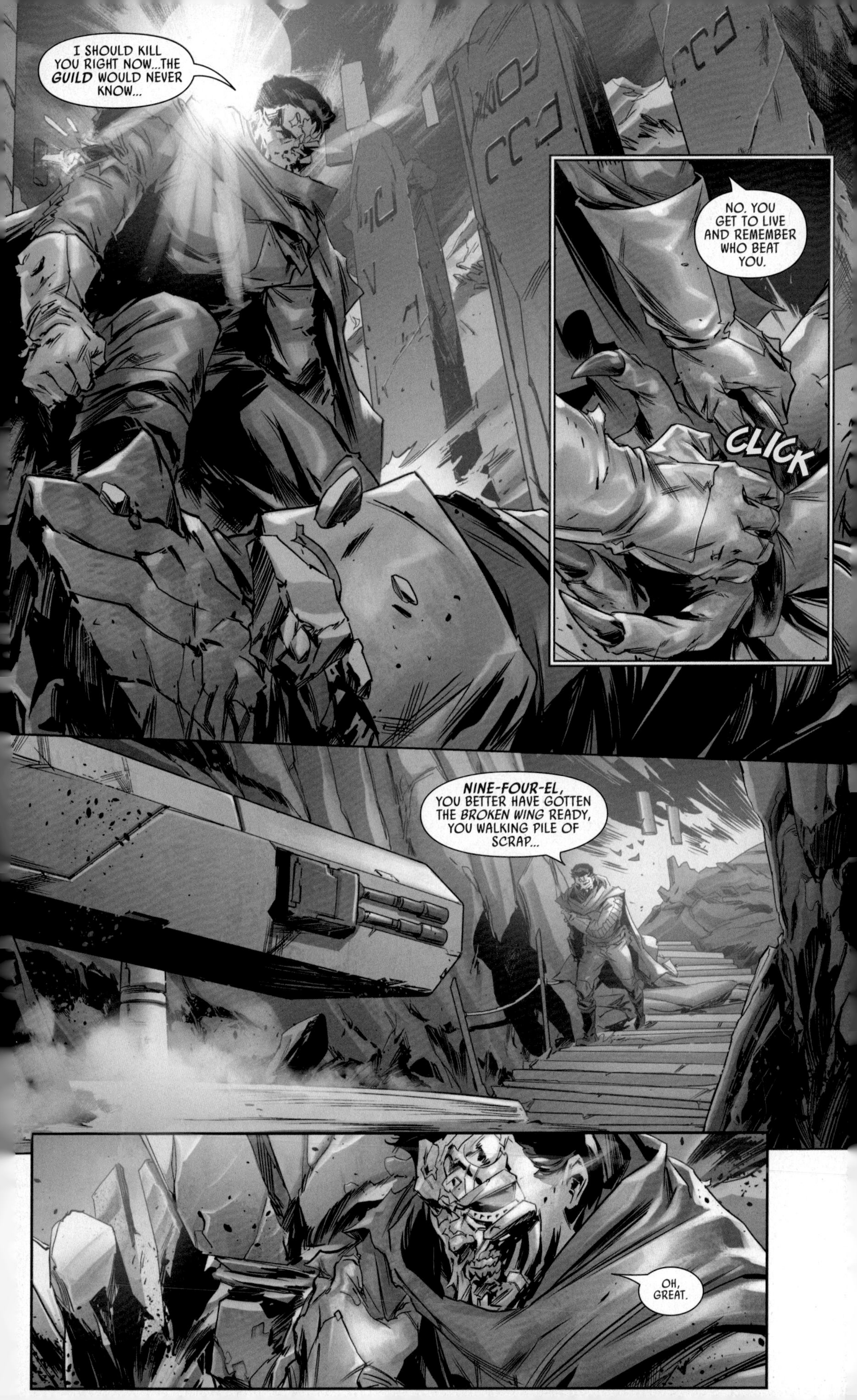
I SHOULD KILL YOU RIGHT NOW...THE GUILD WOULD NEVER KNOW...
NO. YOU GET TO LIVE AND REMEMBER WHO BEAT YOU.
CLICK
NINE-FOUR-EL, YOU BETTER HAVE GOTTEN THE BROKEN WING READY, YOU WALKING PILE OF SCRAP...
OH, GREAT.

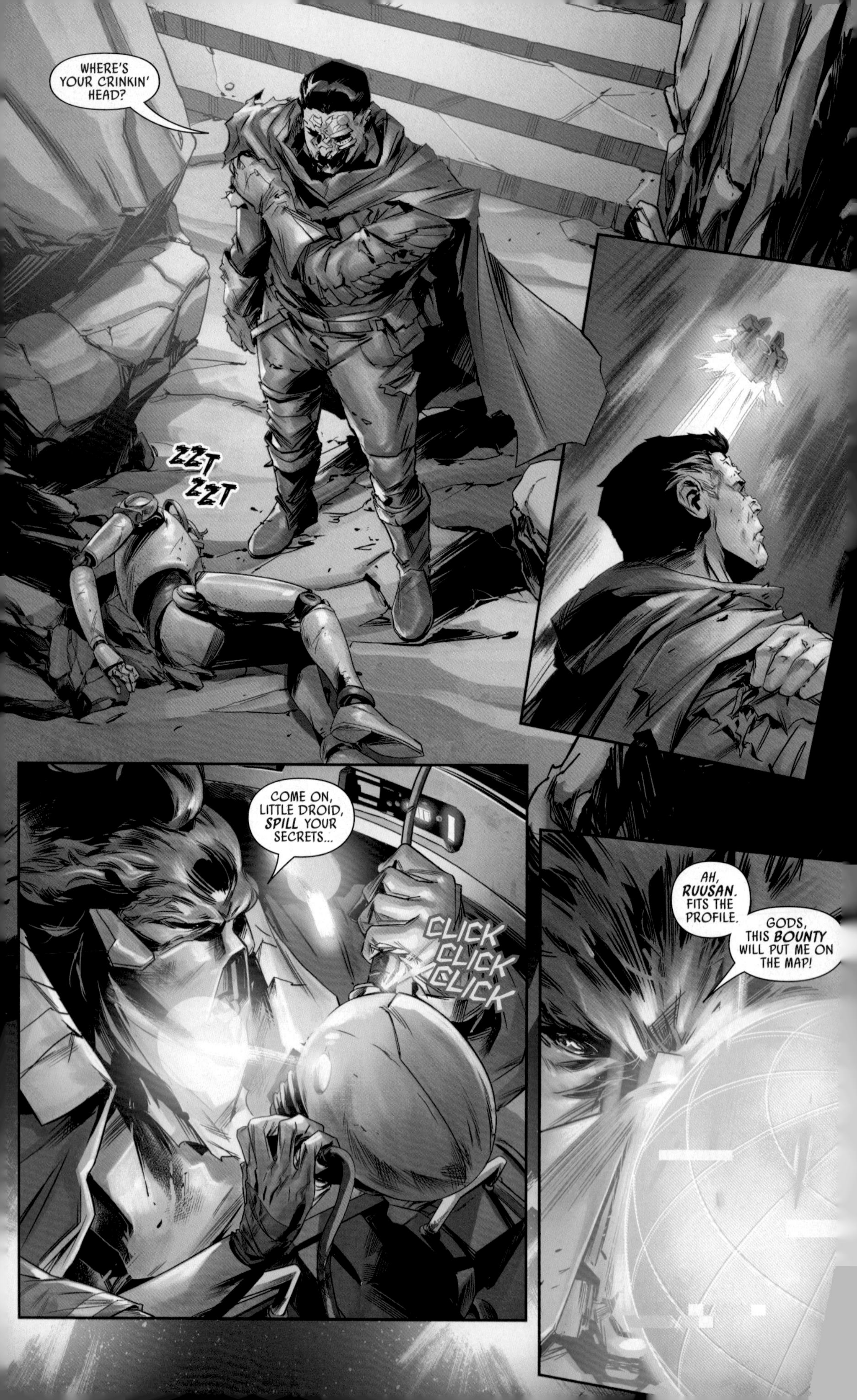
WHERE'S YOUR CRINKIN' HEAD?
ZZT ZZT
COME ON, LITTLE DROID, **SPILL** YOUR SECRETS...
CLICK CLICK CLICK
AH, **RUUSAN**. FITS THE PROFILE.
GODS, THIS **BOUNTY** WILL PUT ME ON THE MAP!

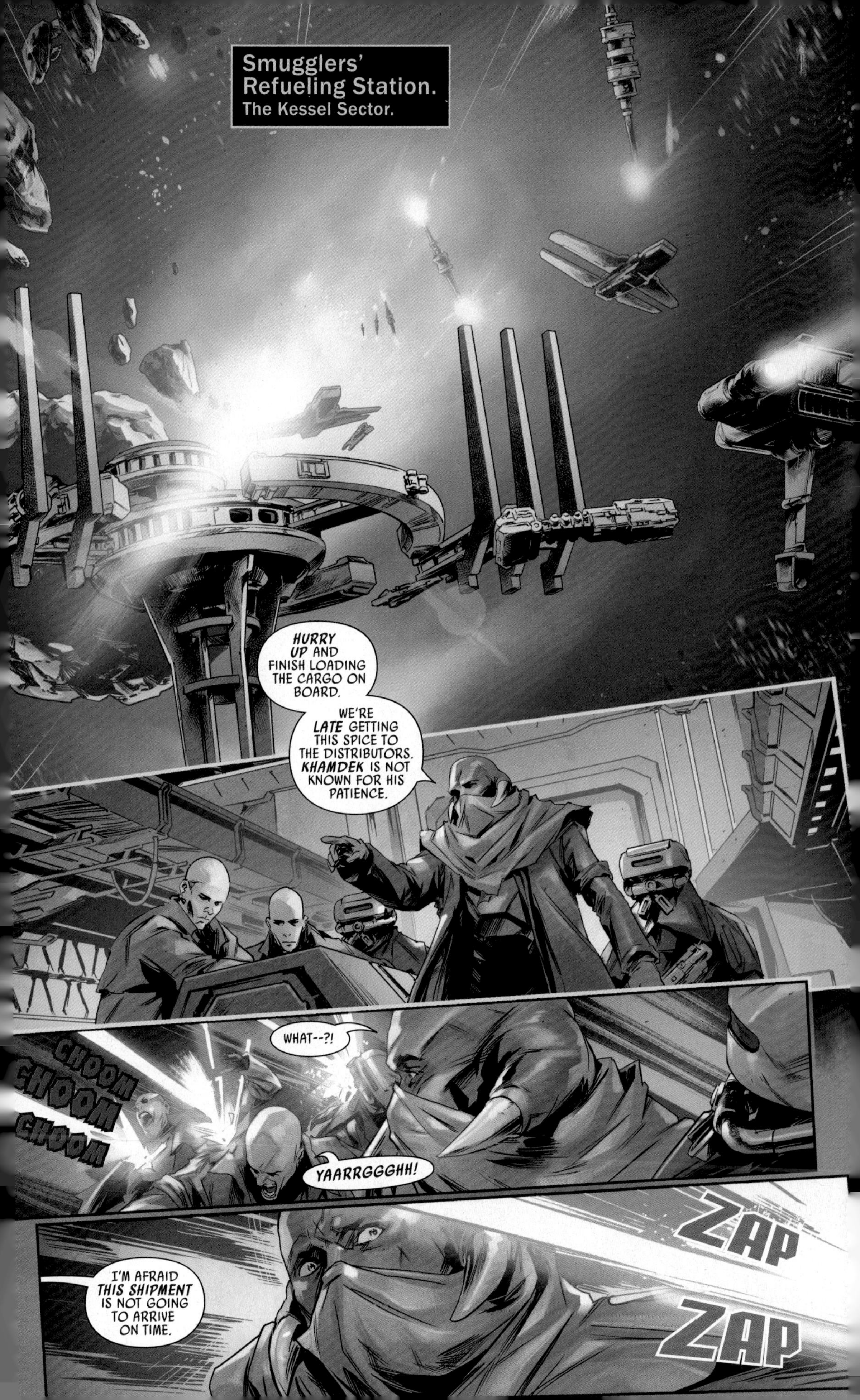
Smugglers' Refueling Station. The Kessel Sector.
HURRY UP AND FINISH LOADING THE CARGO ON BOARD.
WE'RE LATE GETTING THIS SPICE TO THE DISTRIBUTORS. KHAMDEK IS NOT KNOWN FOR HIS PATIENCE.
CHOOM CHOOM CHOOM
WHAT--?!
YAARRGGGHH!
ZAP
ZAP
I'M AFRAID THIS SHIPMENT IS NOT GOING TO ARRIVE ON TIME.

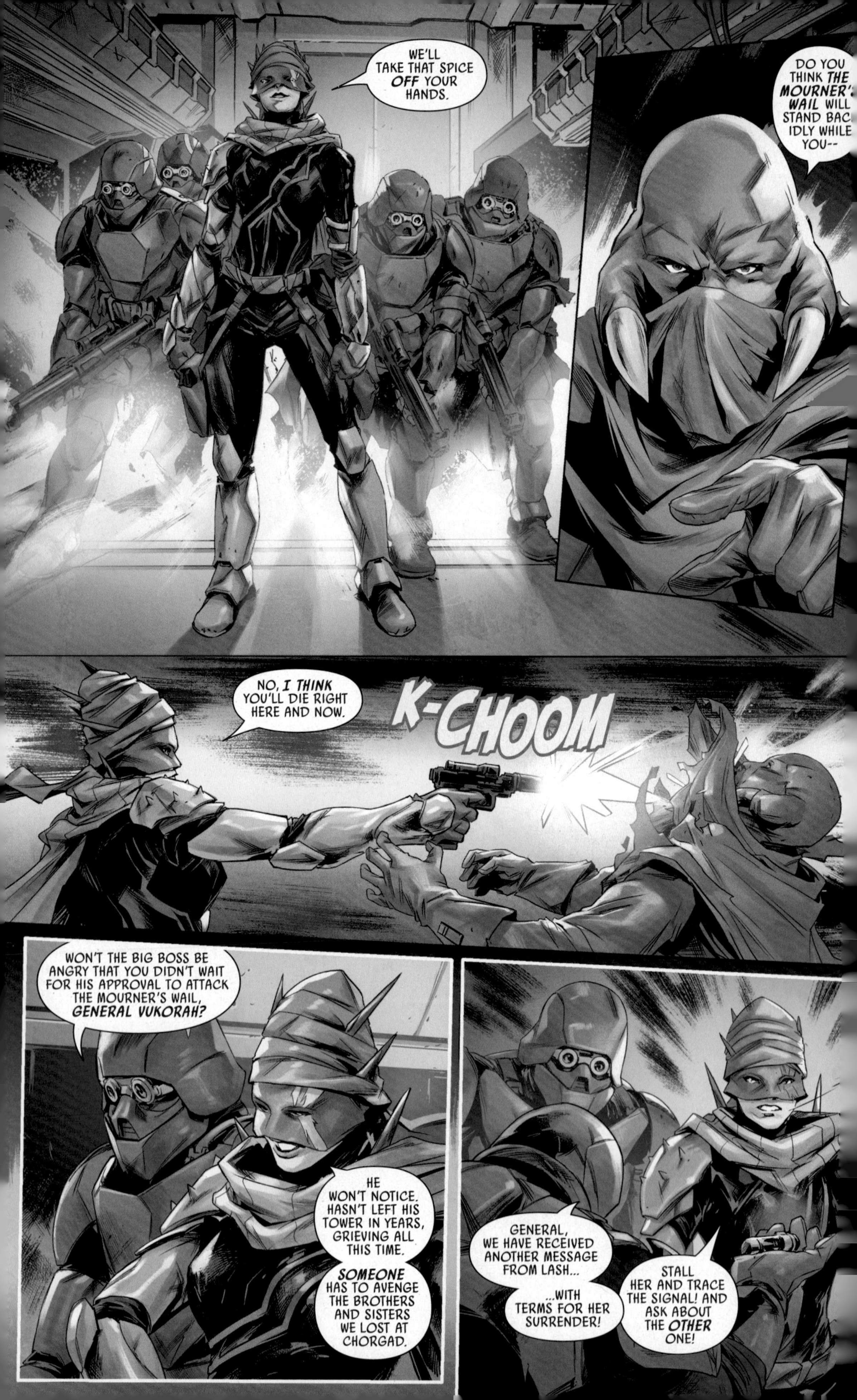
WE'LL TAKE THAT SPICE OFF YOUR HANDS.
DO YOU THINK THE MOURNER'S WAIL WILL STAND BAC IDLY WHILE YOU--
NO, I THINK YOU'LL DIE RIGHT HERE AND NOW.
K-CHOOM
WON'T THE BIG BOSS BE ANGRY THAT YOU DIDN'T WAIT FOR HIS APPROVAL TO ATTACK THE MOURNER'S WAIL, GENERAL VUKORAH?
HE WON'T NOTICE. HASN'T LEFT HIS TOWER IN YEARS, GRIEVING ALL THIS TIME.
SOMEONE HAS TO AVENGE THE BROTHERS AND SISTERS WE LOST AT CHORGAD.
GENERAL, WE HAVE RECEIVED ANOTHER MESSAGE FROM LASH...
...WITH TERMS FOR HER SURRENDER!
STALL HER AND TRACE THE SIGNAL! AND ASK ABOUT THE OTHER ONE!

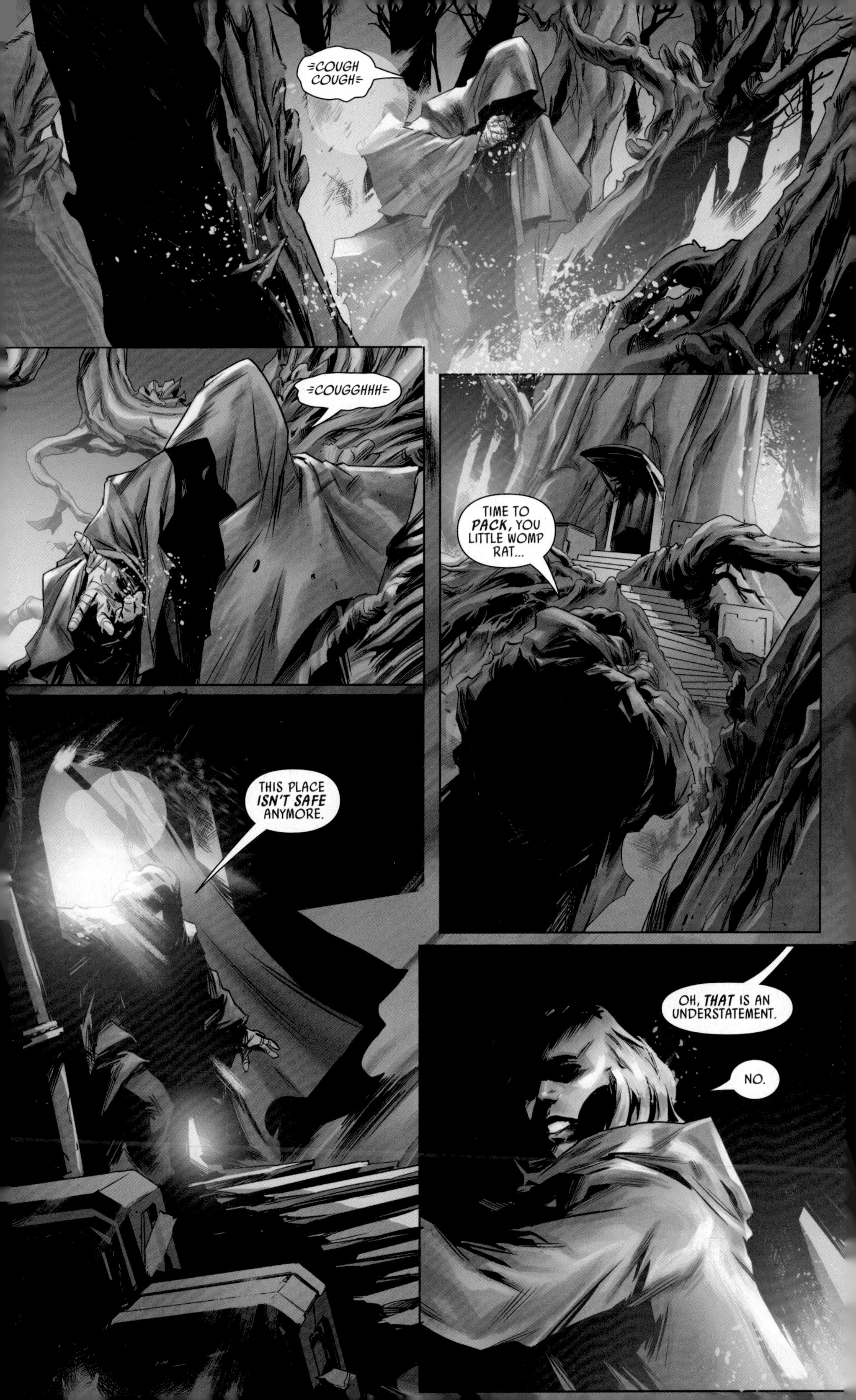
≈COUGH COUGH≈
≈COUGGHHH≈
TIME TO PACK, YOU LITTLE WOMP RAT...
THIS PLACE ISN'T SAFE ANYMORE.
OH, THAT IS AN UNDERSTATEMENT.
NO.

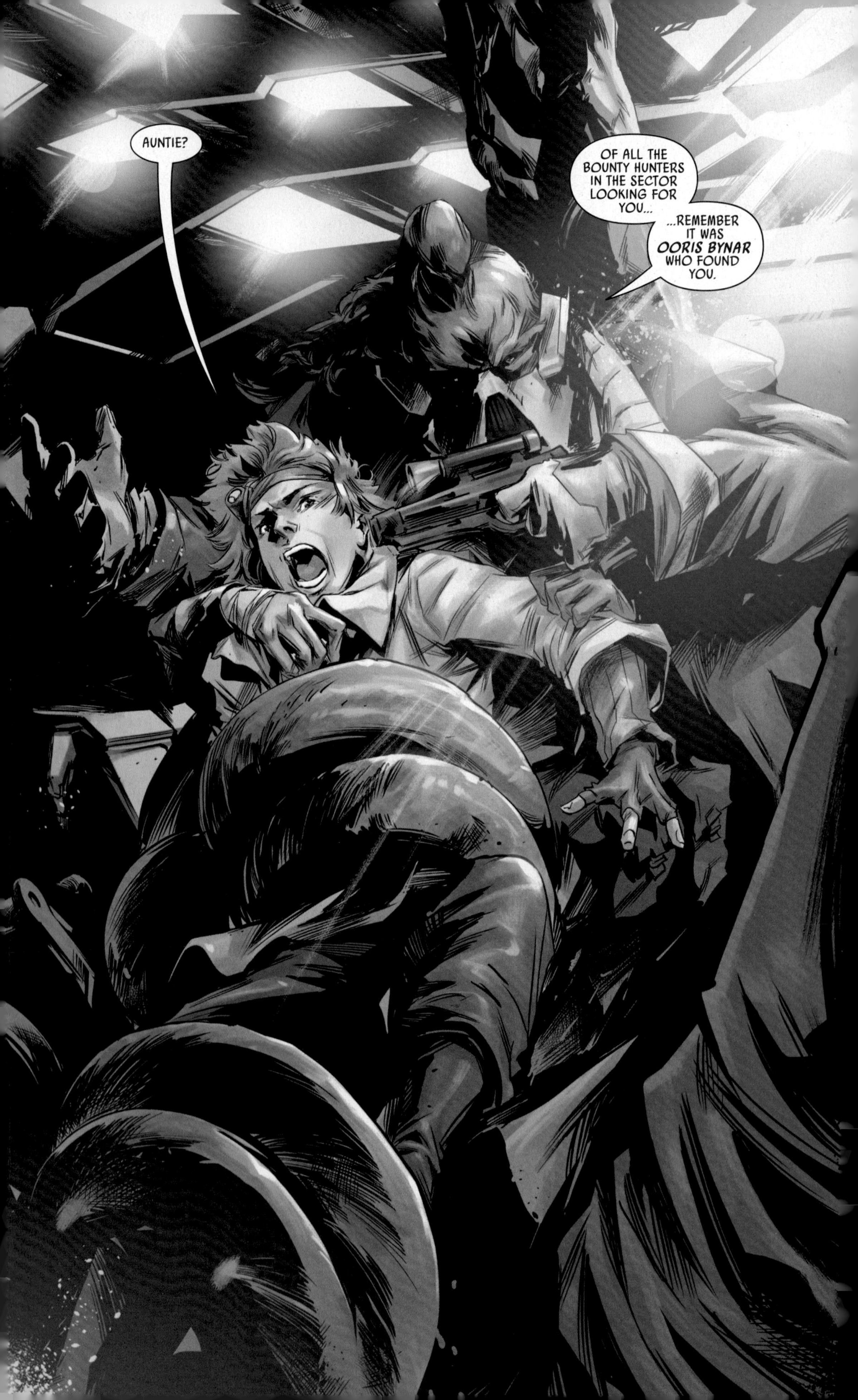
AUNTIE?
OF ALL THE BOUNTY HUNTERS IN THE SECTOR LOOKING FOR YOU...
...REMEMBER IT WAS OORIS BYNAR WHO FOUND YOU.

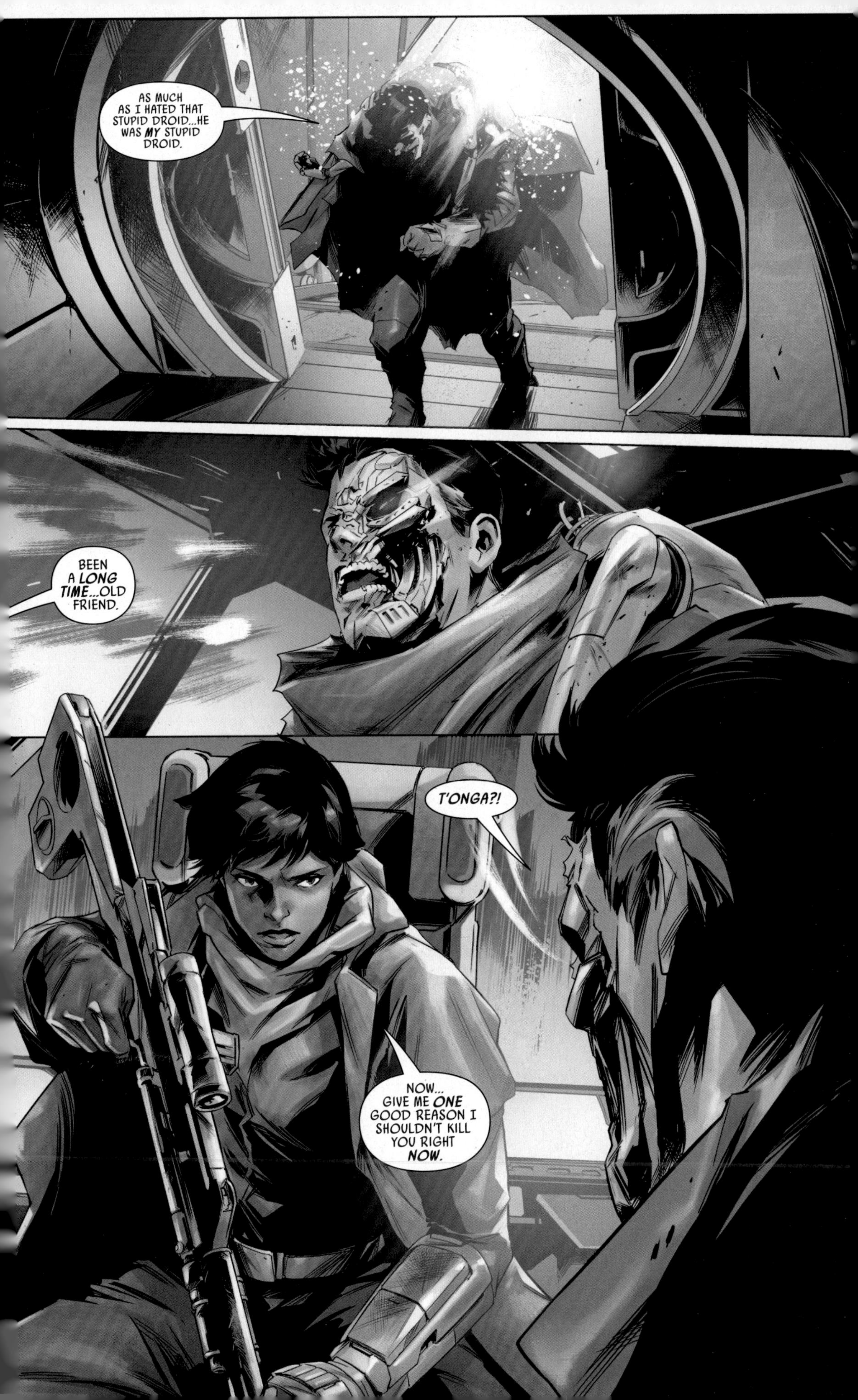
AS MUCH AS I HATED THAT STUPID DROID...HE WAS MY STUPID DROID.
BEEN A LONG TIME...OLD FRIEND.
T'ONGA?!
NOW... GIVE ME ONE GOOD REASON I SHOULDN'T KILL YOU RIGHT NOW.

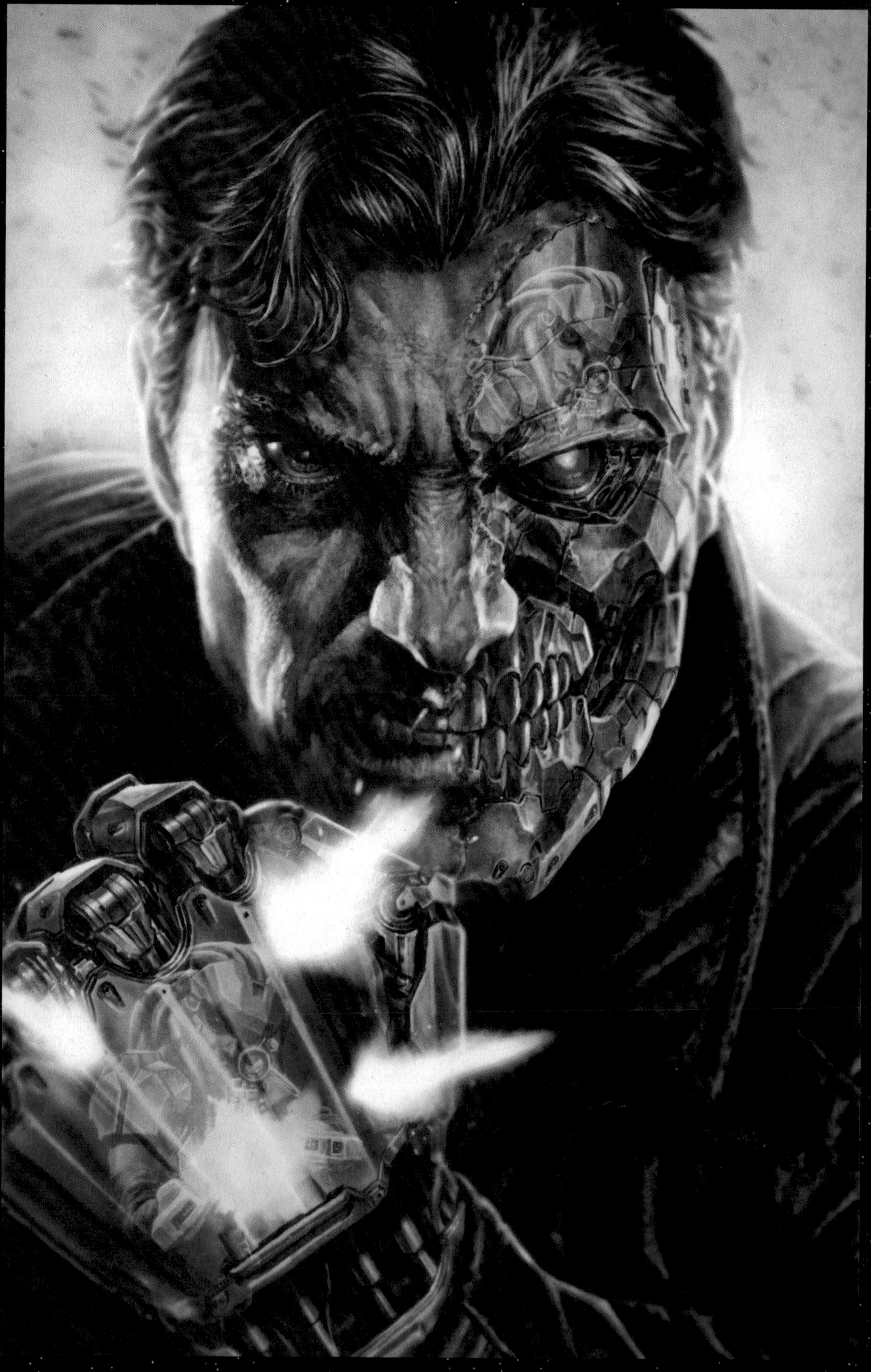

4

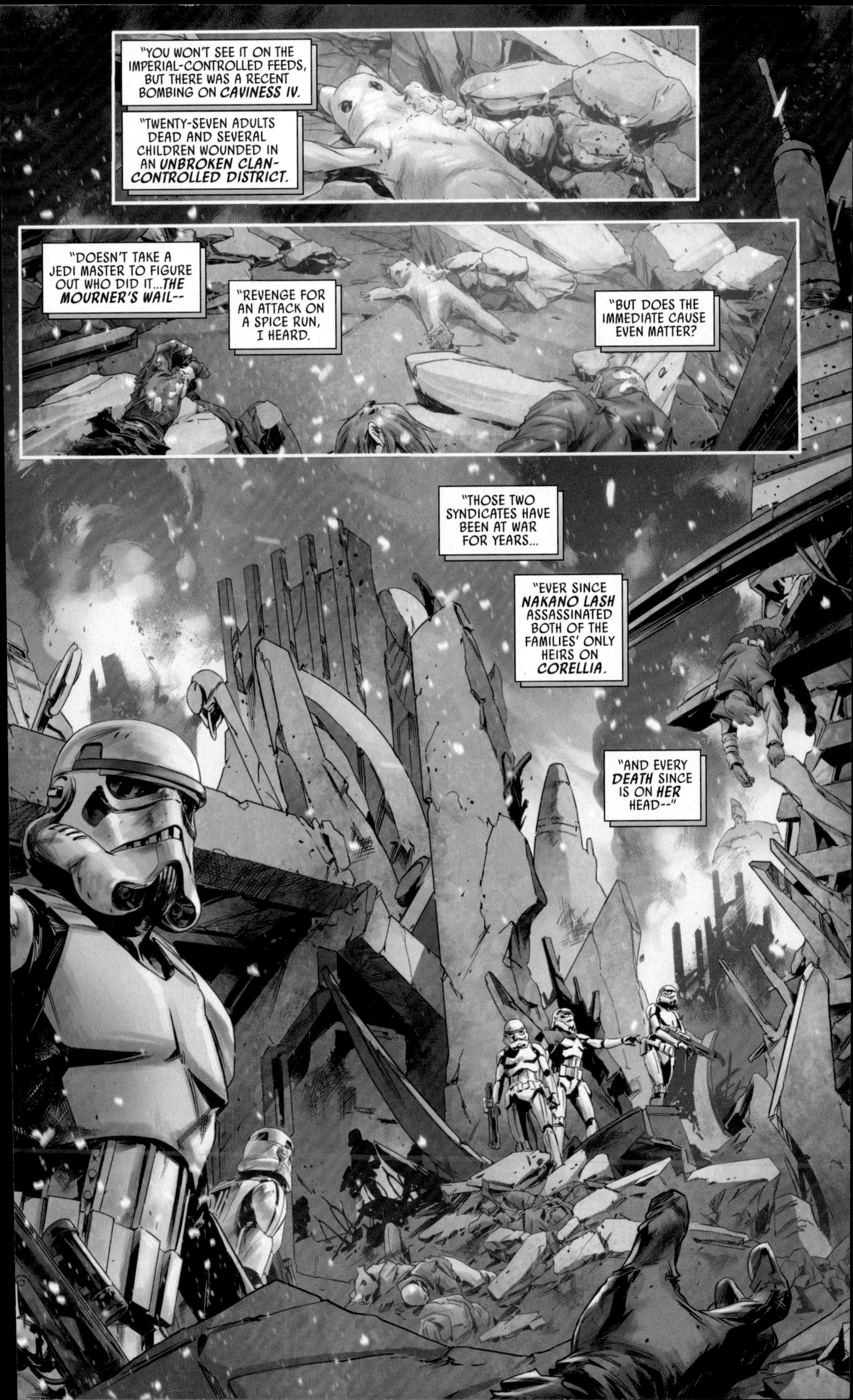
"YOU WON'T SEE IT ON THE IMPERIAL-CONTROLLED FEEDS, BUT THERE WAS A RECENT BOMBING ON CAVINESS IV.
"TWENTY-SEVEN ADULTS DEAD AND SEVERAL CHILDREN WOUNDED IN AN UNBROKEN CLAN-CONTROLLED DISTRICT.
"DOESN'T TAKE A JEDI MASTER TO FIGURE OUT WHO DID IT...THE MOURNER'S WAIL--
"REVENGE FOR AN ATTACK ON A SPICE RUN, I HEARD.
"BUT DOES THE IMMEDIATE CAUSE EVEN MATTER?
"THOSE TWO SYNDICATES HAVE BEEN AT WAR FOR YEARS...
"EVER SINCE NAKANO LASH ASSASSINATED BOTH OF THE FAMILIES' ONLY HEIRS ON CORELLIA.
"AND EVERY DEATH SINCE IS ON HER HEAD--"

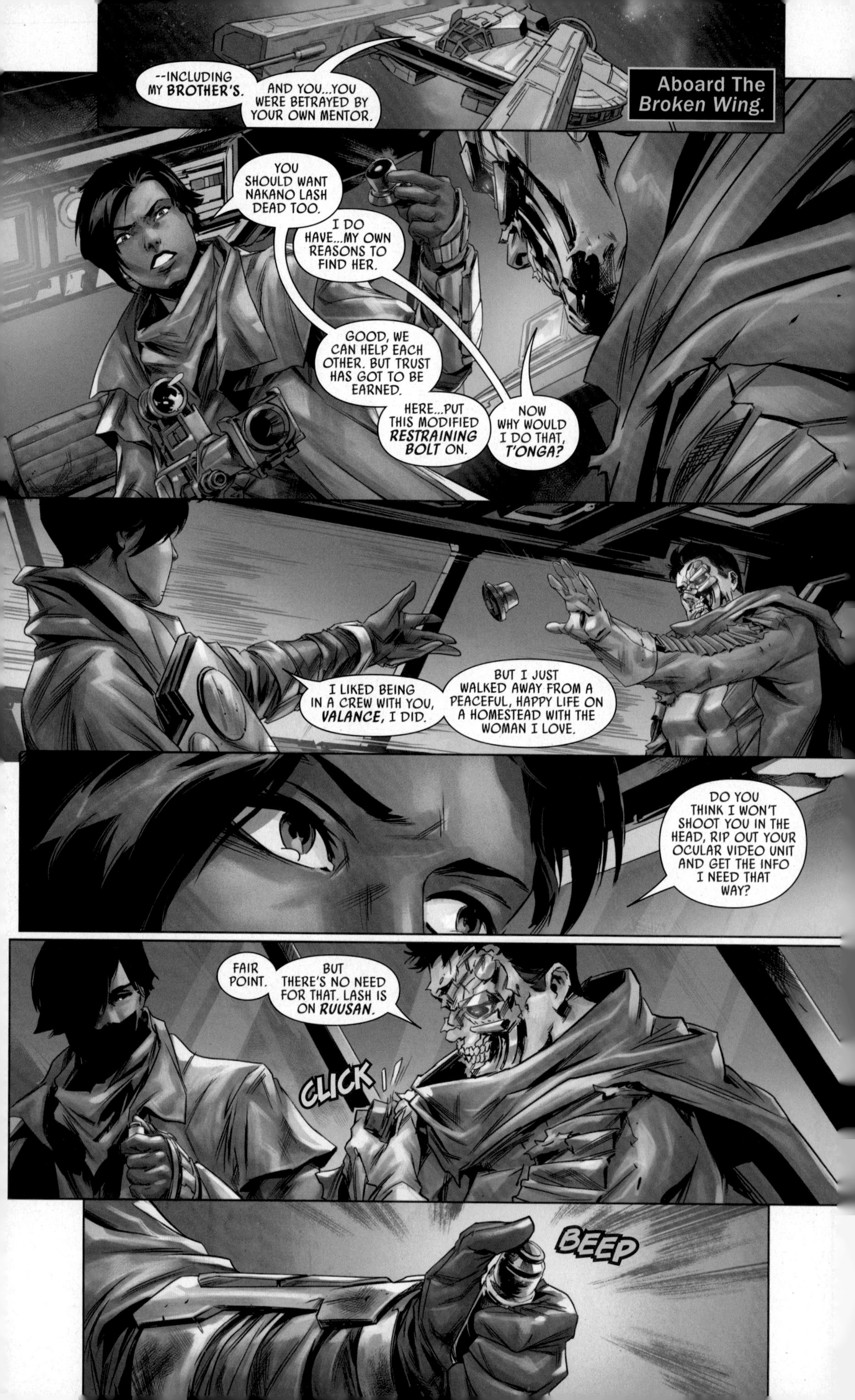
--INCLUDING MY BROTHER'S.
AND YOU...YOU WERE BETRAYED BY YOUR OWN MENTOR.
Aboard The Broken Wing.
YOU SHOULD WANT NAKANO LASH DEAD TOO.
I DO HAVE...MY OWN REASONS TO FIND HER.
GOOD, WE CAN HELP EACH OTHER. BUT TRUST HAS GOT TO BE EARNED.
HERE...PUT THIS MODIFIED RESTRAINING BOLT ON.
NOW WHY WOULD I DO THAT, T'ONGA?
I LIKED BEING IN A CREW WITH YOU, VALANCE, I DID.
BUT I JUST WALKED AWAY FROM A PEACEFUL, HAPPY LIFE ON A HOMESTEAD WITH THE WOMAN I LOVE.
DO YOU THINK I WON'T SHOOT YOU IN THE HEAD, RIP OUT YOUR OCULAR VIDEO UNIT AND GET THE INFO I NEED THAT WAY?
FAIR POINT.
BUT THERE'S NO NEED FOR THAT. LASH IS ON RUUSAN.
CLICK
BEEP

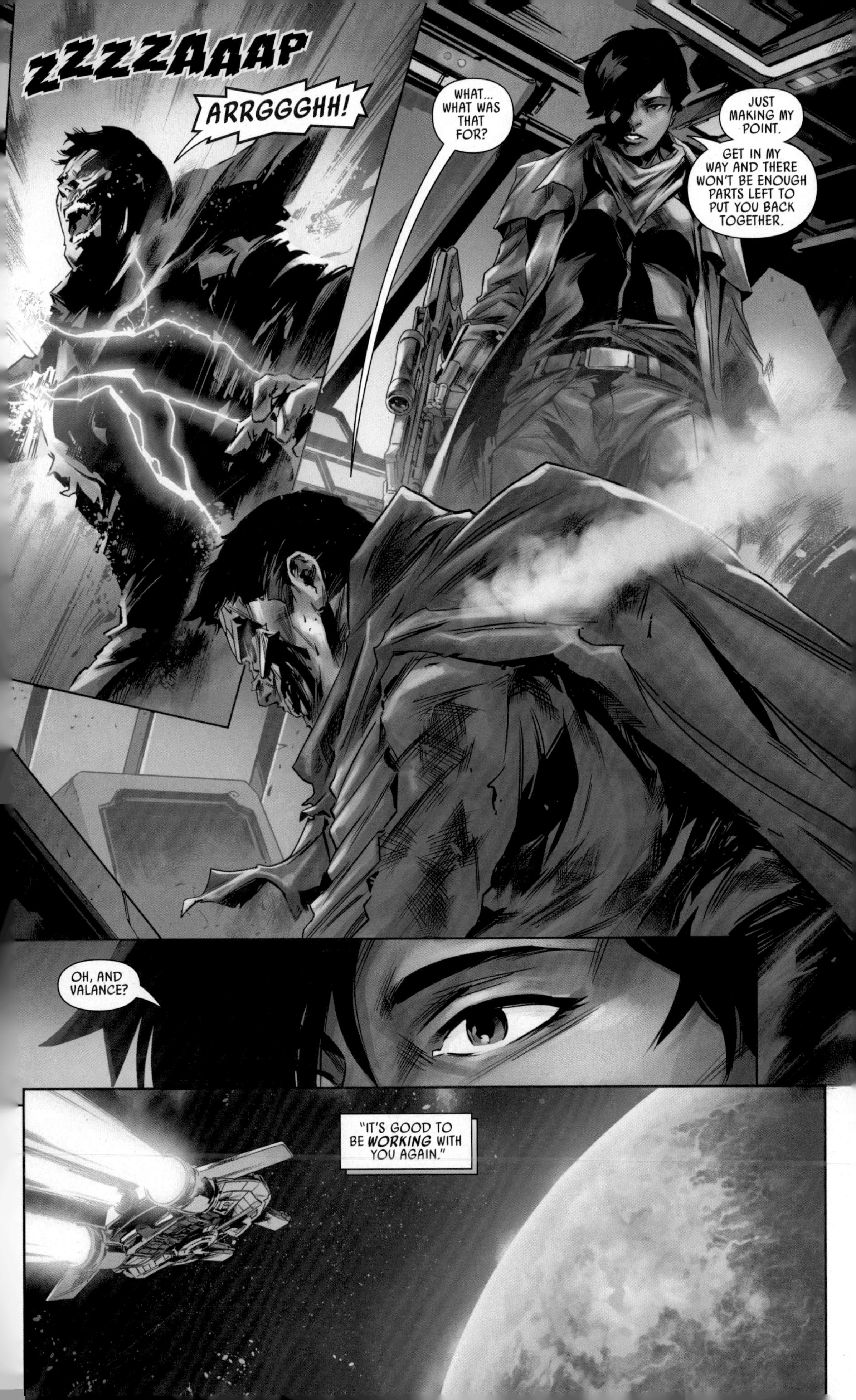
ZZZZZAAAP
ARRGGGHH!
WHAT... WHAT WAS THAT FOR?
JUST MAKING MY POINT.
GET IN MY WAY AND THERE WON'T BE ENOUGH PARTS LEFT TO PUT YOU BACK TOGETHER.
OH, AND VALANCE?
"IT'S GOOD TO BE WORKING WITH YOU AGAIN."

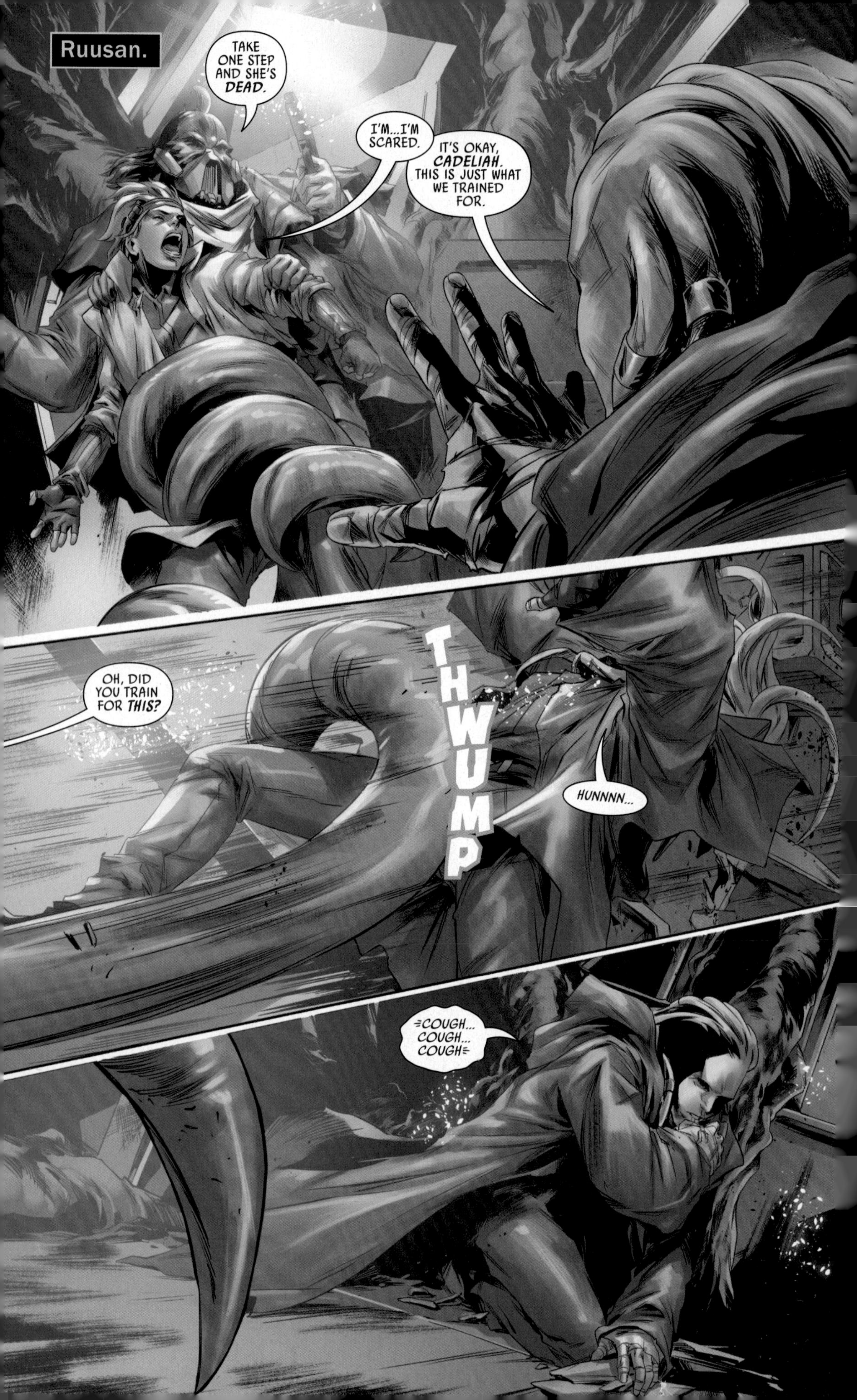
Ruusan.
TAKE ONE STEP AND SHE'S DEAD.
I'M...I'M SCARED.
IT'S OKAY, CADELIAH. THIS IS JUST WHAT WE TRAINED FOR.
OH, DID YOU TRAIN FOR THIS?
THWUMP
HUNNNN...
COUGH... COUGH... COUGH

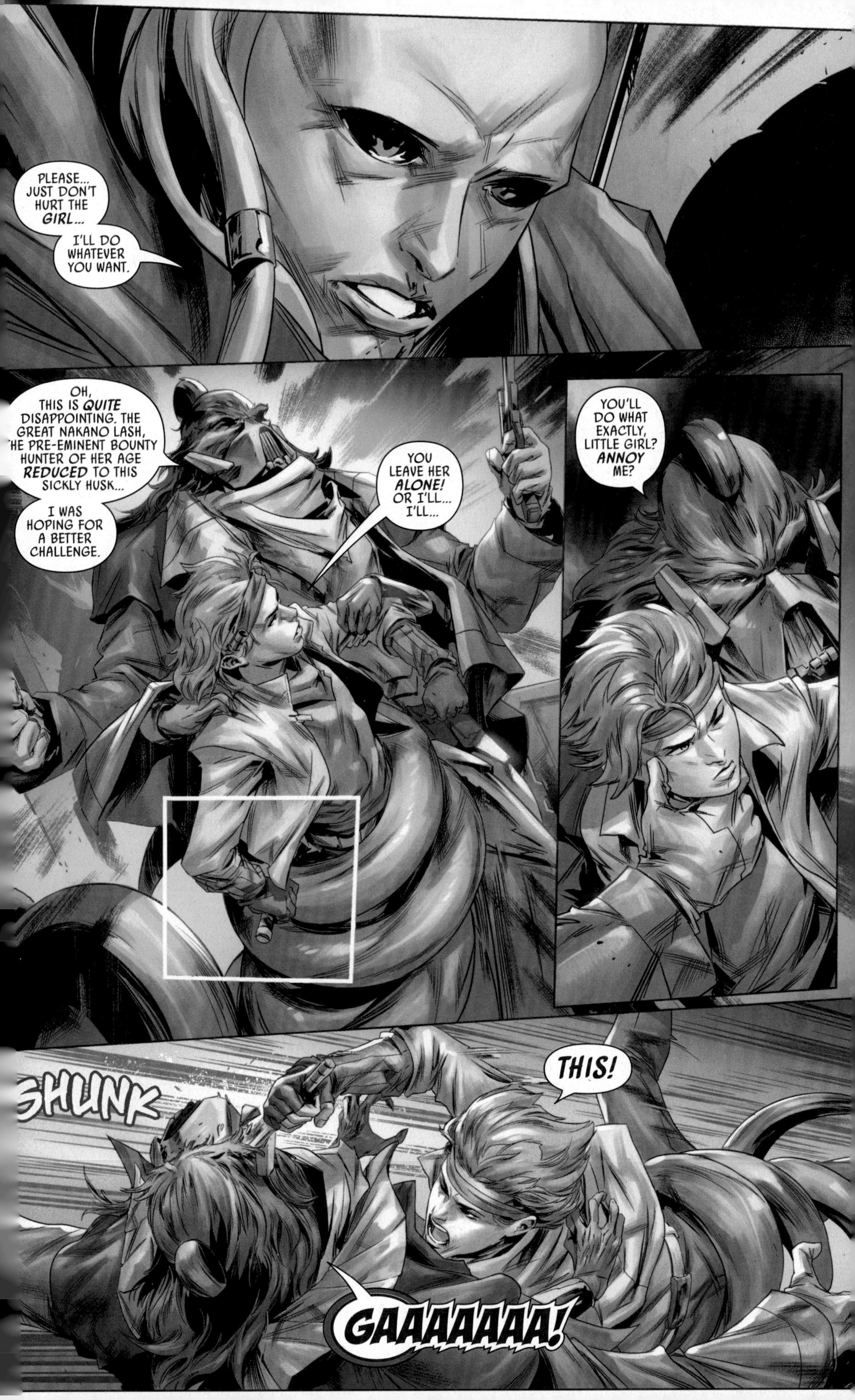
PLEASE... JUST DON'T HURT THE GIRL...
I'LL DO WHATEVER YOU WANT.
OH, THIS IS QUITE DISAPPOINTING. THE GREAT NAKANO LASH, THE PRE-EMINENT BOUNTY HUNTER OF HER AGE REDUCED TO THIS SICKLY HUSK...
I WAS HOPING FOR A BETTER CHALLENGE.
YOU LEAVE HER ALONE! OR I'LL... I'LL...
YOU'LL DO WHAT EXACTLY, LITTLE GIRL? ANNOY ME?
THIS!
SHUNK
GAAAAAAA!

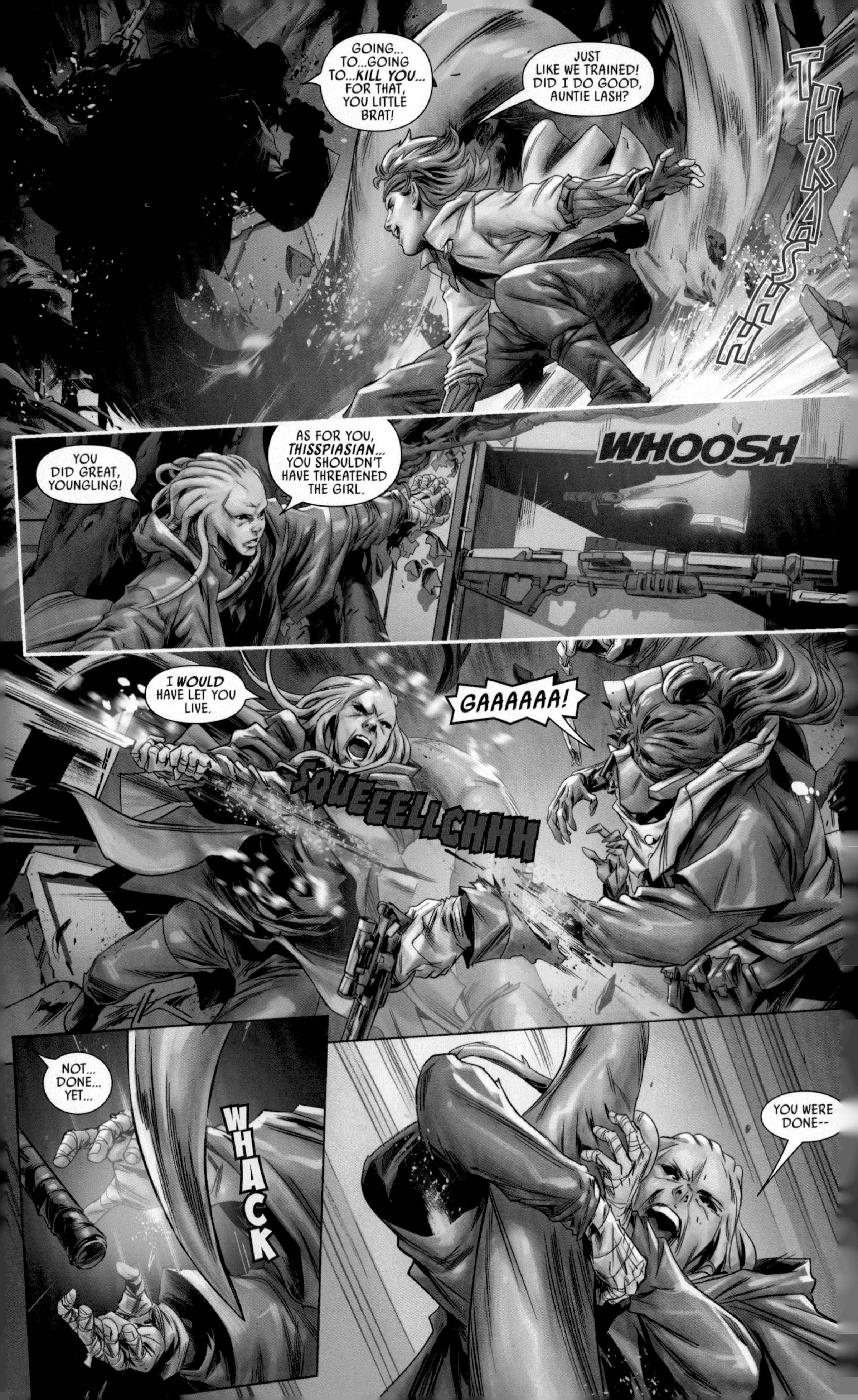
GOING... TO...GOING TO...KILL YOU... FOR THAT, YOU LITTLE BRAT!
JUST LIKE WE TRAINED! DID I DO GOOD, AUNTIE LASH?
THRASHH
YOU DID GREAT, YOUNGLING!
AS FOR YOU, THISSPIASIAN... YOU SHOULDN'T HAVE THREATENED THE GIRL.
WHOOSH
I WOULD HAVE LET YOU LIVE.
GAAAAAA!
SQUEEEELLCHHH
NOT... DONE... YET...
WHACK
YOU WERE DONE--

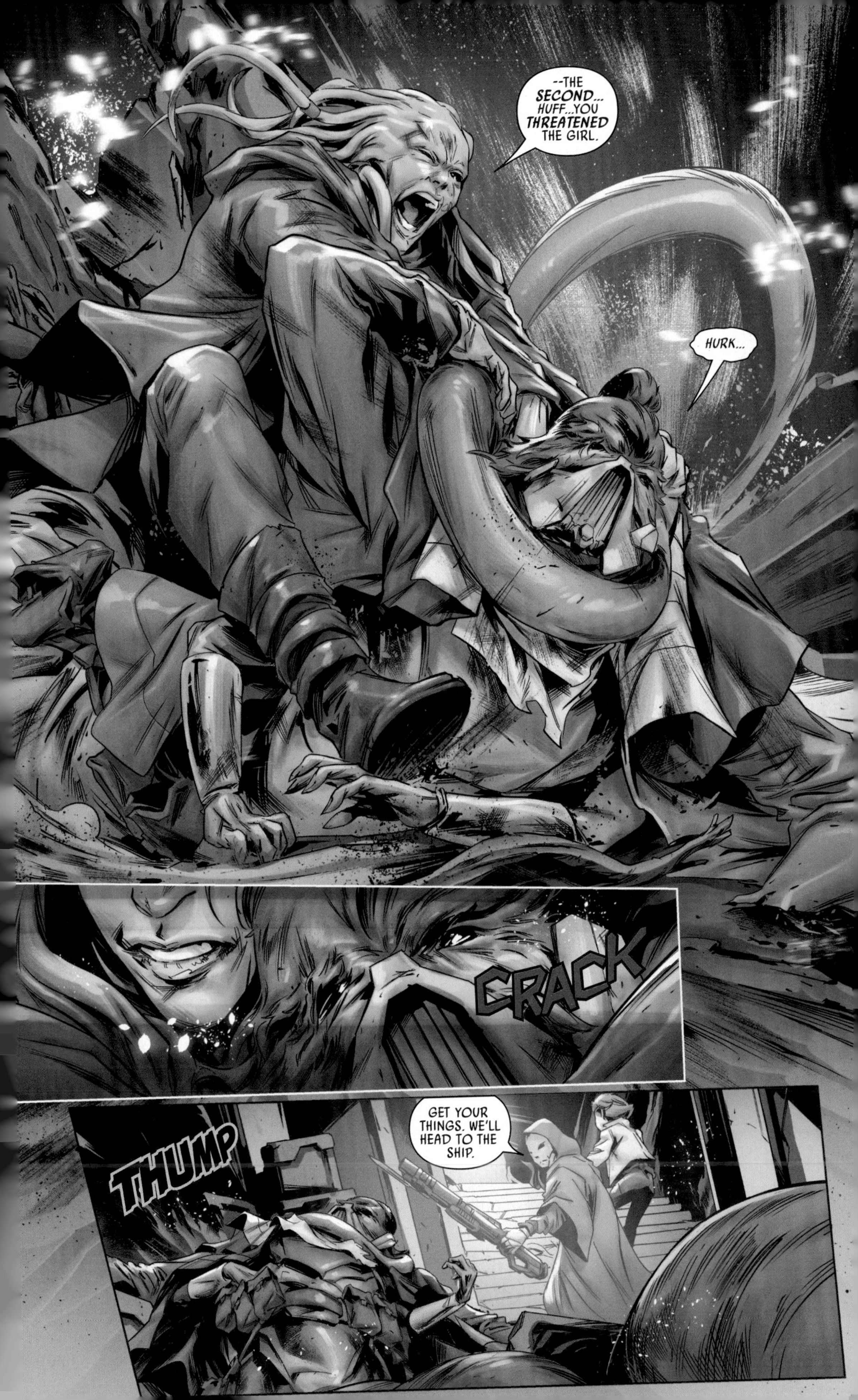

--THE SECOND... HUFF...YOU THREATENED THE GIRL.
HURK...
CRACK
THUMP
GET YOUR THINGS. WE'LL HEAD TO THE SHIP.

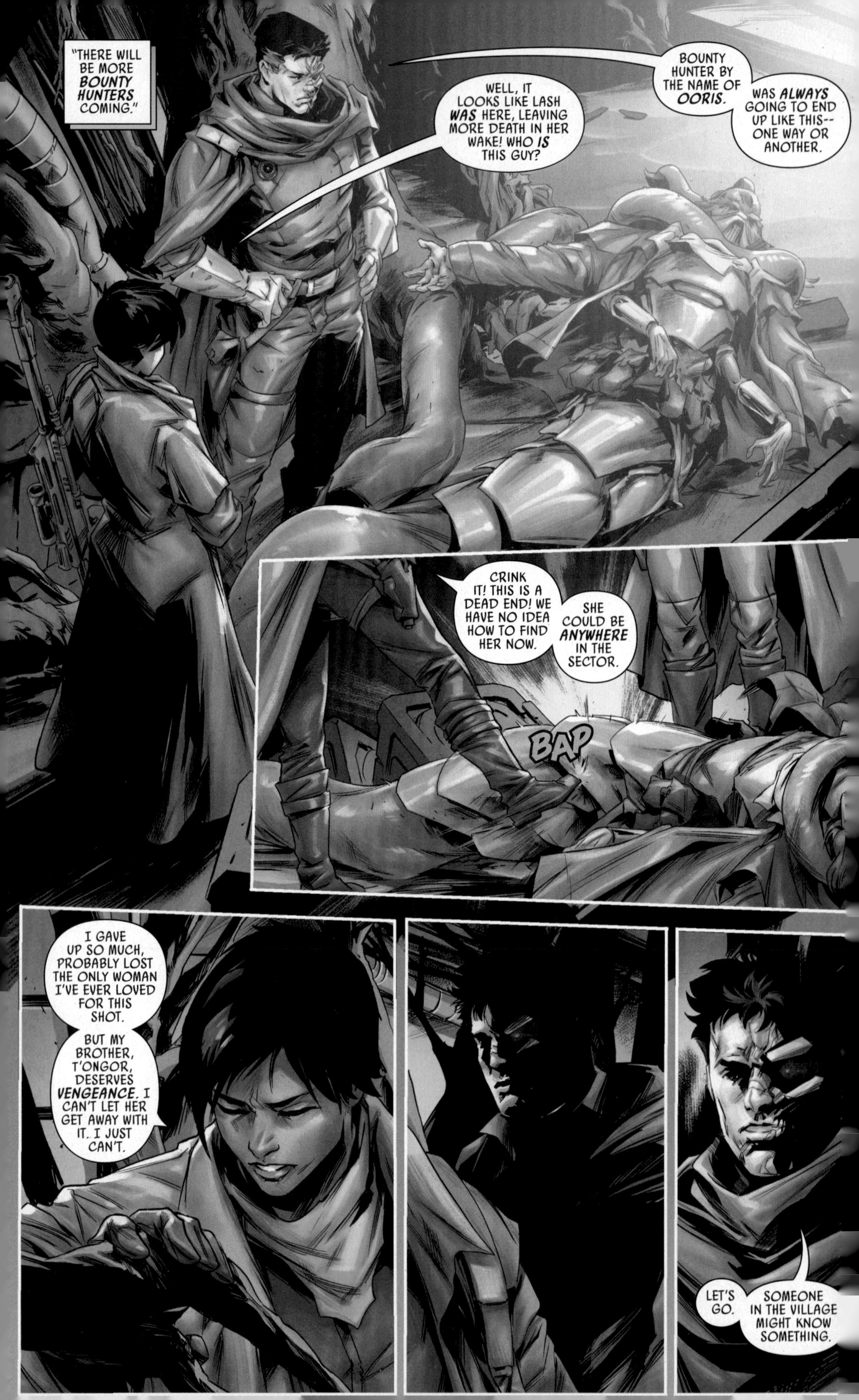
"THERE WILL BE MORE BOUNTY HUNTERS COMING."
WELL, IT LOOKS LIKE LASH WAS HERE, LEAVING MORE DEATH IN HER WAKE! WHO IS THIS GUY?
BOUNTY HUNTER BY THE NAME OF OORIS.
WAS ALWAYS GOING TO END UP LIKE THIS-- ONE WAY OR ANOTHER.
CRINK IT! THIS IS A DEAD END! WE HAVE NO IDEA HOW TO FIND HER NOW.
SHE COULD BE ANYWHERE IN THE SECTOR.
BAP
I GAVE UP SO MUCH, PROBABLY LOST THE ONLY WOMAN I'VE EVER LOVED FOR THIS SHOT.
BUT MY BROTHER, T'ONGOR, DESERVES VENGEANCE. I CAN'T LET HER GET AWAY WITH IT. I JUST CAN'T.
LET'S GO.
SOMEONE IN THE VILLAGE MIGHT KNOW SOMETHING.

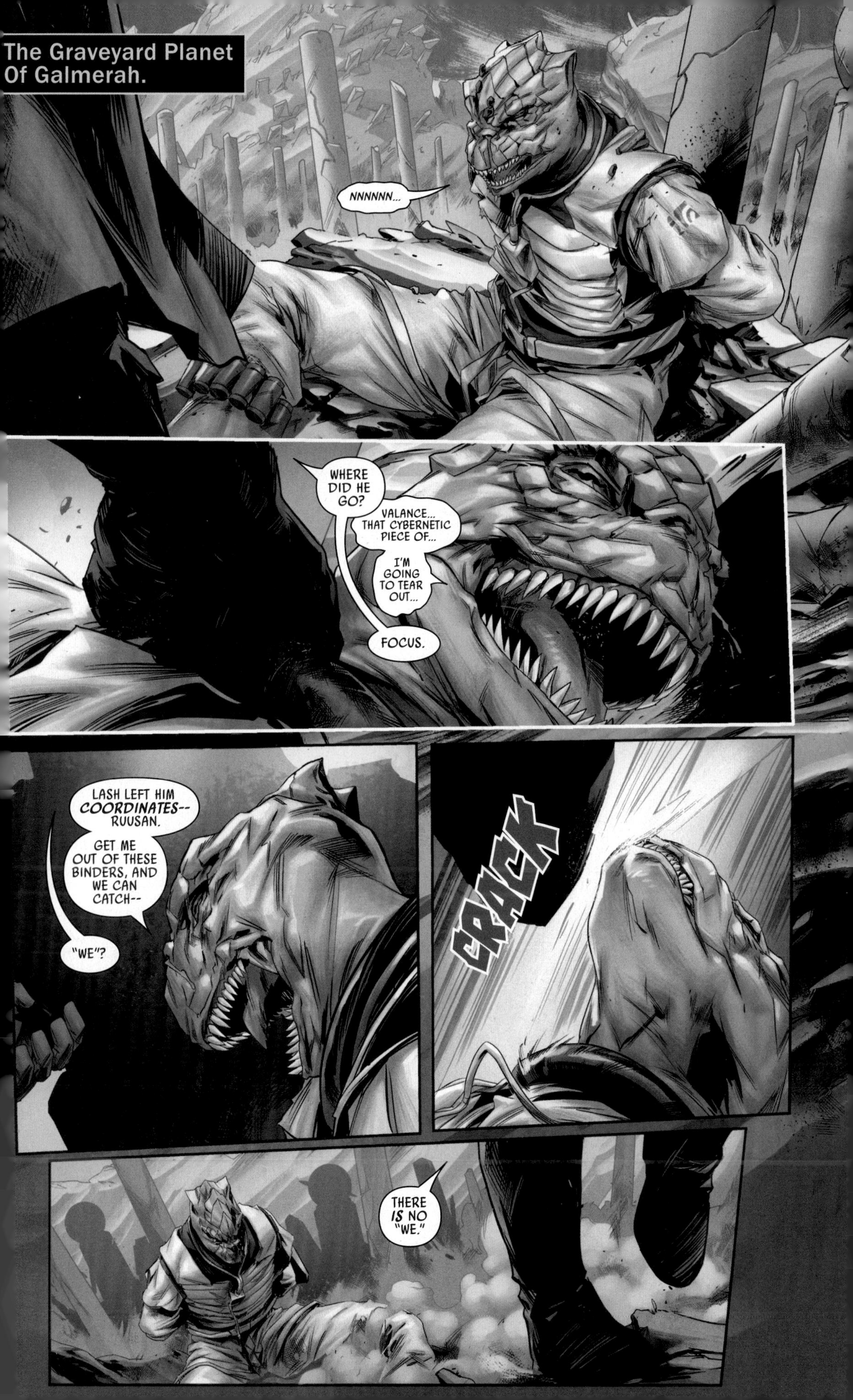
The Graveyard Planet Of Galmerah.
NNNNNN...
WHERE DID HE GO?
VALANCE... THAT CYBERNETIC PIECE OF...
I'M GOING TO TEAR OUT...
FOCUS.
LASH LEFT HIM COORDINATES-- RUUSAN.
GET ME OUT OF THESE BINDERS, AND WE CAN CATCH--
"WE"?
CRACK
THERE IS NO "WE."

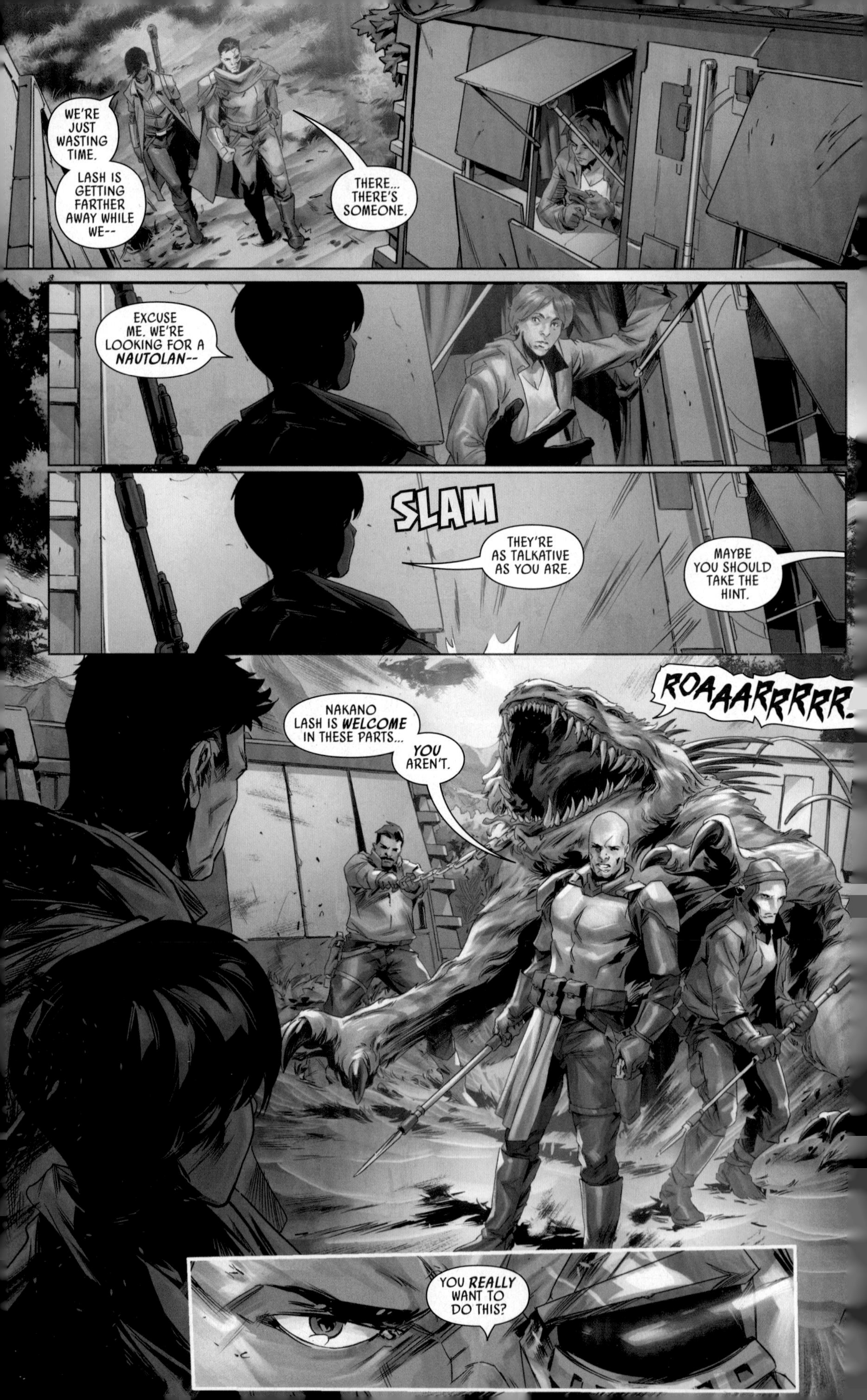
WE'RE JUST WASTING TIME.
LASH IS GETTING FARTHER AWAY WHILE WE--
THERE... THERE'S SOMEONE.
EXCUSE ME. WE'RE LOOKING FOR A NAUTOLAN--
SLAM
THEY'RE AS TALKATIVE AS YOU ARE.
MAYBE YOU SHOULD TAKE THE HINT.
NAKANO LASH IS WELCOME IN THESE PARTS...
YOU AREN'T.
ROAAARRRRR
YOU REALLY WANT TO DO THIS?

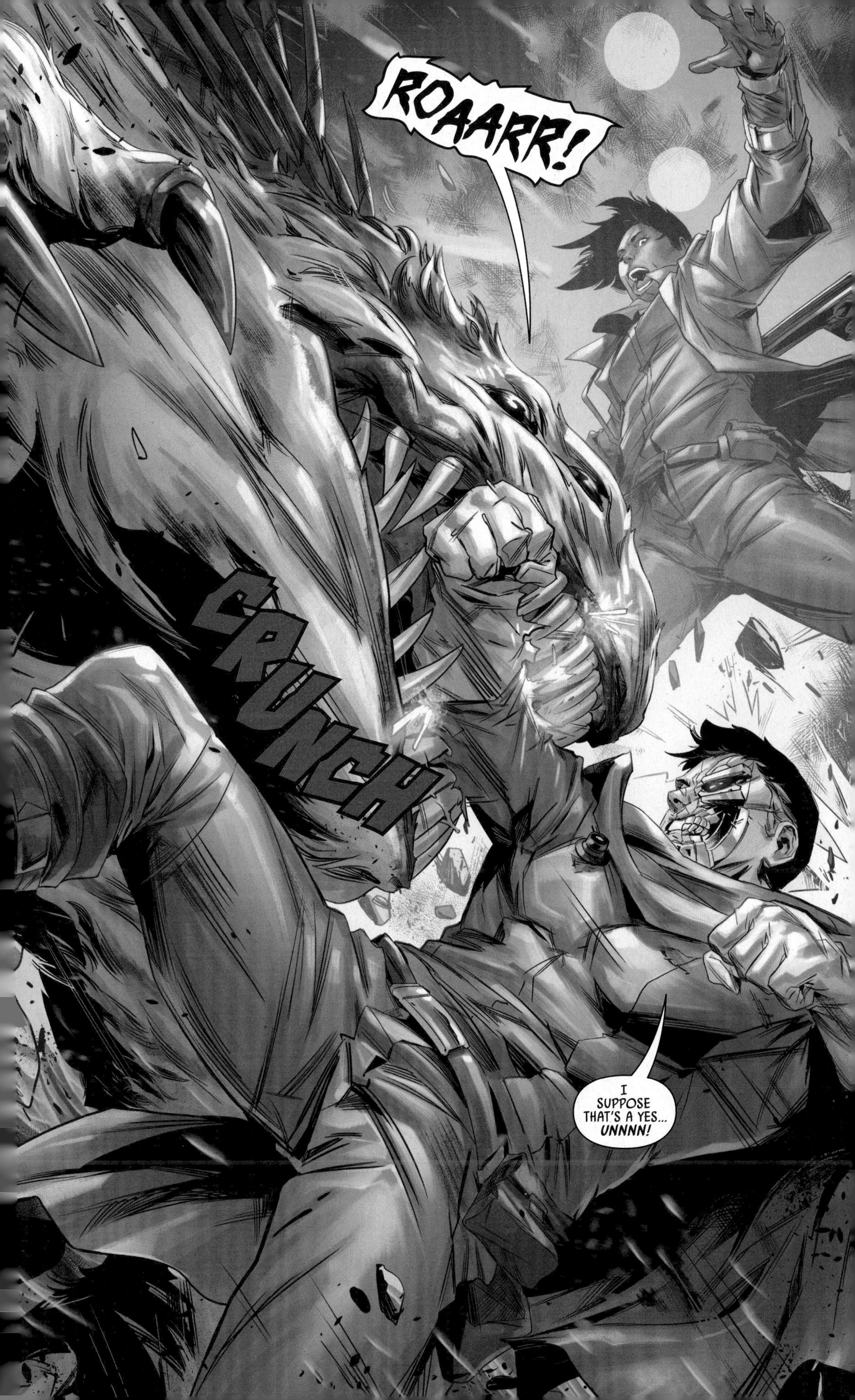
ROAARR!
CRUNCH
I SUPPOSE THAT'S A YES... UNNNN!

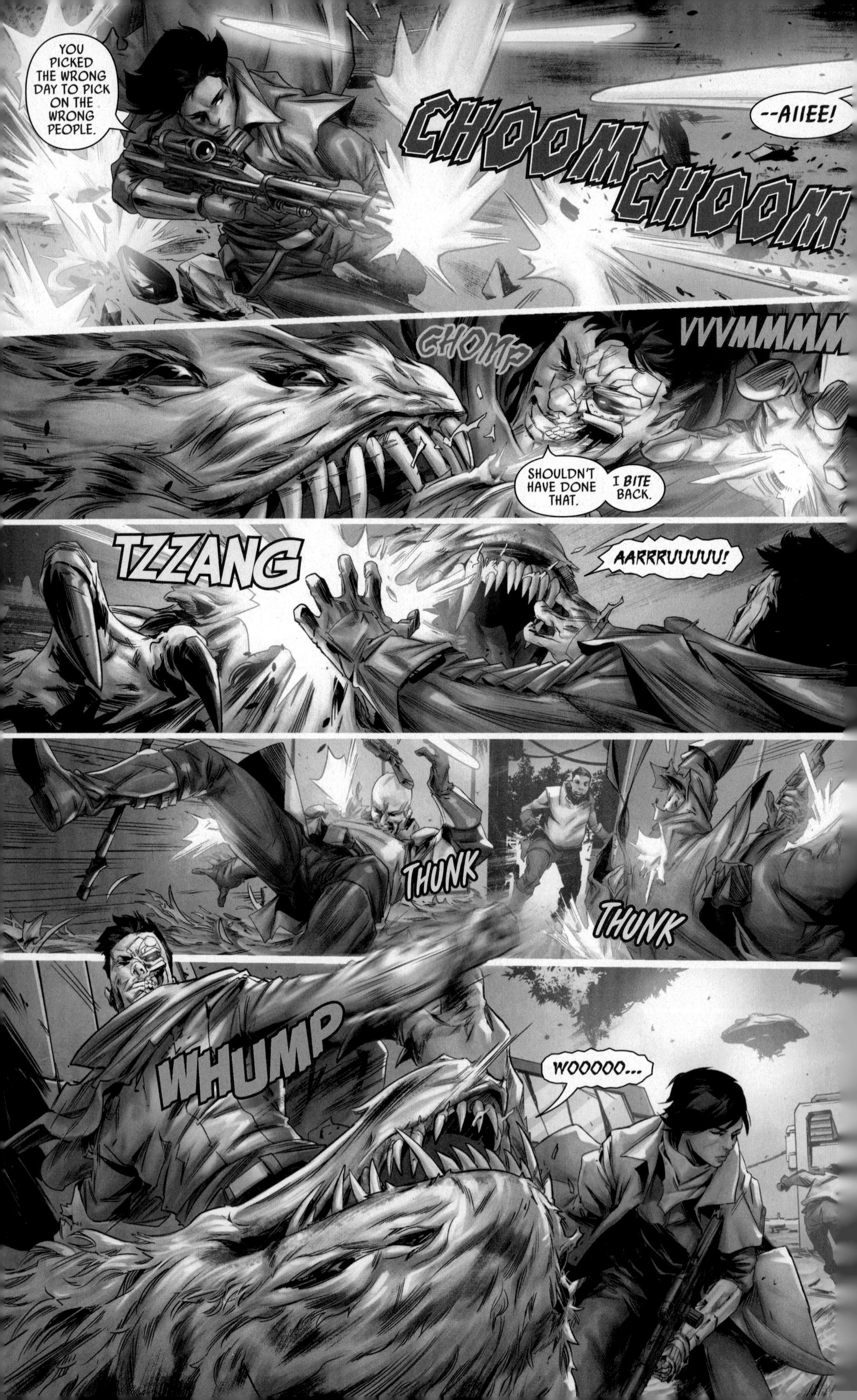
YOU PICKED THE WRONG DAY TO PICK ON THE WRONG PEOPLE.
CHOOM CHOOM
--AIIEE!
CHOMP
VVVMMMMM
SHOULDN'T HAVE DONE THAT.
I BITE BACK.
TZZANG
AARRRUUUUU!
THUNK
THUNK
WHUMP
WOOOOO...

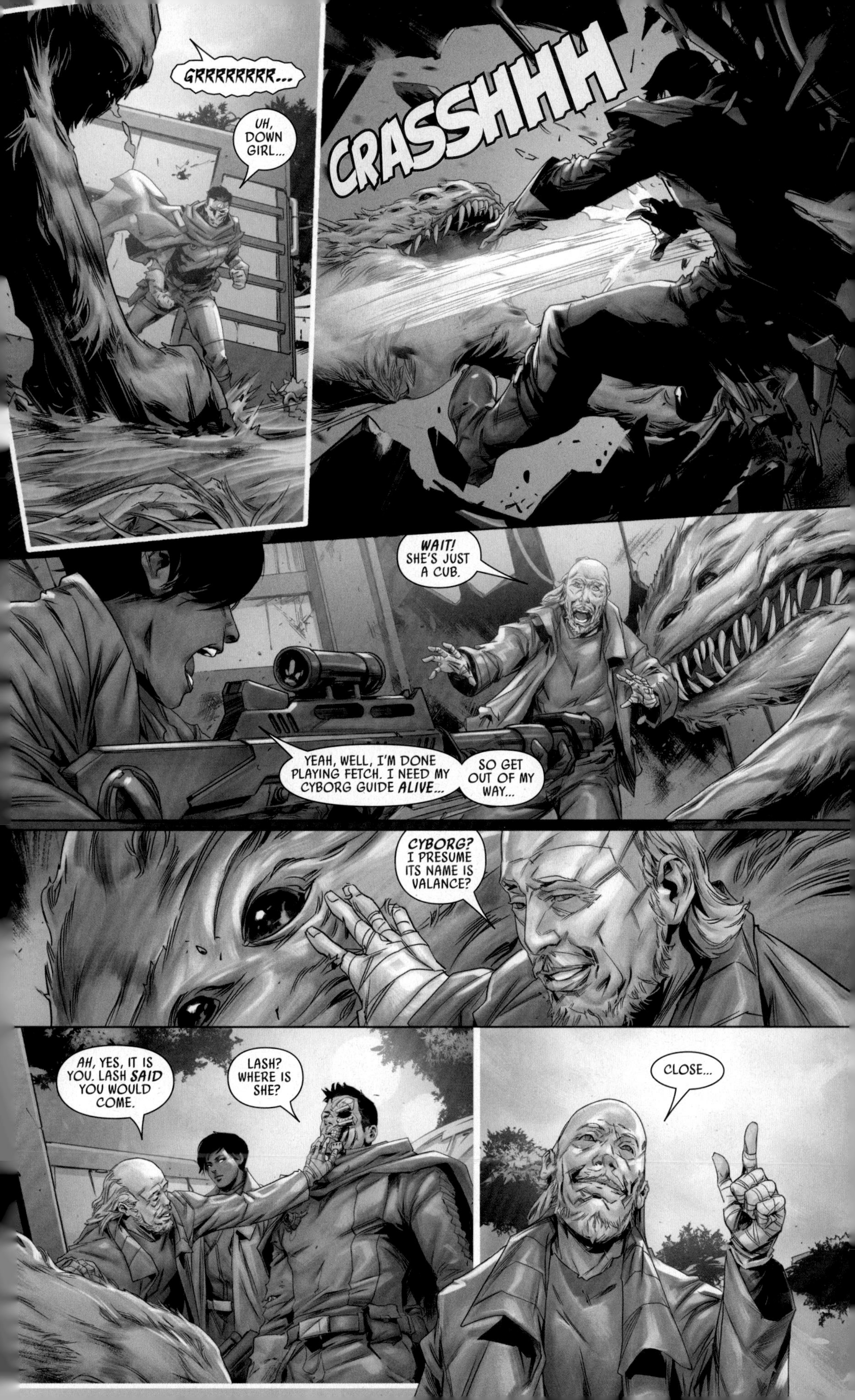
GRRRRRRRR...
UH, DOWN GIRL...
CRASSHHH
WAIT! SHE'S JUST A CUB.
YEAH, WELL, I'M DONE PLAYING FETCH. I NEED MY CYBORG GUIDE ALIVE...
SO GET OUT OF MY WAY...
CYBORG? I PRESUME ITS NAME IS VALANCE?
AH, YES, IT IS YOU. LASH SAID YOU WOULD COME.
LASH? WHERE IS SHE?
CLOSE...

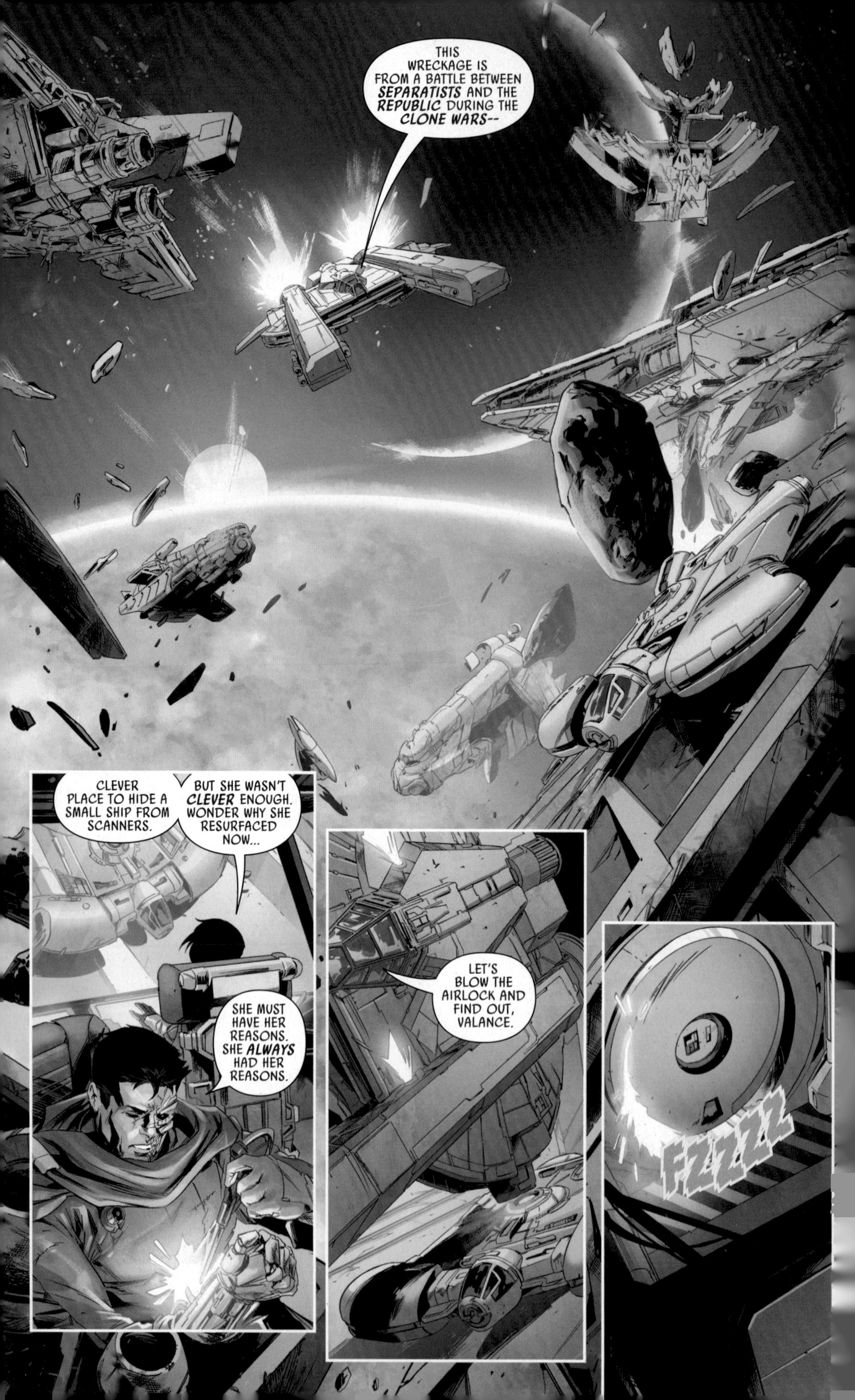
THIS WRECKAGE IS FROM A BATTLE BETWEEN SEPARATISTS AND THE REPUBLIC DURING THE CLONE WARS--
CLEVER PLACE TO HIDE A SMALL SHIP FROM SCANNERS.
BUT SHE WASN'T CLEVER ENOUGH. WONDER WHY SHE RESURFACED NOW...
SHE MUST HAVE HER REASONS. SHE ALWAYS HAD HER REASONS.
LET'S BLOW THE AIRLOCK AND FIND OUT, VALANCE.
FZZZZ

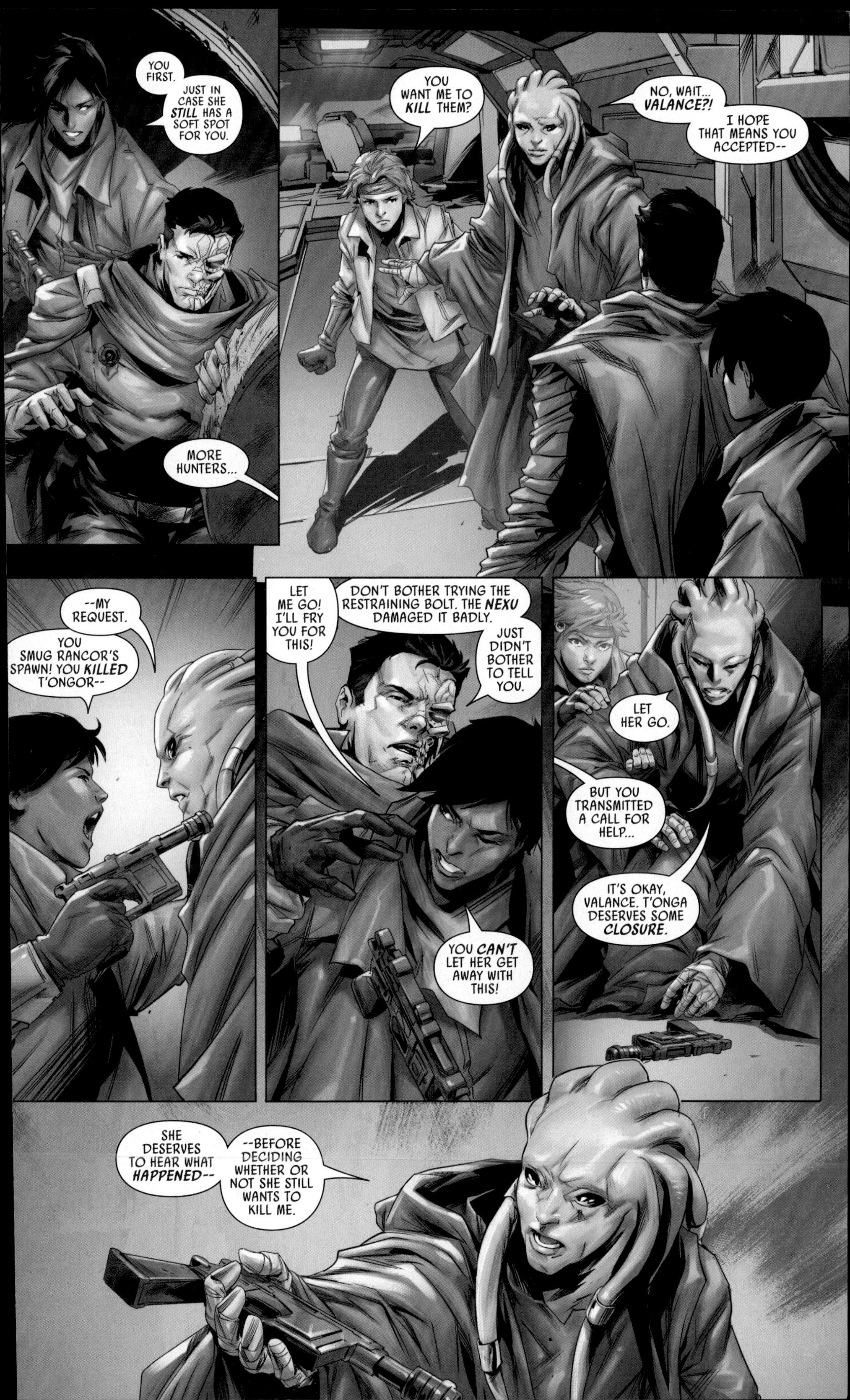
YOU FIRST.
JUST IN CASE SHE STILL HAS A SOFT SPOT FOR YOU.
MORE HUNTERS...
YOU WANT ME TO KILL THEM?
NO, WAIT... VALANCE?!
I HOPE THAT MEANS YOU ACCEPTED--
--MY REQUEST.
YOU SMUG RANCOR'S SPAWN! YOU KILLED T'ONGOR--
LET ME GO! I'LL FRY YOU FOR THIS!
DON'T BOTHER TRYING THE RESTRAINING BOLT. THE NEXU DAMAGED IT BADLY.
JUST DIDN'T BOTHER TO TELL YOU.
YOU CAN'T LET HER GET AWAY WITH THIS!
LET HER GO.
BUT YOU TRANSMITTED A CALL FOR HELP...
IT'S OKAY, VALANCE. T'ONGA DESERVES SOME CLOSURE.
SHE DESERVES TO HEAR WHAT HAPPENED--
--BEFORE DECIDING WHETHER OR NOT SHE STILL WANTS TO KILL ME.

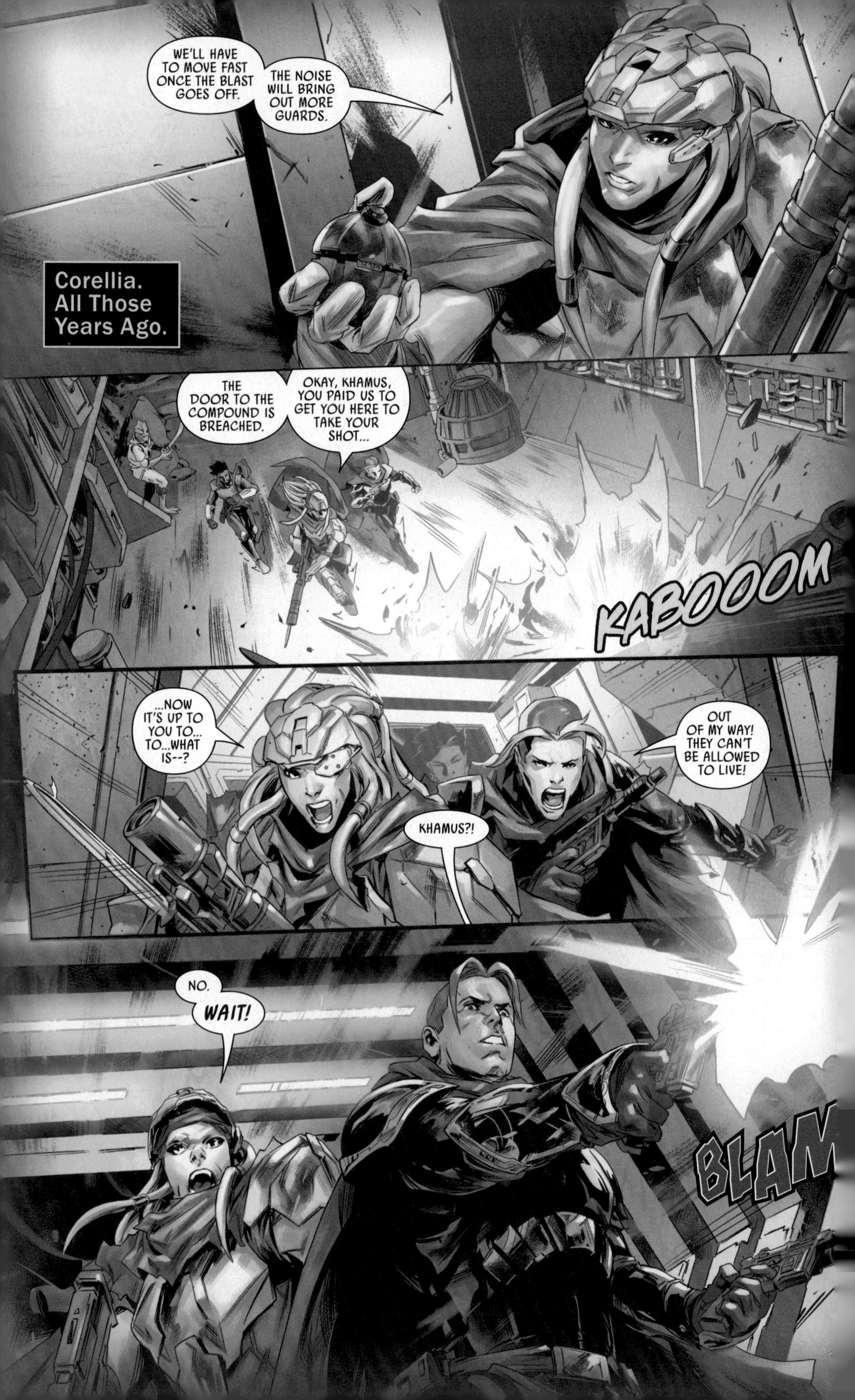

WE'LL HAVE TO MOVE FAST ONCE THE BLAST GOES OFF.
THE NOISE WILL BRING OUT MORE GUARDS.
Corellia. All Those Years Ago.
THE DOOR TO THE COMPOUND IS BREACHED.
OKAY, KHAMUS, YOU PAID US TO GET YOU HERE TO TAKE YOUR SHOT...
KABOOOM
...NOW IT'S UP TO YOU TO... TO...WHAT IS--?
OUT OF MY WAY! THEY CAN'T BE ALLOWED TO LIVE!
KHAMUS?!
NO.
WAIT!
BLAM

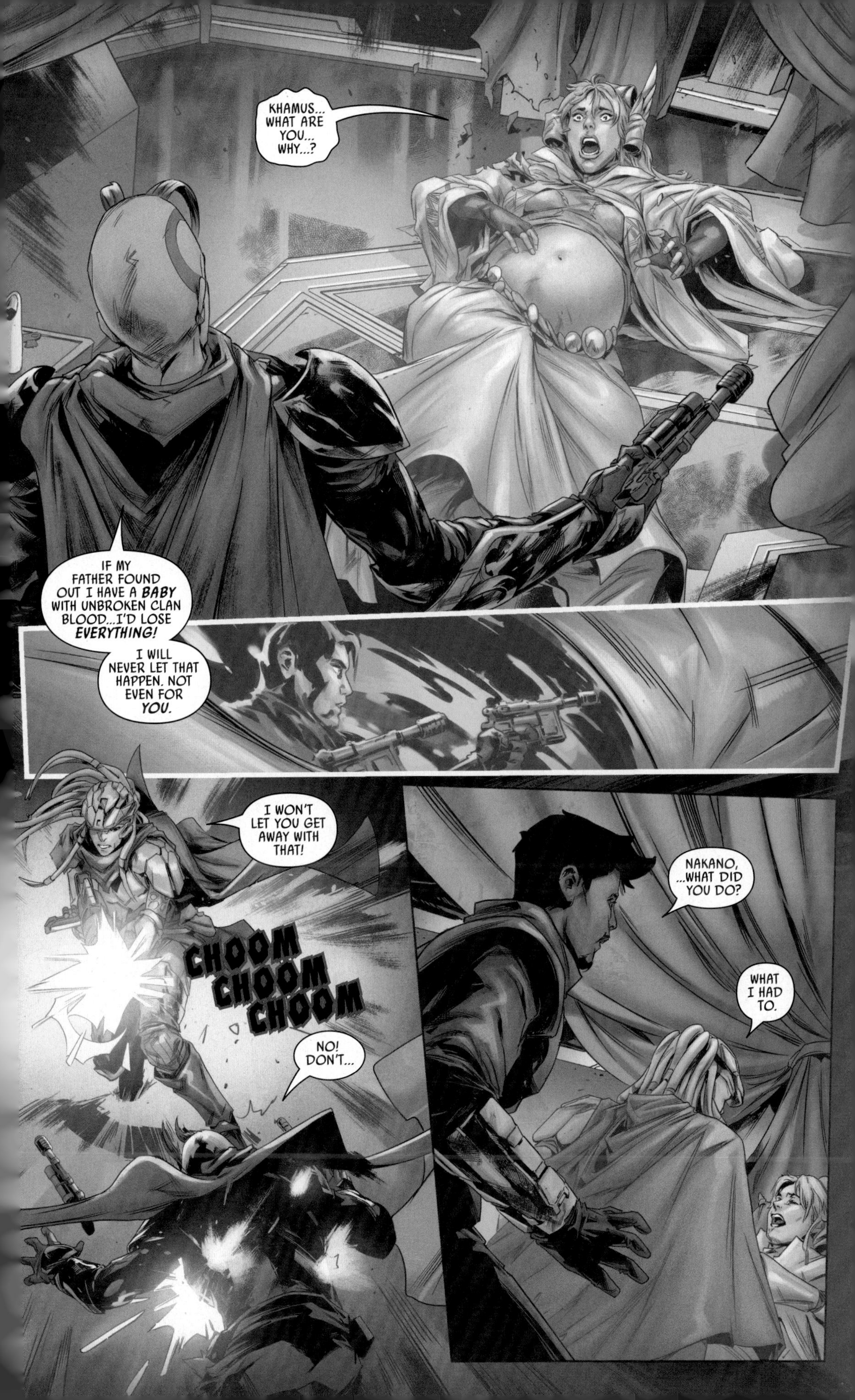
KHAMUS... WHAT ARE YOU... WHY...?
IF MY FATHER FOUND OUT I HAVE A BABY WITH UNBROKEN CLAN BLOOD...I'D LOSE EVERYTHING!
I WILL NEVER LET THAT HAPPEN. NOT EVEN FOR YOU.
I WON'T LET YOU GET AWAY WITH THAT!
CHOOM CHOOM CHOOM
NO! DON'T...
NAKANO, ...WHAT DID YOU DO?
WHAT I HAD TO.

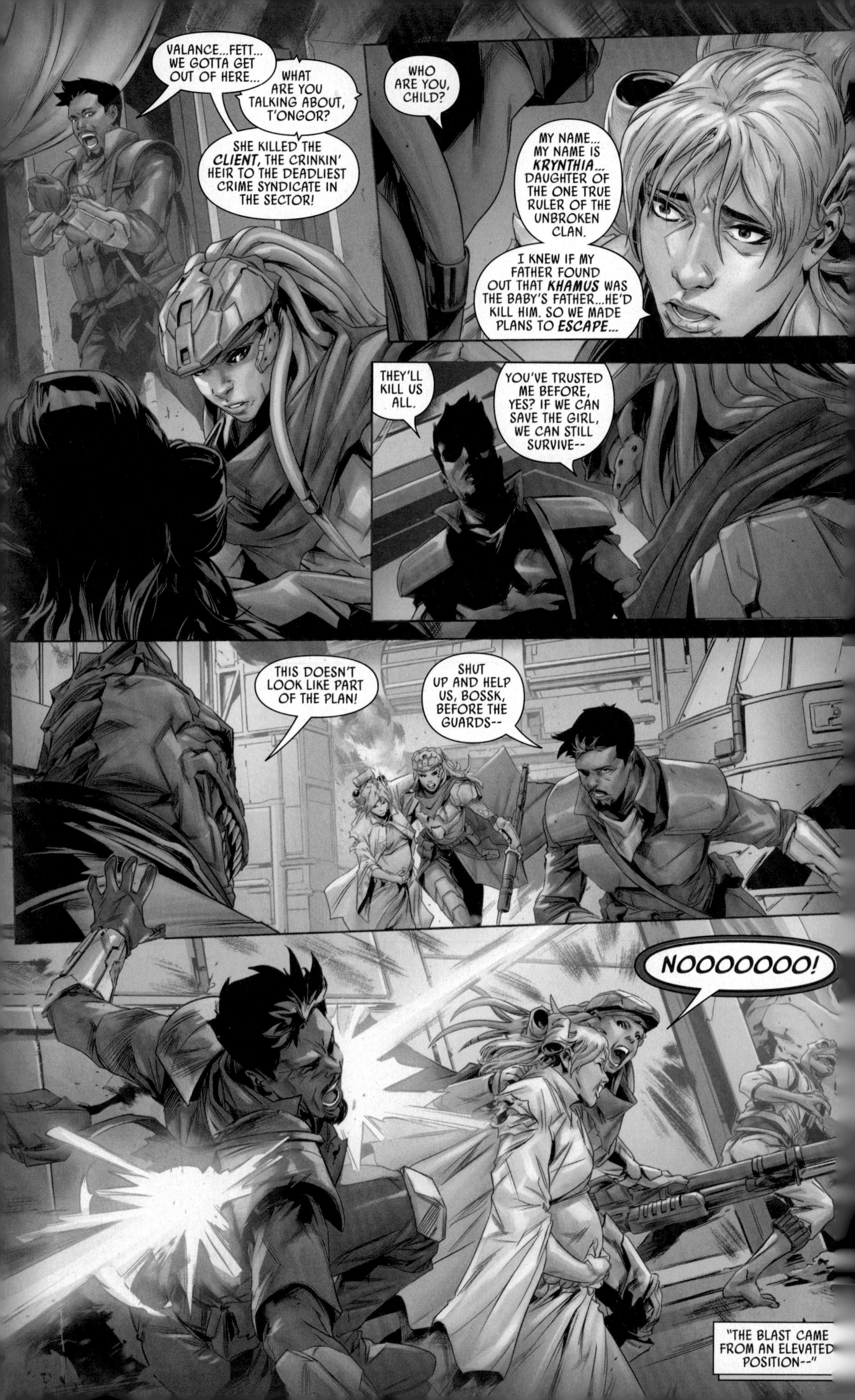
VALANCE...FETT... WE GOTTA GET OUT OF HERE...
WHAT ARE YOU TALKING ABOUT, T'ONGOR?
SHE KILLED THE **CLIENT**, THE CRINKIN' HEIR TO THE DEADLIEST CRIME SYNDICATE IN THE SECTOR!
WHO ARE YOU, CHILD?
MY NAME... MY NAME IS **KRYNTHIA**... DAUGHTER OF THE ONE TRUE RULER OF THE UNBROKEN CLAN.
I KNEW IF MY FATHER FOUND OUT THAT **KHAMUS** WAS THE BABY'S FATHER...HE'D KILL HIM. SO WE MADE PLANS TO **ESCAPE**...
THEY'LL KILL US ALL.
YOU'VE TRUSTED ME BEFORE, YES? IF WE CAN SAVE THE GIRL, WE CAN STILL SURVIVE--
THIS DOESN'T LOOK LIKE PART OF THE PLAN!
SHUT UP AND HELP US, BOSSK, BEFORE THE GUARDS--
NOOOOOOO!
"THE BLAST CAME FROM AN ELEVATED POSITION--"

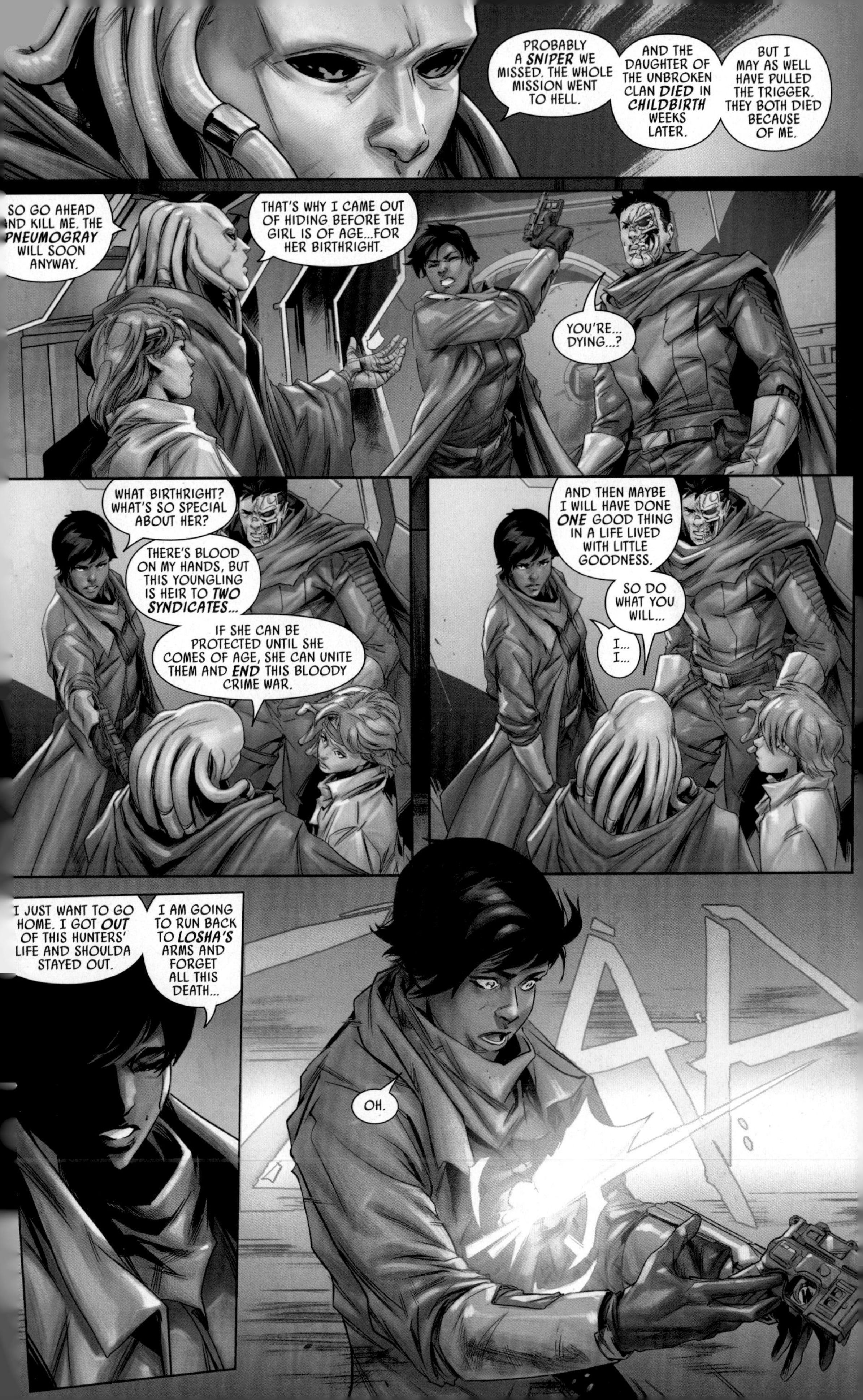
PROBABLY A SNIPER WE MISSED. THE WHOLE MISSION WENT TO HELL.
AND THE DAUGHTER OF THE UNBROKEN CLAN DIED IN CHILDBIRTH WEEKS LATER.
BUT I MAY AS WELL HAVE PULLED THE TRIGGER. THEY BOTH DIED BECAUSE OF ME.
SO GO AHEAD AND KILL ME. THE PNEUMOGRAY WILL SOON ANYWAY.
THAT'S WHY I CAME OUT OF HIDING BEFORE THE GIRL IS OF AGE...FOR HER BIRTHRIGHT.
YOU'RE... DYING...?
WHAT BIRTHRIGHT? WHAT'S SO SPECIAL ABOUT HER?
THERE'S BLOOD ON MY HANDS, BUT THIS YOUNGLING IS HEIR TO TWO SYNDICATES...
IF SHE CAN BE PROTECTED UNTIL SHE COMES OF AGE, SHE CAN UNITE THEM AND END THIS BLOODY CRIME WAR.
AND THEN MAYBE I WILL HAVE DONE ONE GOOD THING IN A LIFE LIVED WITH LITTLE GOODNESS.
SO DO WHAT YOU WILL...
I... I...
I JUST WANT TO GO HOME. I GOT OUT OF THIS HUNTERS' LIFE AND SHOULDA STAYED OUT.
I AM GOING TO RUN BACK TO LOSHA'S ARMS AND FORGET ALL THIS DEATH...
OH.

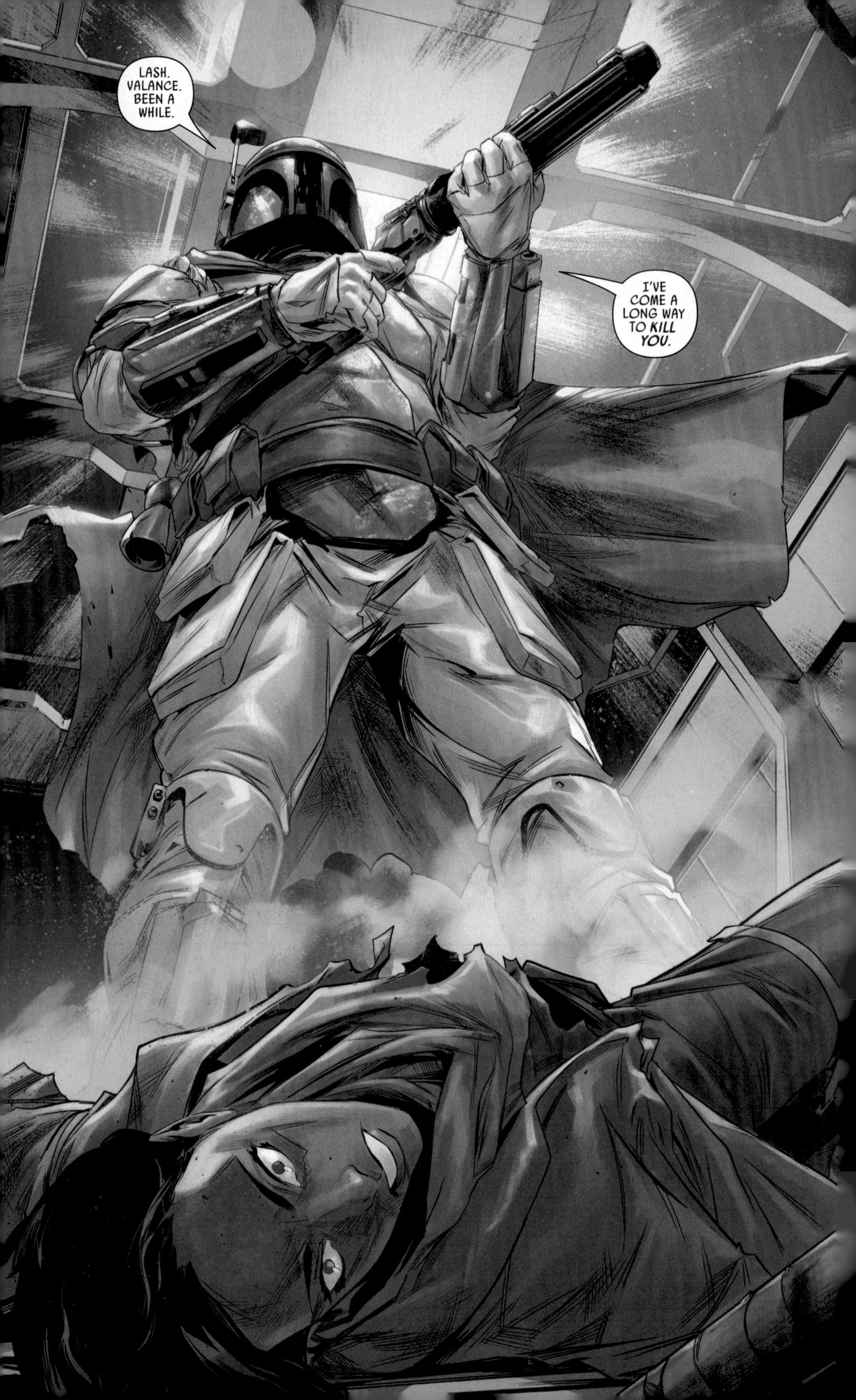
LASH. VALANCE. BEEN A WHILE.
I'VE COME A LONG WAY TO *KILL YOU*.

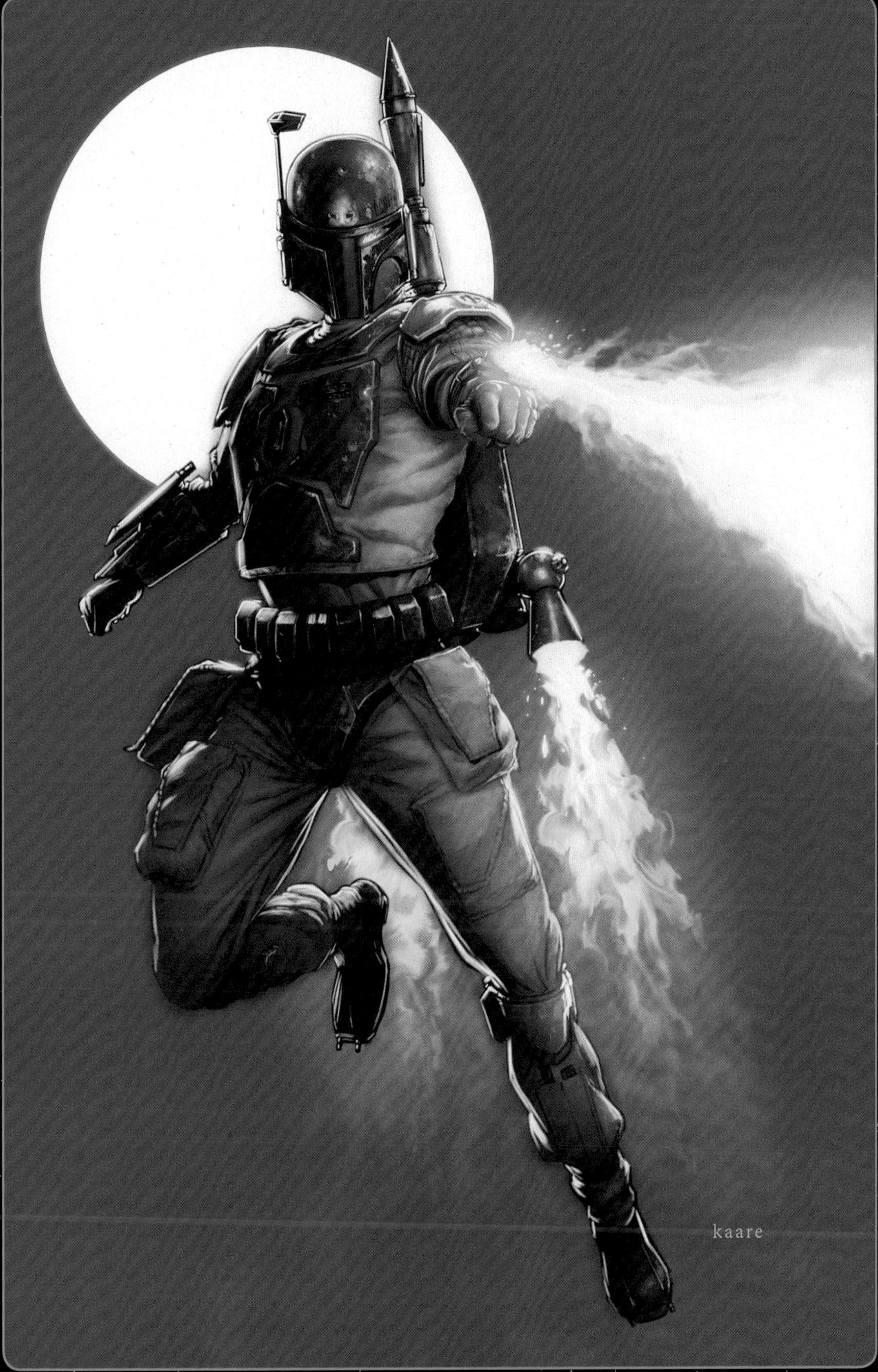
kaare

#1 Variant by
KAARE ANDREWS

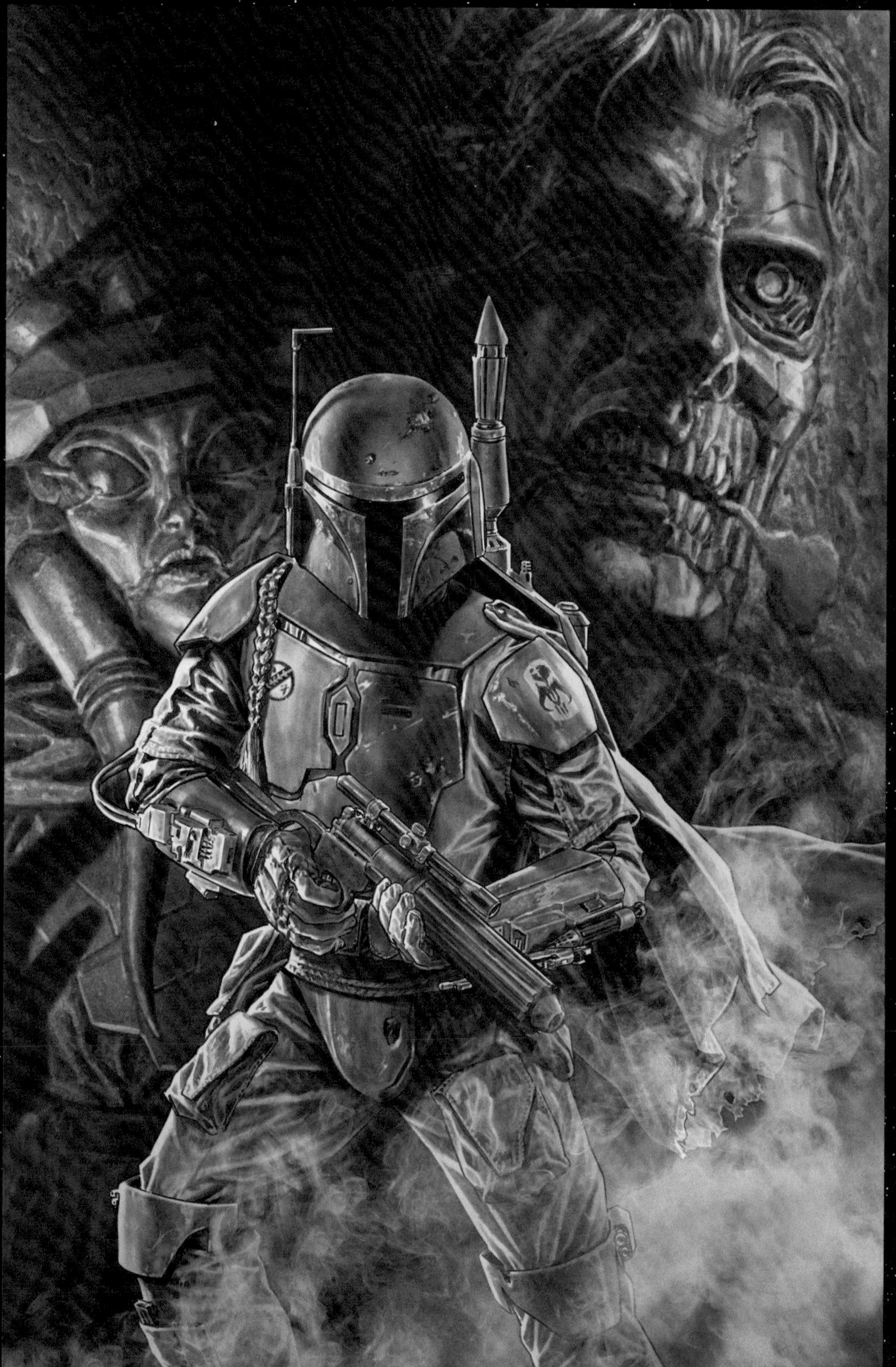

5

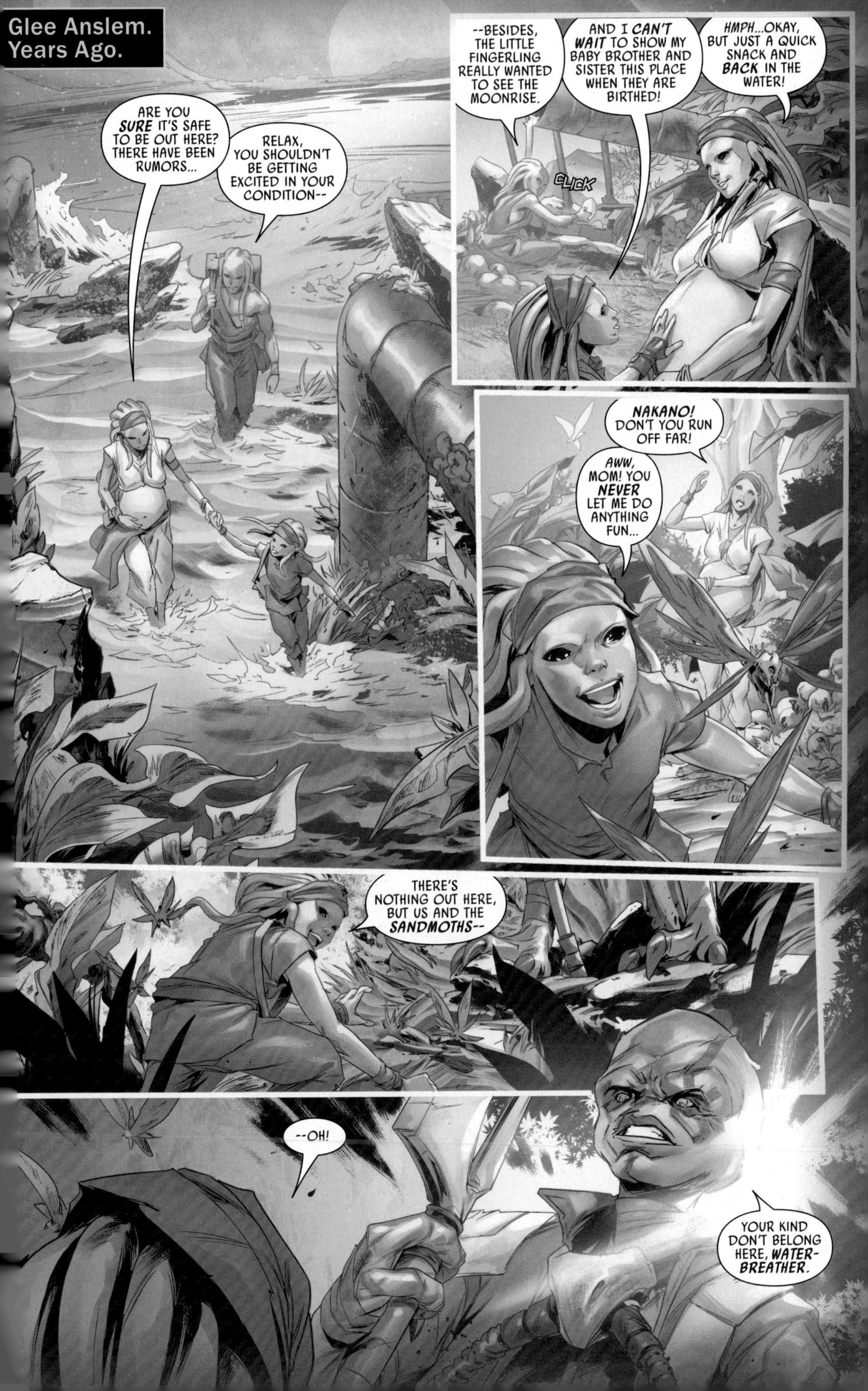
Glee Anslem. Years Ago.
ARE YOU SURE IT'S SAFE TO BE OUT HERE? THERE HAVE BEEN RUMORS...
RELAX, YOU SHOULDN'T BE GETTING EXCITED IN YOUR CONDITION--
--BESIDES, THE LITTLE FINGERLING REALLY WANTED TO SEE THE MOONRISE.
AND I CAN'T WAIT TO SHOW MY BABY BROTHER AND SISTER THIS PLACE WHEN THEY ARE BIRTHED!
HMPH...OKAY, BUT JUST A QUICK SNACK AND BACK IN THE WATER!
CLICK
NAKANO! DON'T YOU RUN OFF FAR!
AWW, MOM! YOU NEVER LET ME DO ANYTHING FUN...
THERE'S NOTHING OUT HERE, BUT US AND THE SANDMOTHS--
--OH!
YOUR KIND DON'T BELONG HERE, WATER-BREATHER.

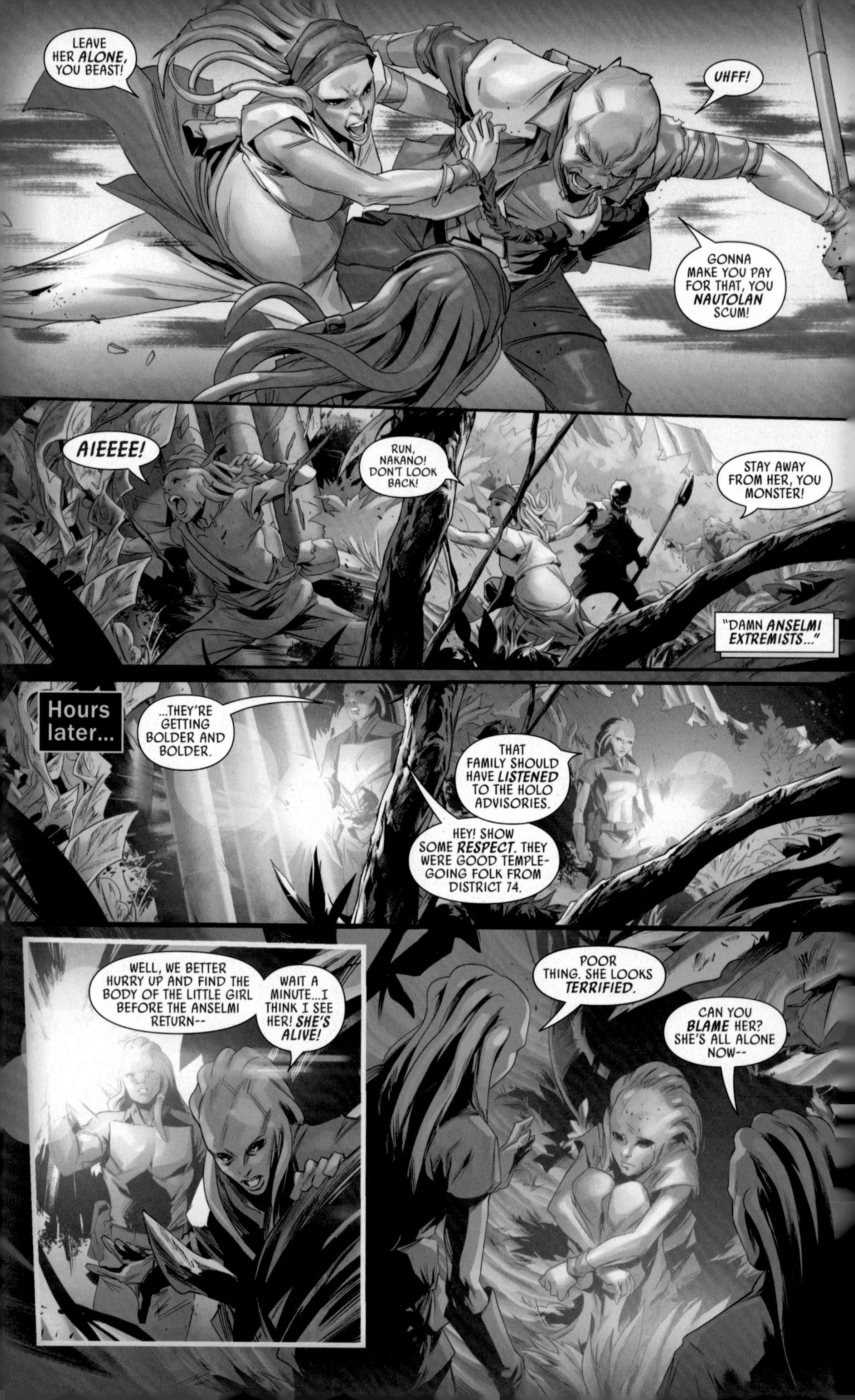
LEAVE HER ALONE, YOU BEAST!
UHFF!
GONNA MAKE YOU PAY FOR THAT, YOU NAUTOLAN SCUM!
AIEEEE!
RUN, NAKANO! DON'T LOOK BACK!
STAY AWAY FROM HER, YOU MONSTER!
"DAMN ANSELMI EXTREMISTS..."
Hours later...
...THEY'RE GETTING BOLDER AND BOLDER.
THAT FAMILY SHOULD HAVE LISTENED TO THE HOLO ADVISORIES.
HEY! SHOW SOME RESPECT. THEY WERE GOOD TEMPLE-GOING FOLK FROM DISTRICT 74.
WELL, WE BETTER HURRY UP AND FIND THE BODY OF THE LITTLE GIRL BEFORE THE ANSELMI RETURN--
WAIT A MINUTE...I THINK I SEE HER! SHE'S ALIVE!
POOR THING. SHE LOOKS TERRIFIED.
CAN YOU BLAME HER? SHE'S ALL ALONE NOW--

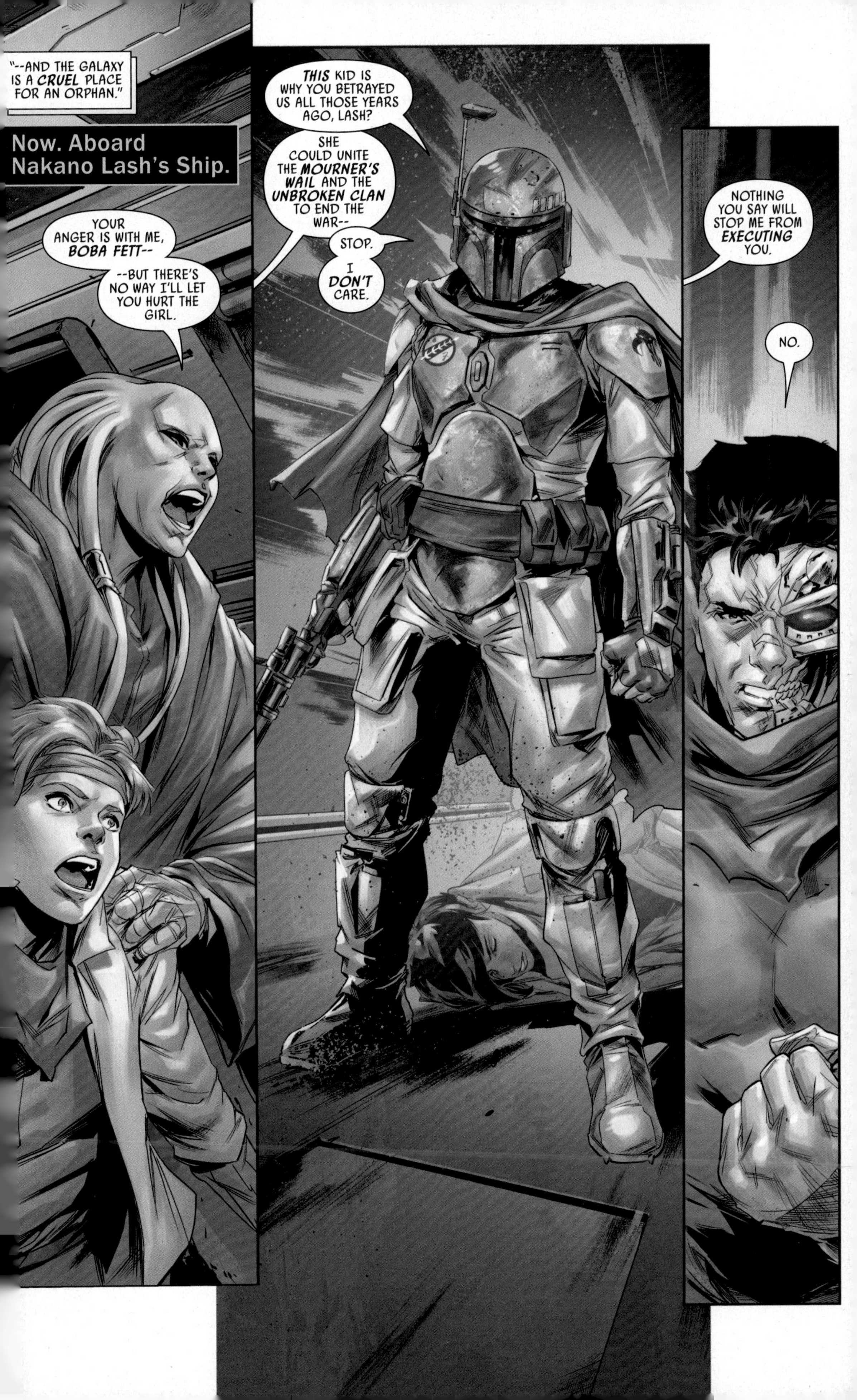
"--AND THE GALAXY IS A CRUEL PLACE FOR AN ORPHAN."
Now. Aboard Nakano Lash's Ship.
YOUR ANGER IS WITH ME, BOBA FETT--
--BUT THERE'S NO WAY I'LL LET YOU HURT THE GIRL.
THIS KID IS WHY YOU BETRAYED US ALL THOSE YEARS AGO, LASH?
SHE COULD UNITE THE MOURNER'S WAIL AND THE UNBROKEN CLAN TO END THE WAR--
STOP.
I DON'T CARE.
NOTHING YOU SAY WILL STOP ME FROM EXECUTING YOU.
NO.

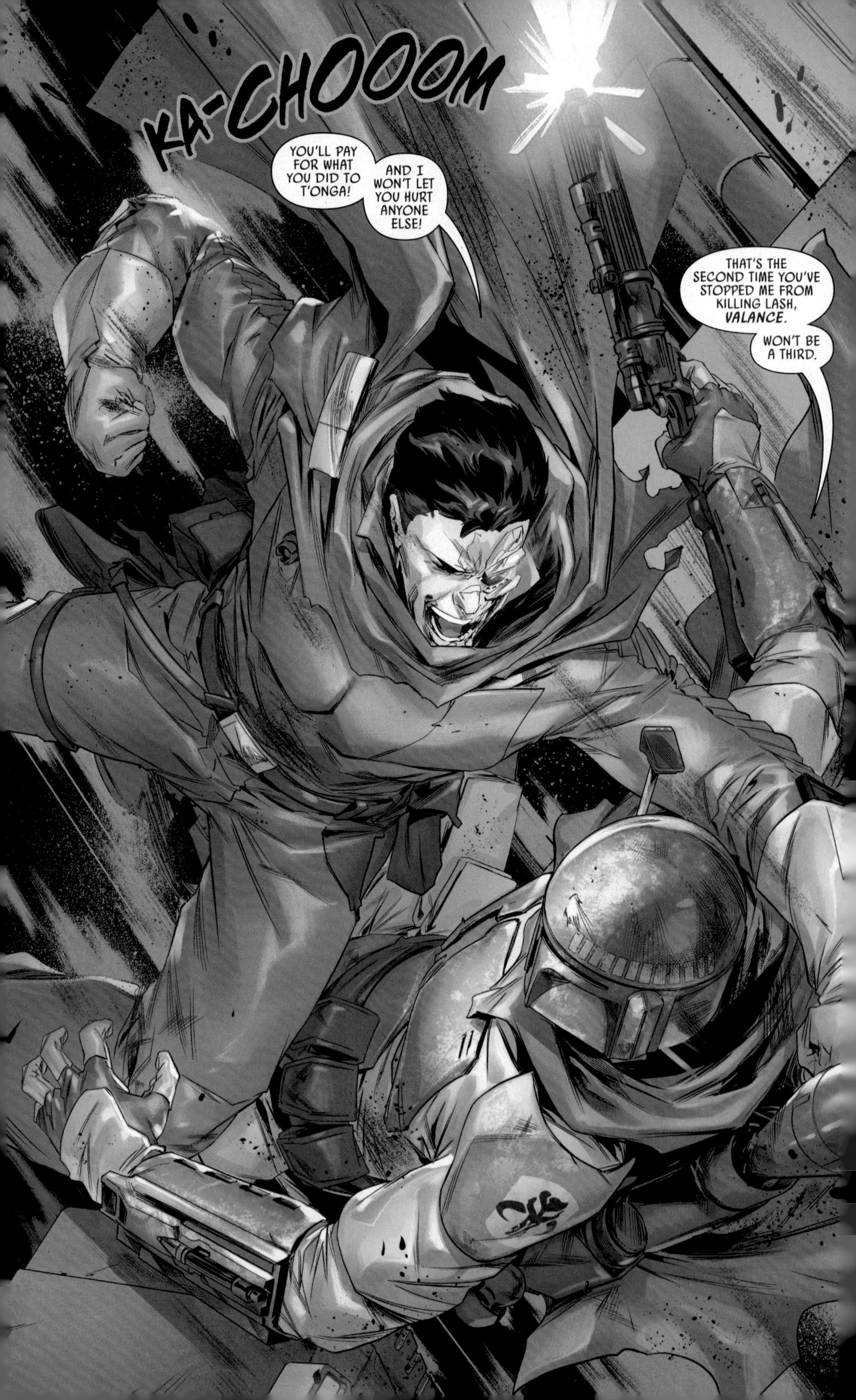
KA-CHOOOM
YOU'LL PAY FOR WHAT YOU DID TO T'ONGA!
AND I WON'T LET YOU HURT ANYONE ELSE!
THAT'S THE SECOND TIME YOU'VE STOPPED ME FROM KILLING LASH, VALANCE.
WON'T BE A THIRD.

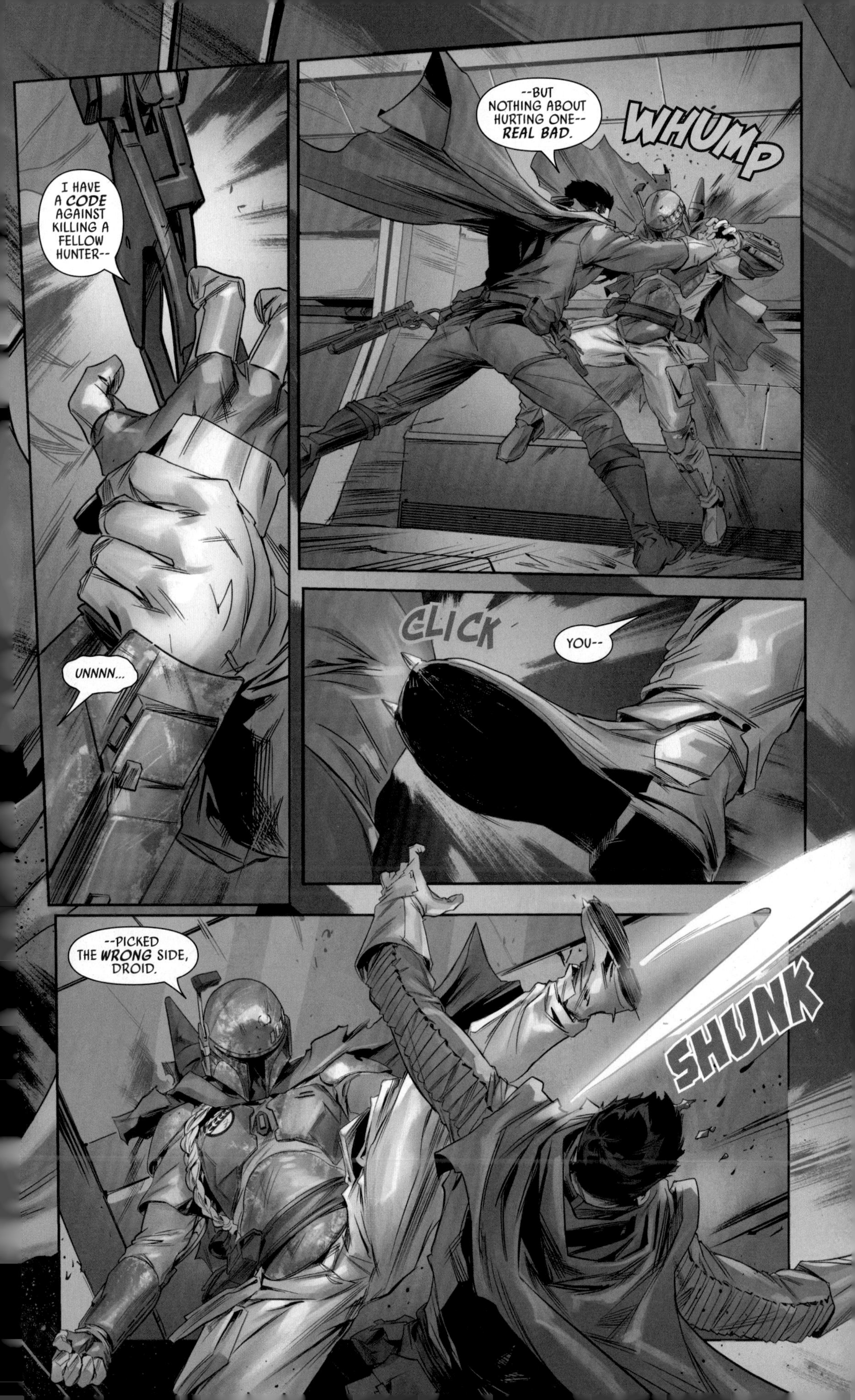
I HAVE A CODE AGAINST KILLING A FELLOW HUNTER--
--BUT NOTHING ABOUT HURTING ONE-- REAL BAD.
WHUMP
UNNNN...
CLICK
YOU--
--PICKED THE WRONG SIDE, DROID.
SHUNK

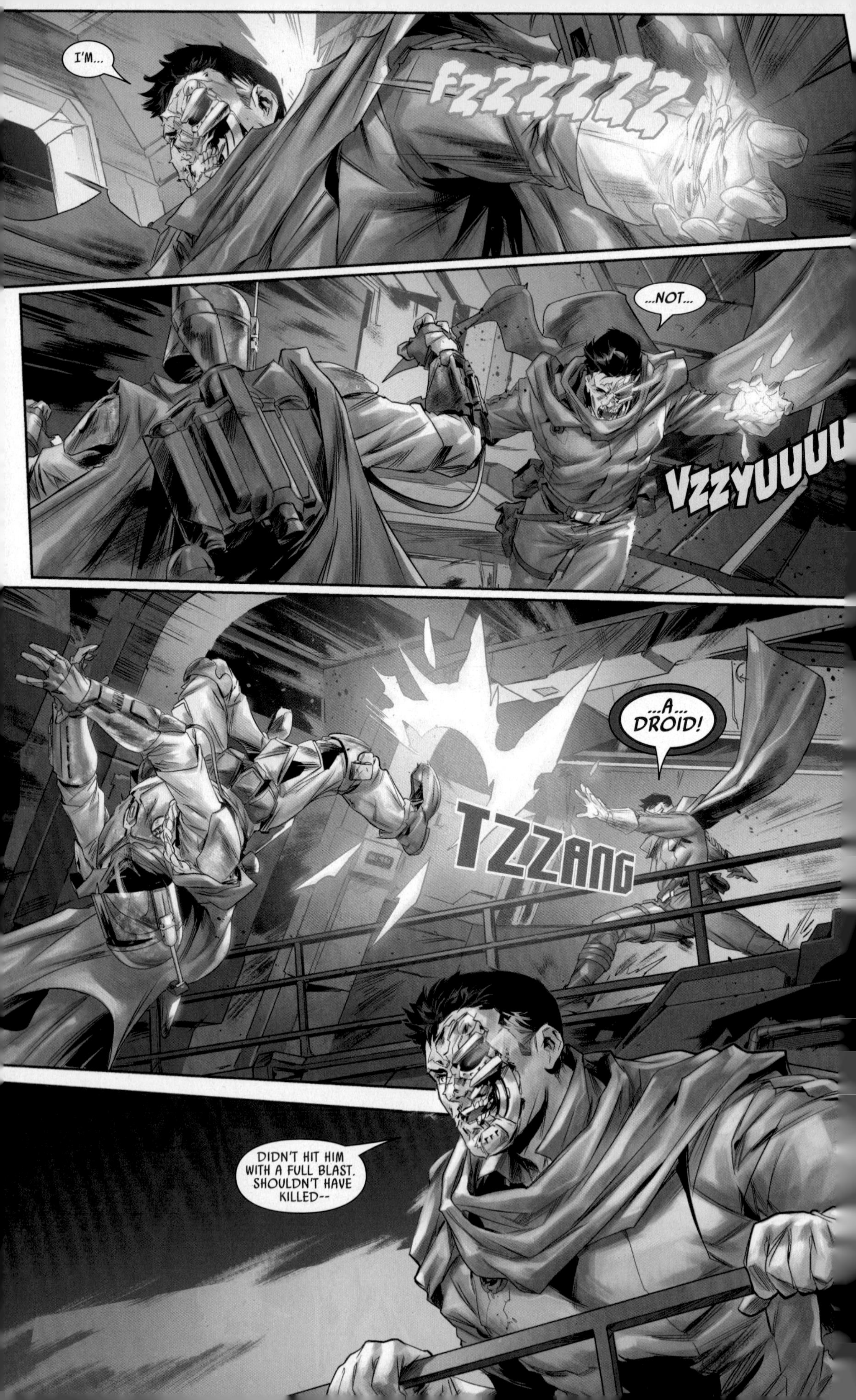
I'M...
FZZZZZZZ
...NOT...
VZZYUUUU
...A... DROID!
TZZANG
DIDN'T HIT HIM WITH A FULL BLAST. SHOULDN'T HAVE KILLED--

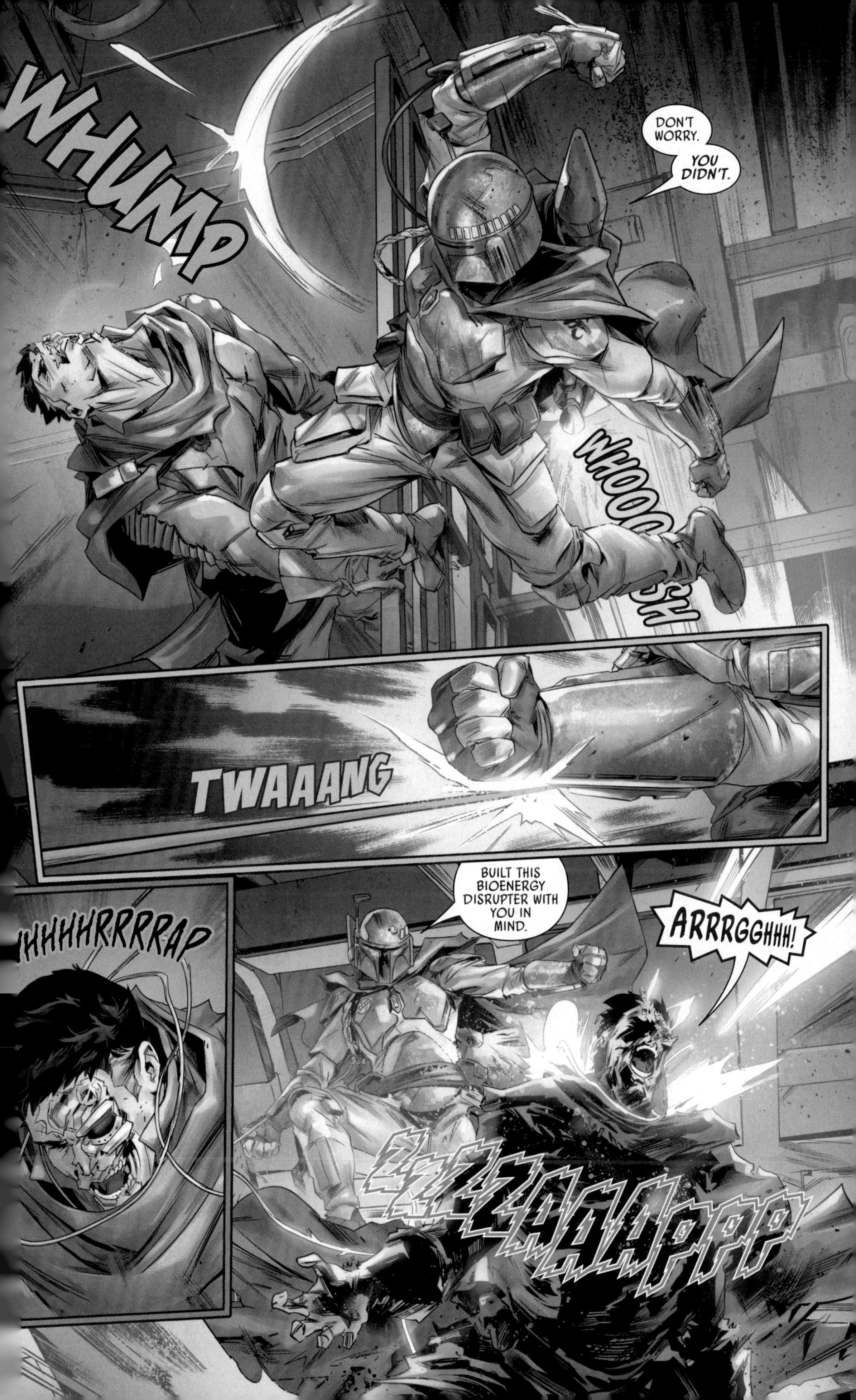
WHUMP
DON'T WORRY.
YOU DIDN'T.
TWAAANG
BUILT THIS BIOENERGY DISRUPTER WITH YOU IN MIND.
ARRRGGHHH!

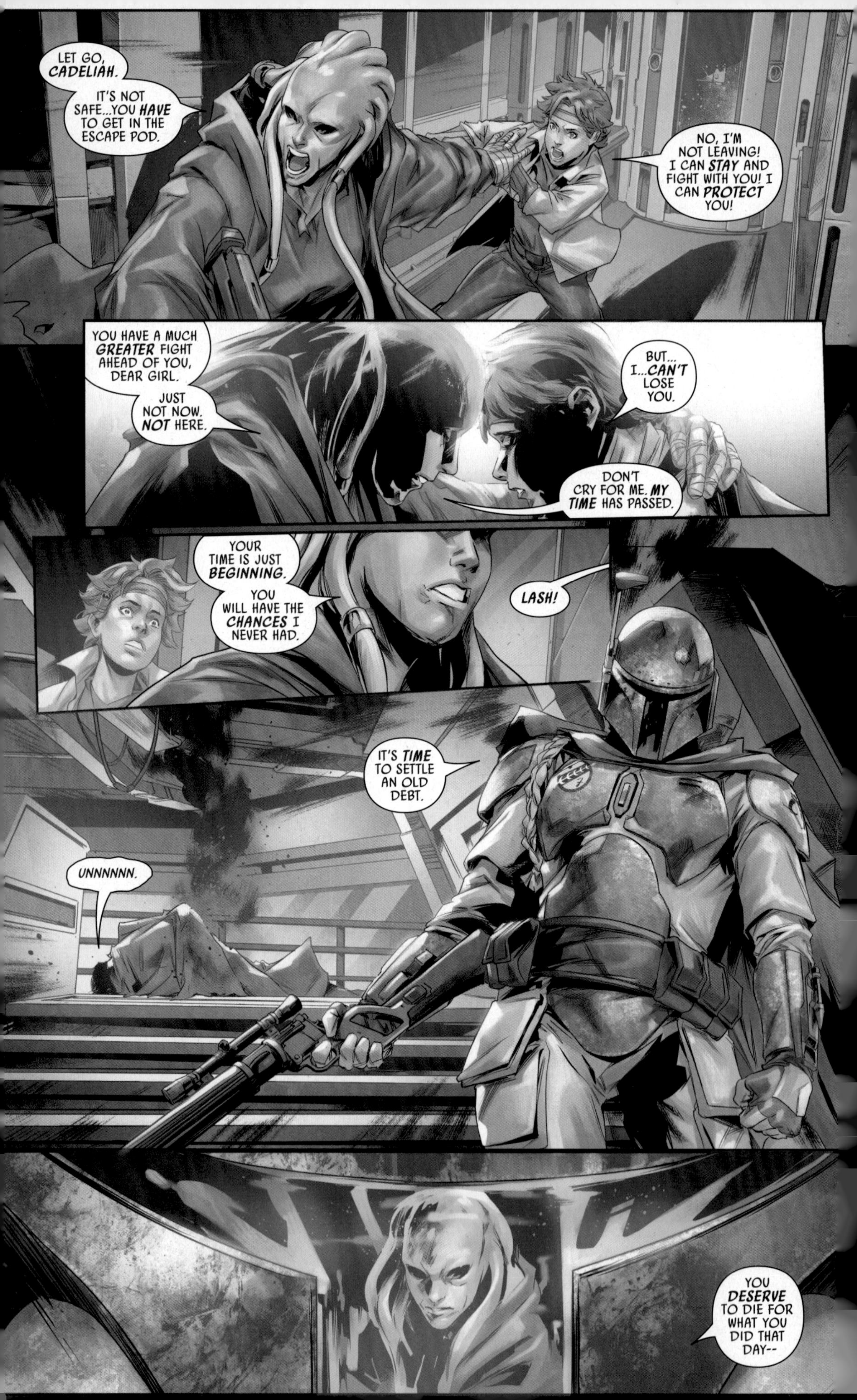
LET GO, CADELIAH.
IT'S NOT SAFE...YOU HAVE TO GET IN THE ESCAPE POD.
NO, I'M NOT LEAVING! I CAN STAY AND FIGHT WITH YOU! I CAN PROTECT YOU!
YOU HAVE A MUCH GREATER FIGHT AHEAD OF YOU, DEAR GIRL.
JUST NOT NOW. NOT HERE.
BUT... I...CAN'T LOSE YOU.
DON'T CRY FOR ME. MY TIME HAS PASSED.
YOUR TIME IS JUST BEGINNING.
YOU WILL HAVE THE CHANCES I NEVER HAD.
LASH!
IT'S TIME TO SETTLE AN OLD DEBT.
UNNNNNN.
YOU DESERVE TO DIE FOR WHAT YOU DID THAT DAY--

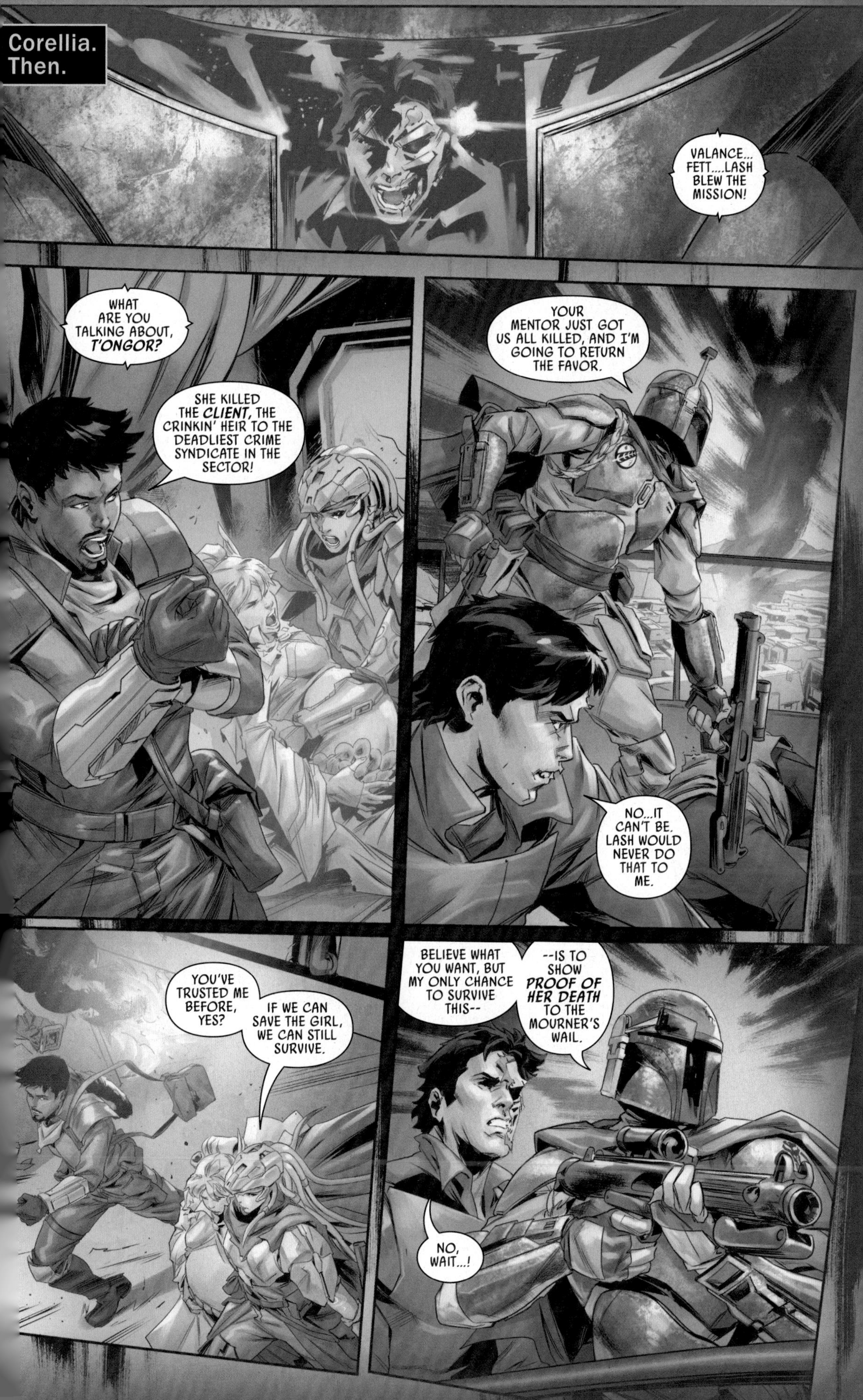
Corellia. Then.
VALANCE... FETT....LASH BLEW THE MISSION!
WHAT ARE YOU TALKING ABOUT, T'ONGOR?
SHE KILLED THE CLIENT, THE CRINKIN' HEIR TO THE DEADLIEST CRIME SYNDICATE IN THE SECTOR!
YOUR MENTOR JUST GOT US ALL KILLED, AND I'M GOING TO RETURN THE FAVOR.
NO...IT CAN'T BE. LASH WOULD NEVER DO THAT TO ME.
YOU'VE TRUSTED ME BEFORE, YES?
IF WE CAN SAVE THE GIRL, WE CAN STILL SURVIVE.
BELIEVE WHAT YOU WANT, BUT MY ONLY CHANCE TO SURVIVE THIS--
--IS TO SHOW PROOF OF HER DEATH TO THE MOURNER'S WAIL.
NO, WAIT...!

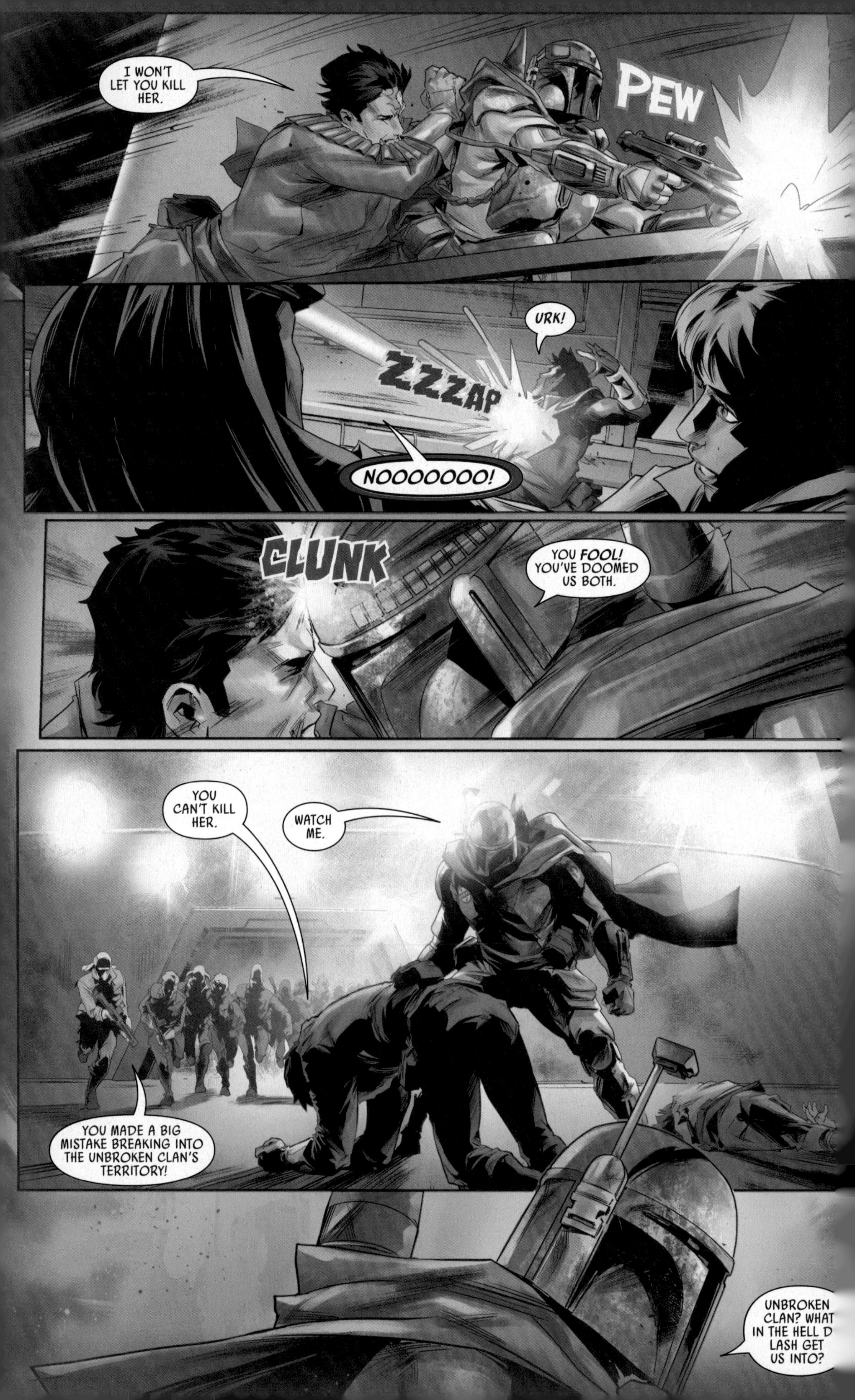
I WON'T LET YOU KILL HER.
PEW
URK!
ZZZAP
NOOOOOOO!
CLUNK
YOU FOOL! YOU'VE DOOMED US BOTH.
YOU CAN'T KILL HER.
WATCH ME.
YOU MADE A BIG MISTAKE BREAKING INTO THE UNBROKEN CLAN'S TERRITORY!
UNBROKEN CLAN? WHAT IN THE HELL D LASH GET US INTO?

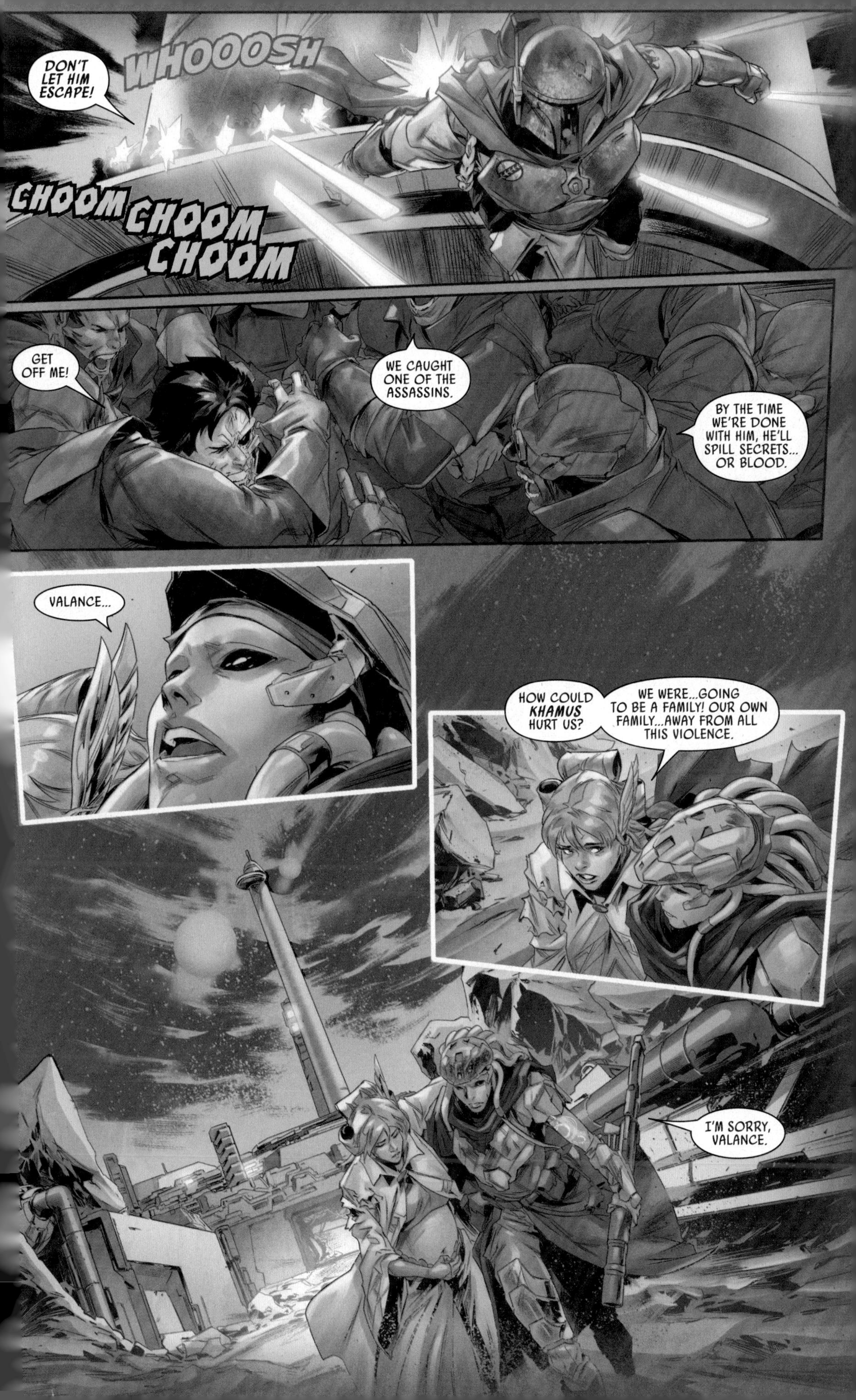
DON'T LET HIM ESCAPE!
WHOOOSH
CHOOM CHOOM CHOOM
GET OFF ME!
WE CAUGHT ONE OF THE ASSASSINS.
BY THE TIME WE'RE DONE WITH HIM, HE'LL SPILL SECRETS... OR BLOOD.
VALANCE...
HOW COULD KHAMUS HURT US?
WE WERE...GOING TO BE A FAMILY! OUR OWN FAMILY...AWAY FROM ALL THIS VIOLENCE.
I'M SORRY, VALANCE.

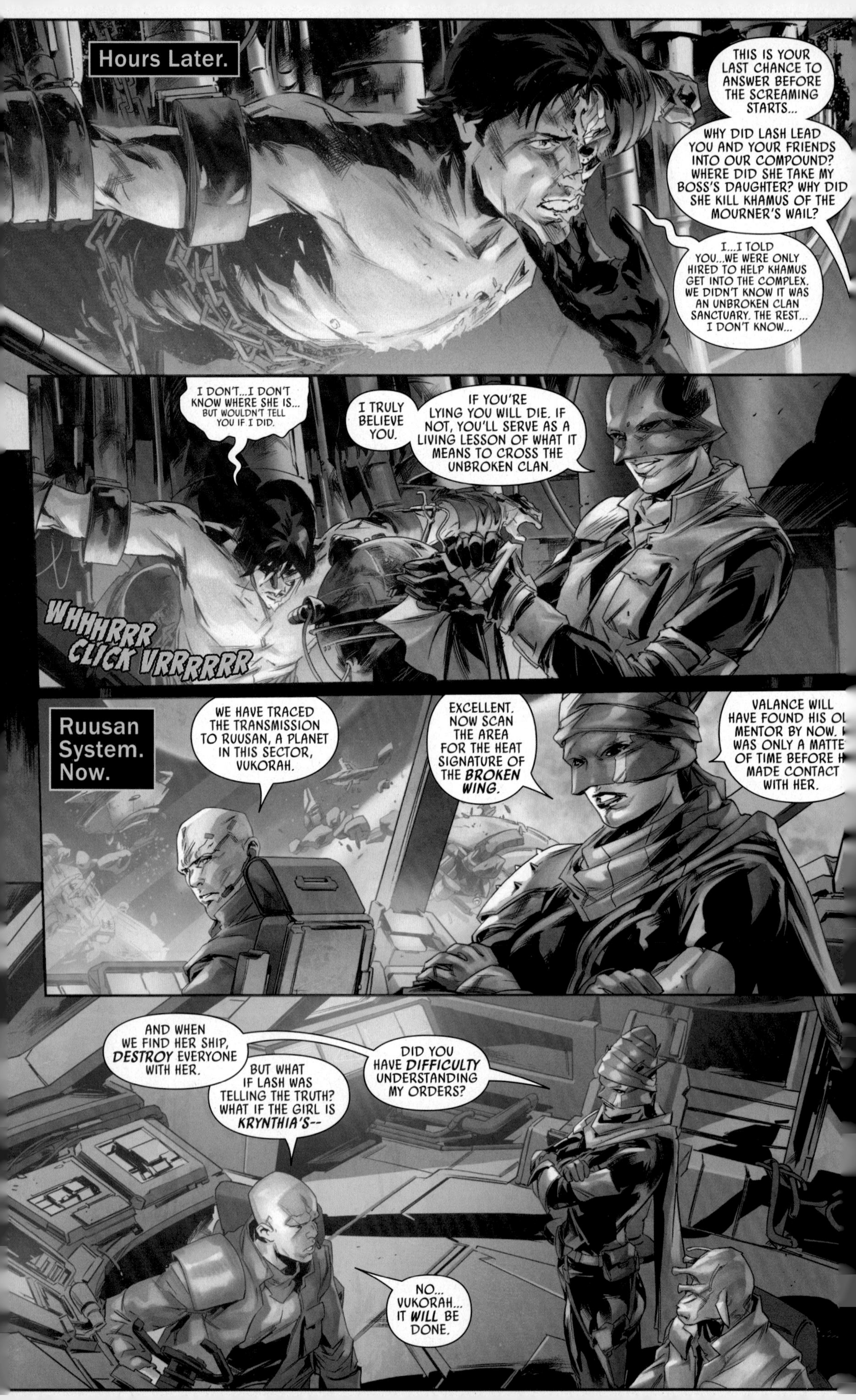
Hours Later.
THIS IS YOUR LAST CHANCE TO ANSWER BEFORE THE SCREAMING STARTS...
WHY DID LASH LEAD YOU AND YOUR FRIENDS INTO OUR COMPOUND? WHERE DID SHE TAKE MY BOSS'S DAUGHTER? WHY DID SHE KILL KHAMUS OF THE MOURNER'S WAIL?
I...I TOLD YOU...WE WERE ONLY HIRED TO HELP KHAMUS GET INTO THE COMPLEX. WE DIDN'T KNOW IT WAS AN UNBROKEN CLAN SANCTUARY. THE REST... I DON'T KNOW...
I DON'T...I DON'T KNOW WHERE SHE IS... BUT WOULDN'T TELL YOU IF I DID.
I TRULY BELIEVE YOU.
IF YOU'RE LYING YOU WILL DIE. IF NOT, YOU'LL SERVE AS A LIVING LESSON OF WHAT IT MEANS TO CROSS THE UNBROKEN CLAN.
WHHHRRR CLICK VRRRRRR
Ruusan System. Now.
WE HAVE TRACED THE TRANSMISSION TO RUUSAN, A PLANET IN THIS SECTOR, VUKORAH.
EXCELLENT. NOW SCAN THE AREA FOR THE HEAT SIGNATURE OF THE BROKEN WING.
VALANCE WILL HAVE FOUND HIS OL MENTOR BY NOW. WAS ONLY A MATTE OF TIME BEFORE H MADE CONTACT WITH HER.
AND WHEN WE FIND HER SHIP, DESTROY EVERYONE WITH HER.
BUT WHAT IF LASH WAS TELLING THE TRUTH? WHAT IF THE GIRL IS KRYNTHIA'S--
DID YOU HAVE DIFFICULTY UNDERSTANDING MY ORDERS?
NO... VUKORAH... IT WILL BE DONE.

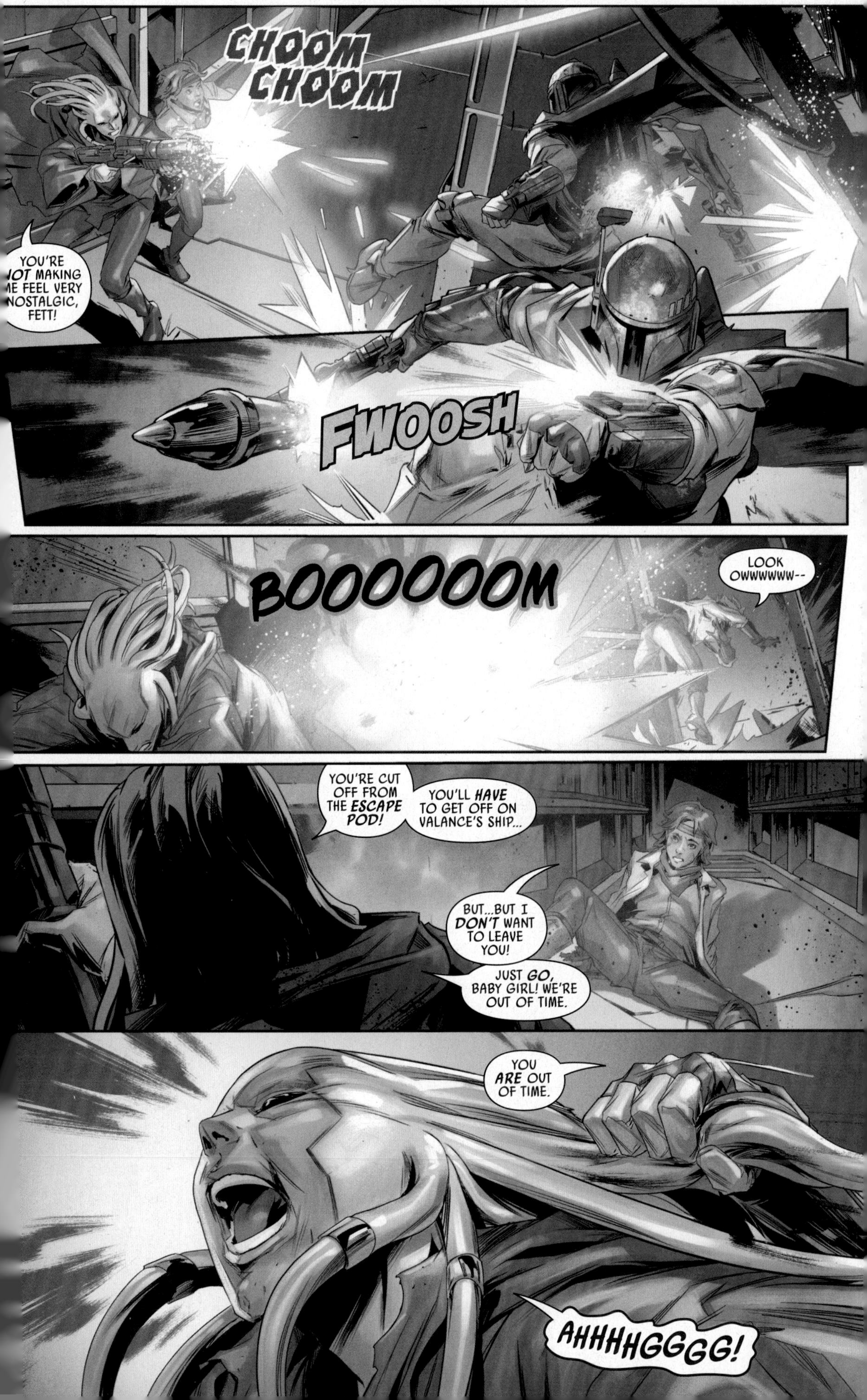
CHOOM CHOOM
YOU'RE NOT MAKING ME FEEL VERY NOSTALGIC, FETT!
FWOOSH
BOOOOOOM
LOOK OWWWWWW--
YOU'RE CUT OFF FROM THE ESCAPE POD!
YOU'LL HAVE TO GET OFF ON VALANCE'S SHIP...
BUT...BUT I DON'T WANT TO LEAVE YOU!
JUST GO, BABY GIRL! WE'RE OUT OF TIME.
YOU ARE OUT OF TIME.
AHHHHGGGGG!

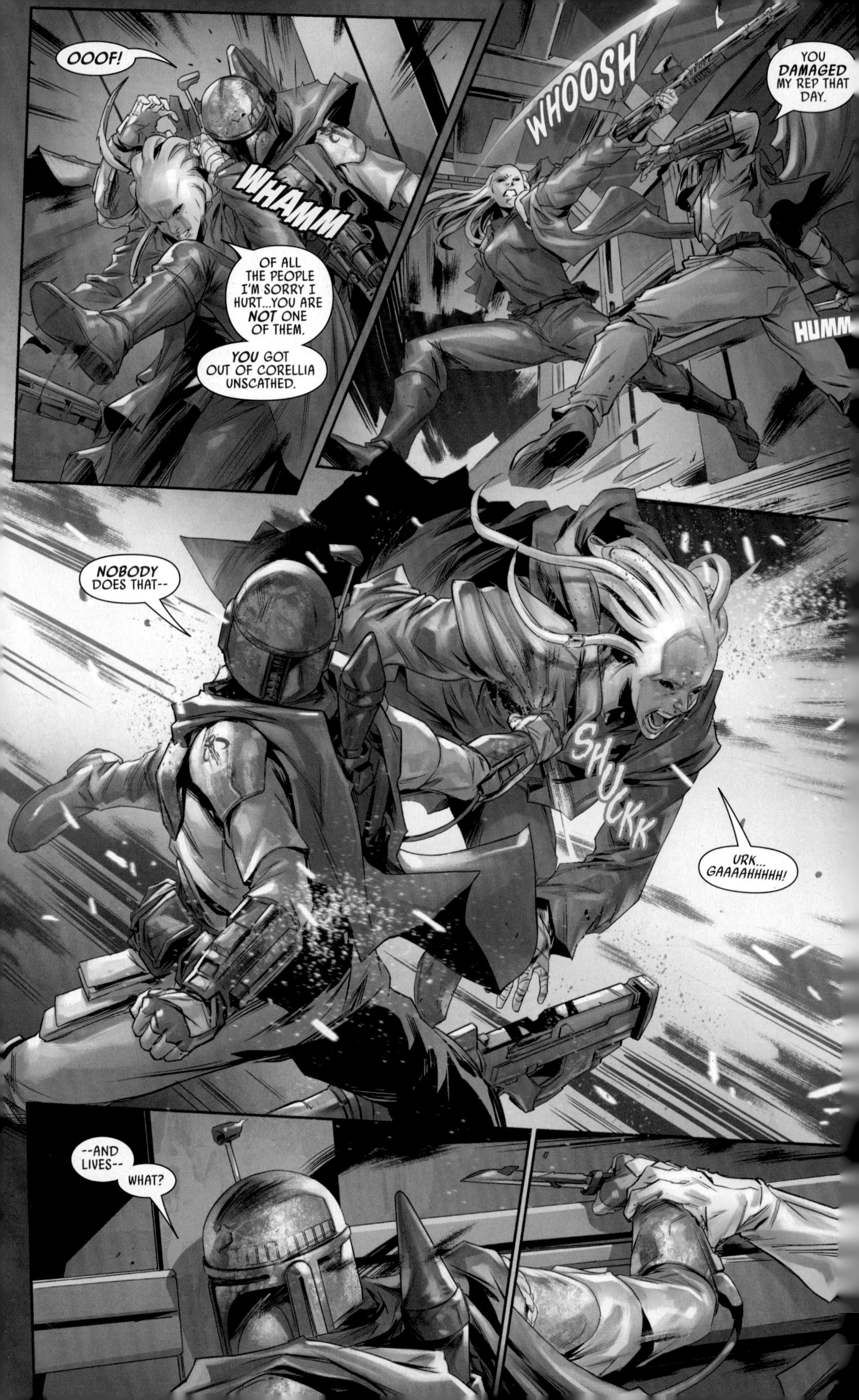
OOOF!
WHAMM
OF ALL THE PEOPLE I'M SORRY I HURT...YOU ARE NOT ONE OF THEM.
YOU GOT OUT OF CORELLIA UNSCATHED.
WHOOSH
YOU DAMAGED MY REP THAT DAY.
HUMM
NOBODY DOES THAT--
SHUCKK
URK... GAAAAHHHHH!
--AND LIVES--
WHAT?

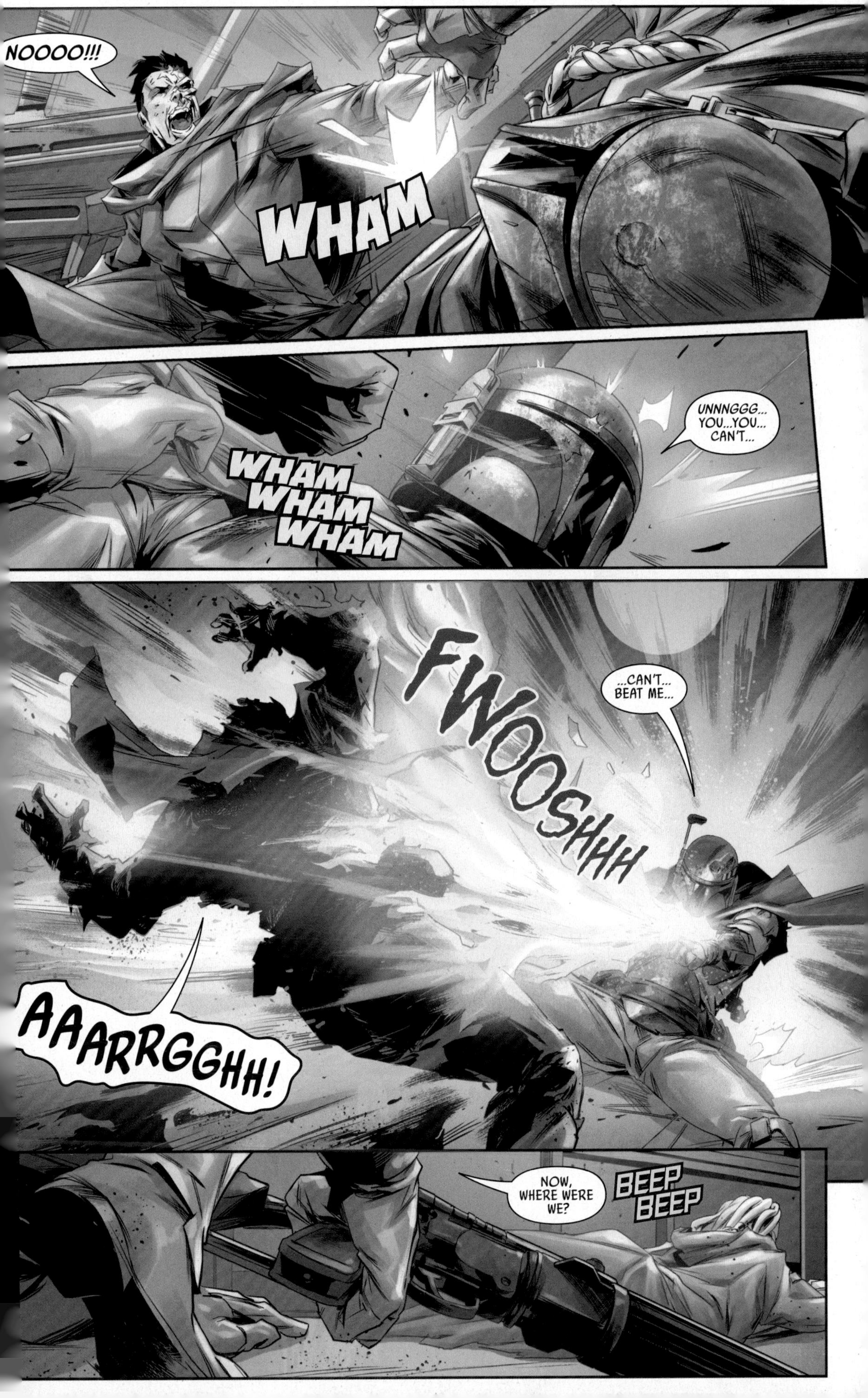
NOOOO!!!
WHAM
WHAM
WHAM
WHAM
UNNNGGG... YOU...YOU... CAN'T...
FWOOSHHH
...CAN'T... BEAT ME...
AAARRGGHH!
NOW, WHERE WERE WE?
BEEP BEEP

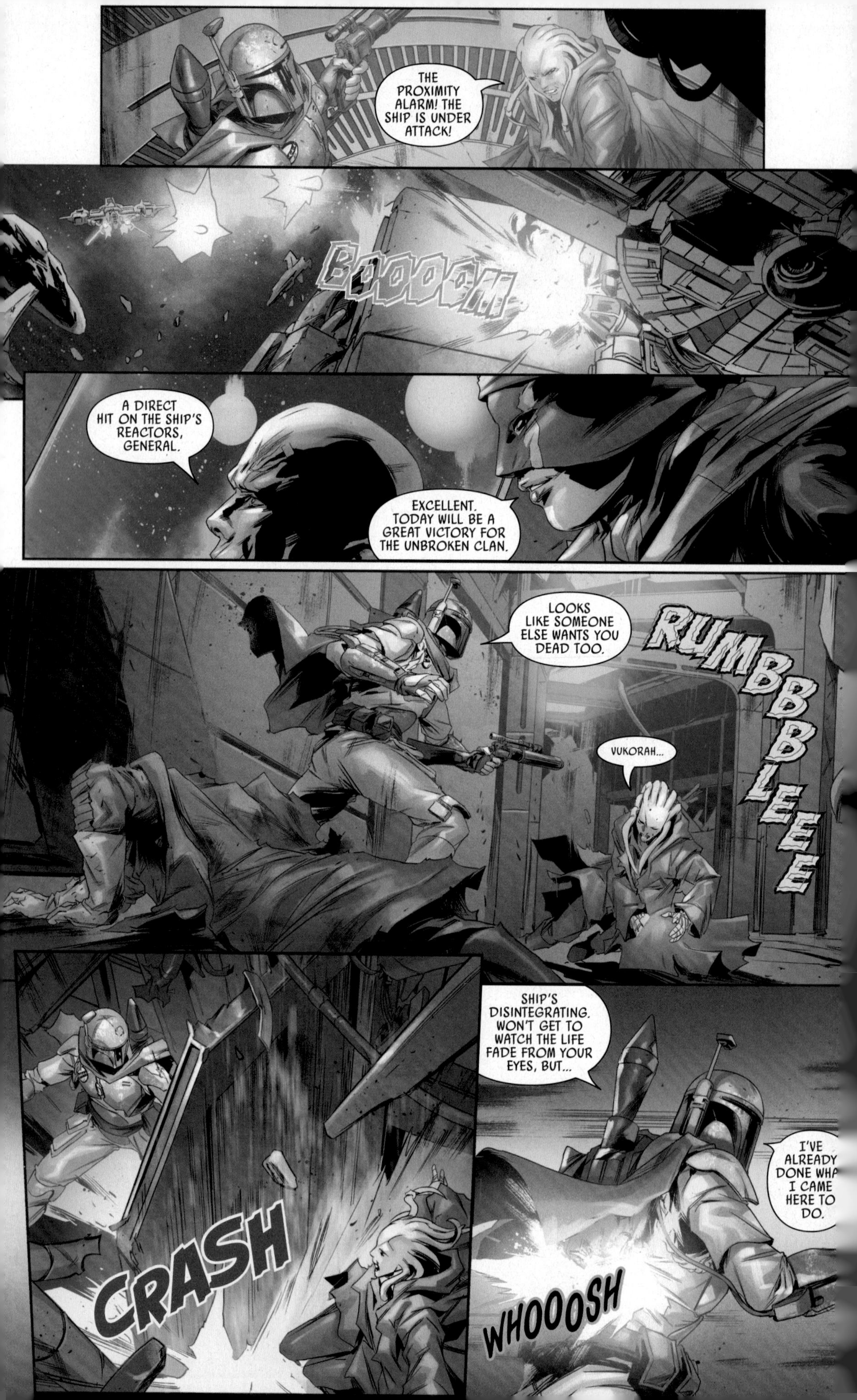
THE PROXIMITY ALARM! THE SHIP IS UNDER ATTACK!
BOOOOOM
A DIRECT HIT ON THE SHIP'S REACTORS, GENERAL.
EXCELLENT. TODAY WILL BE A GREAT VICTORY FOR THE UNBROKEN CLAN.
LOOKS LIKE SOMEONE ELSE WANTS YOU DEAD TOO.
RUMBBBLEEE
VUKORAH...
SHIP'S DISINTEGRATING. WON'T GET TO WATCH THE LIFE FADE FROM YOUR EYES, BUT...
I'VE ALREADY DONE WHA I CAME HERE TO DO.
CRASH
WHOOOSH

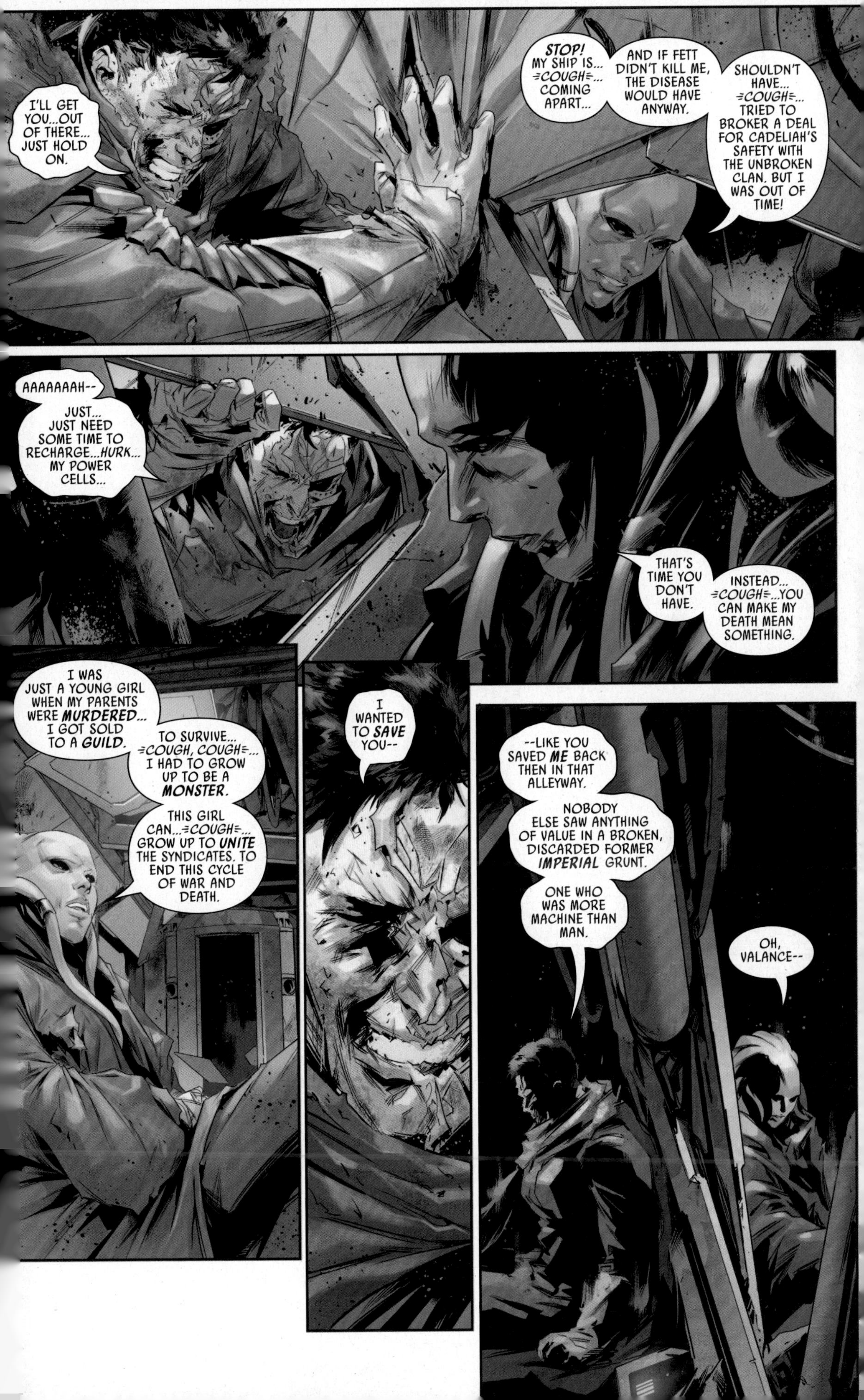
I'LL GET YOU...OUT OF THERE... JUST HOLD ON.
STOP! MY SHIP IS... =COUGH=... COMING APART...
AND IF FETT DIDN'T KILL ME, THE DISEASE WOULD HAVE ANYWAY.
SHOULDN'T HAVE... =COUGH=... TRIED TO BROKER A DEAL FOR CADELIAH'S SAFETY WITH THE UNBROKEN CLAN. BUT I WAS OUT OF TIME!
AAAAAAAH--
JUST... JUST NEED SOME TIME TO RECHARGE...HURK... MY POWER CELLS...
THAT'S TIME YOU DON'T HAVE.
INSTEAD... =COUGH=...YOU CAN MAKE MY DEATH MEAN SOMETHING.
I WAS JUST A YOUNG GIRL WHEN MY PARENTS WERE MURDERED... I GOT SOLD TO A GUILD.
TO SURVIVE... =COUGH, COUGH=... I HAD TO GROW UP TO BE A MONSTER.
THIS GIRL CAN... =COUGH=... GROW UP TO UNITE THE SYNDICATES. TO END THIS CYCLE OF WAR AND DEATH.
I WANTED TO SAVE YOU--
--LIKE YOU SAVED ME BACK THEN IN THAT ALLEYWAY.
NOBODY ELSE SAW ANYTHING OF VALUE IN A BROKEN, DISCARDED FORMER IMPERIAL GRUNT.
ONE WHO WAS MORE MACHINE THAN MAN.
OH, VALANCE--

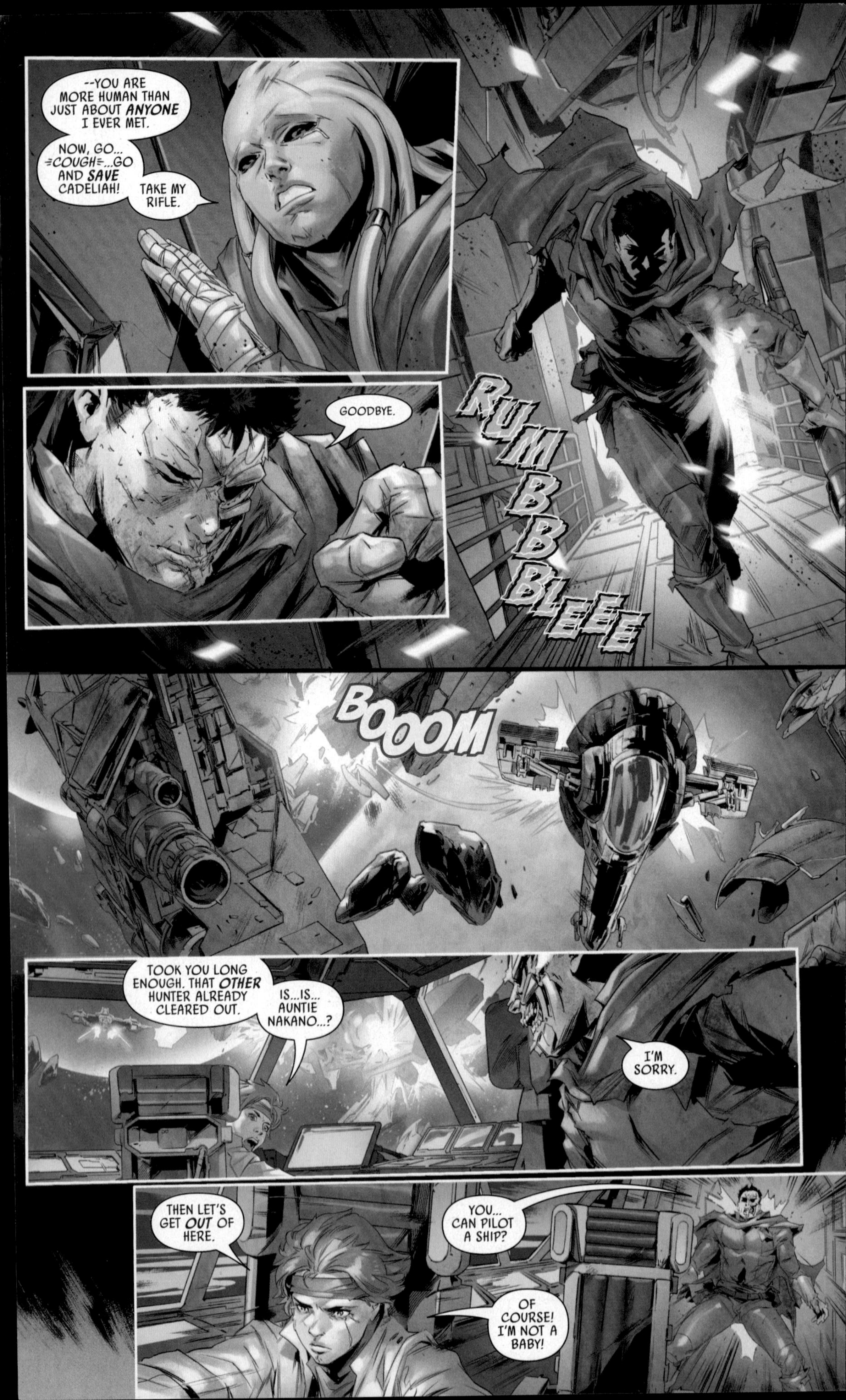
--YOU ARE MORE HUMAN THAN JUST ABOUT ANYONE I EVER MET.
NOW, GO... =COUGH=...GO AND SAVE CADELIAH!
TAKE MY RIFLE.
GOODBYE.
RUMBBBLEEE
BOOOM
TOOK YOU LONG ENOUGH. THAT OTHER HUNTER ALREADY CLEARED OUT.
IS...IS... AUNTIE NAKANO...?
I'M SORRY.
THEN LET'S GET OUT OF HERE.
YOU... CAN PILOT A SHIP?
OF COURSE! I'M NOT A BABY!

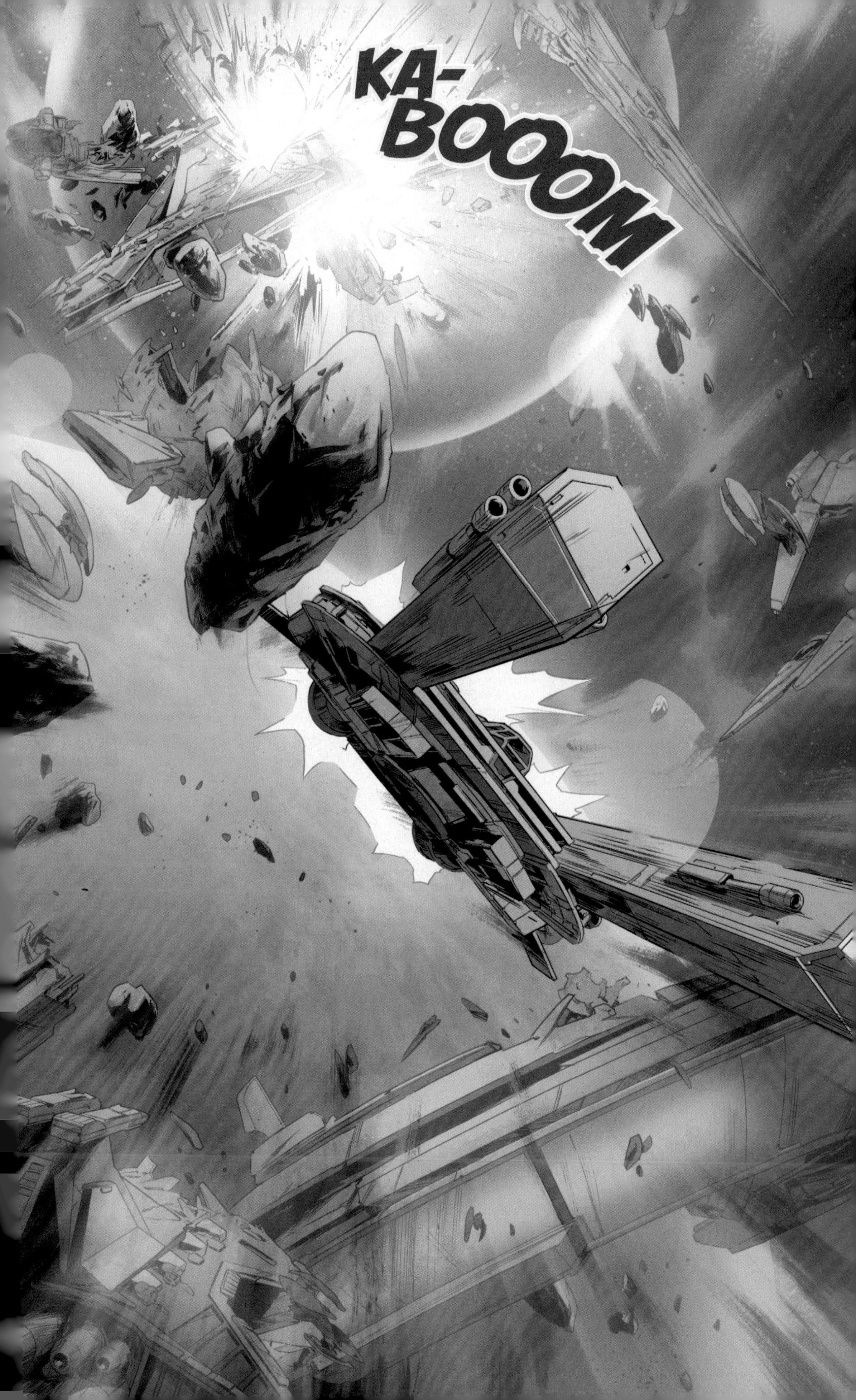
KA-
BOOOOM

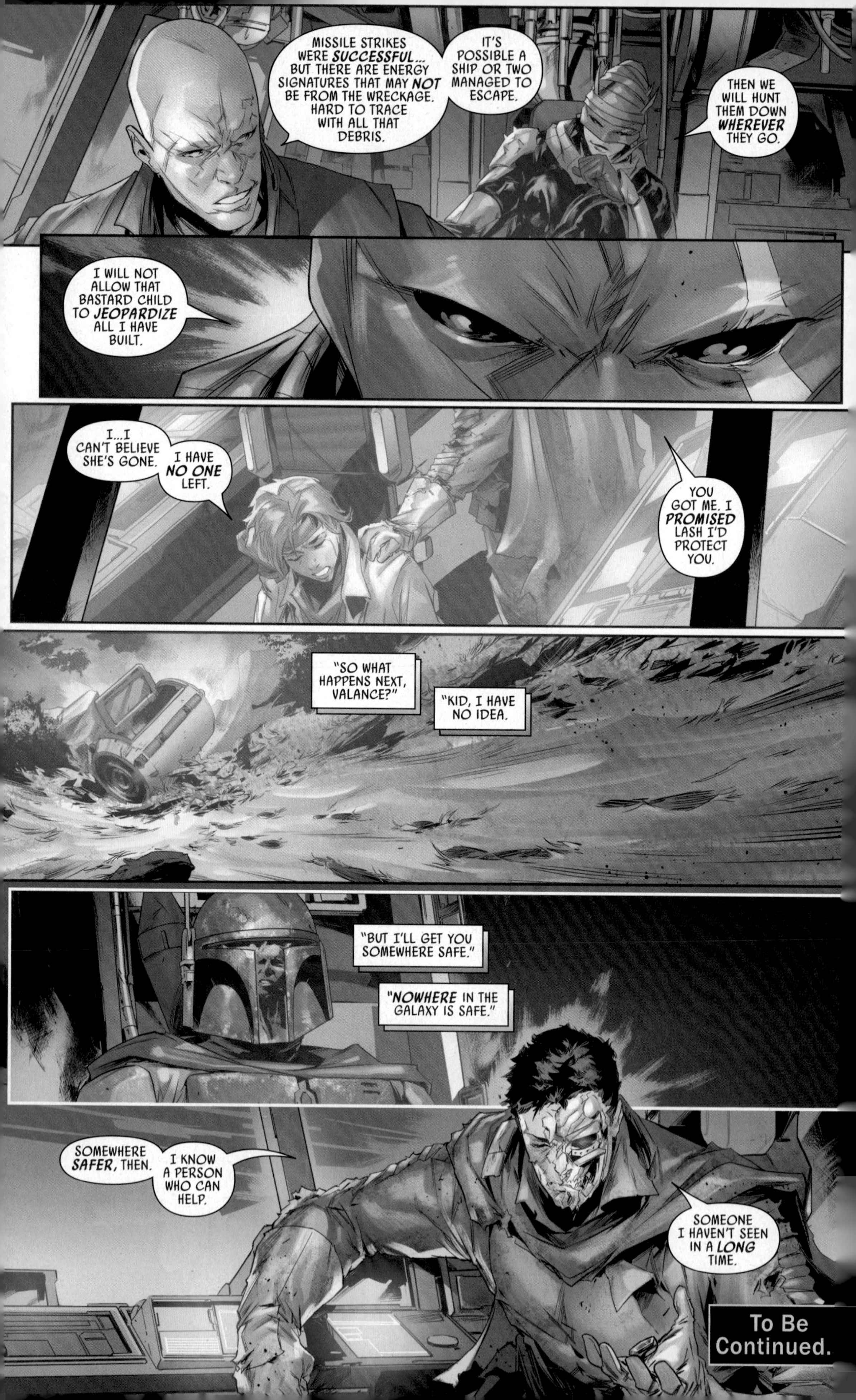
MISSILE STRIKES WERE SUCCESSFUL... BUT THERE ARE ENERGY SIGNATURES THAT MAY NOT BE FROM THE WRECKAGE. HARD TO TRACE WITH ALL THAT DEBRIS.
IT'S POSSIBLE A SHIP OR TWO MANAGED TO ESCAPE.
THEN WE WILL HUNT THEM DOWN WHEREVER THEY GO.
I WILL NOT ALLOW THAT BASTARD CHILD TO JEOPARDIZE ALL I HAVE BUILT.
I...I CAN'T BELIEVE SHE'S GONE.
I HAVE NO ONE LEFT.
YOU GOT ME. I PROMISED LASH I'D PROTECT YOU.
"SO WHAT HAPPENS NEXT, VALANCE?"
"KID, I HAVE NO IDEA.
"BUT I'LL GET YOU SOMEWHERE SAFE."
"NOWHERE IN THE GALAXY IS SAFE."
SOMEWHERE SAFER, THEN.
I KNOW A PERSON WHO CAN HELP.
SOMEONE I HAVEN'T SEEN IN A LONG TIME.
To Be Continued.

VALANCE

Believing in the cause of the Empire, Beilert Valance set out from his homeworld, the mining planet of Chorin, to enlist as a TIE fighter pilot. His ideals, however, were crushed along with his body in an explosion during an Imperial incursion on Mimban. Cast out of the Imperial service after command deemed it not worth the cost of fully repairing him, Valance was left more machine than man and struggling to find his place in the galaxy.

After a chance encounter with the famed Nakano Lash and her crew, Valance found a new calling as a bounty hunter, ready to take out his anger on scum who deserve it. Over time, he has augmented the cheaper system installed by his Imperial doctors with superior cybernetic tech, turning him into a much more formidable warrior.

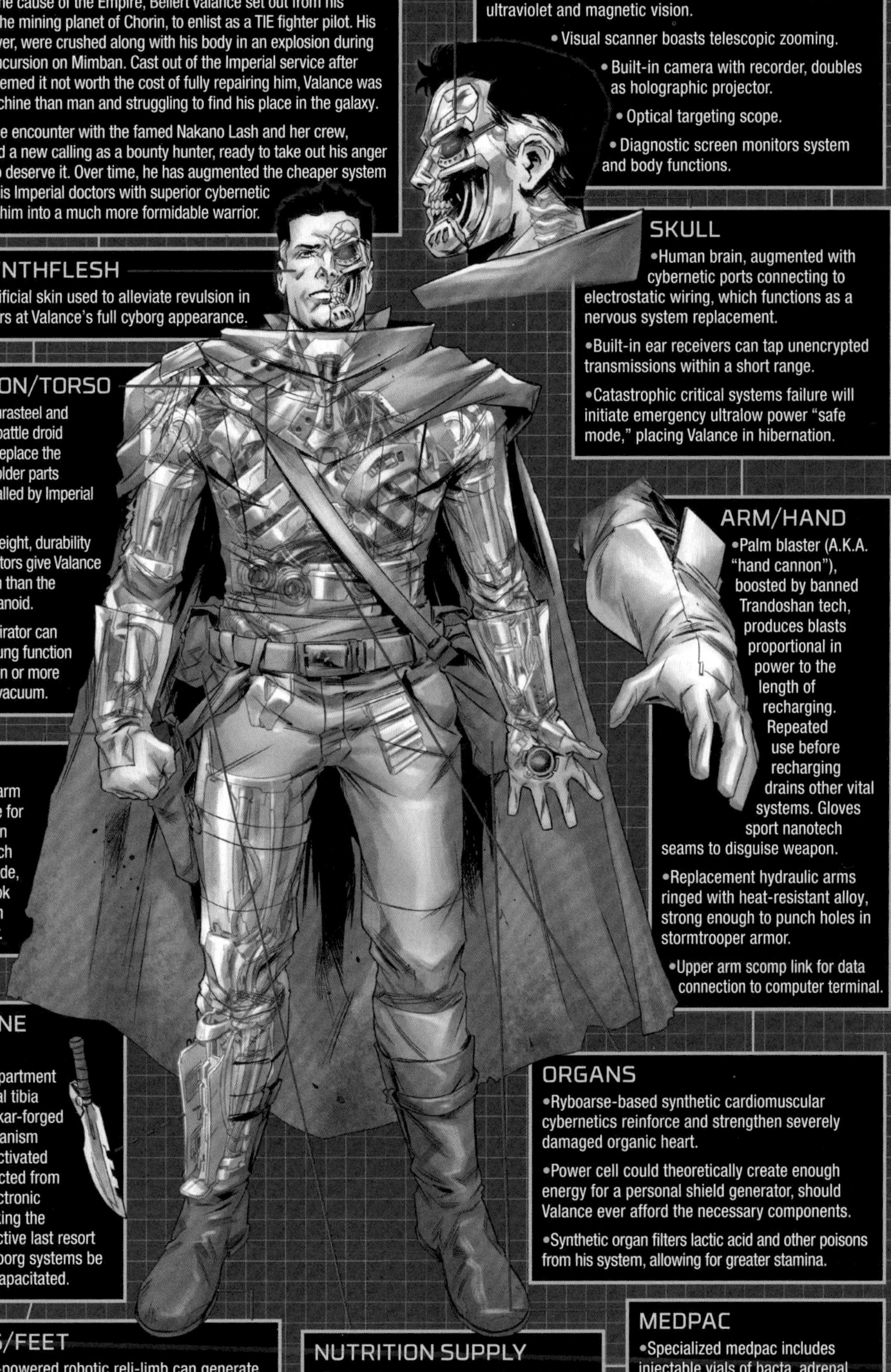

CYBERNETIC EYE

- Advanced photoreceptor capable of infrared, night, ultraviolet and magnetic vision.
- Visual scanner boasts telescopic zooming.
- Built-in camera with recorder, doubles as holographic projector.
- Optical targeting scope.
- Diagnostic screen monitors system and body functions.

SKULL

- Human brain, augmented with cybernetic ports connecting to electrostatic wiring, which functions as a nervous system replacement.
- Built-in ear receivers can tap unencrypted transmissions within a short range.
- Catastrophic critical systems failure will initiate emergency ultralow power "safe mode," placing Valance in hibernation.

SYNTHFLESH

- Artificial skin used to alleviate revulsion in others at Valance's full cyborg appearance.

SKELETON/TORSO

- Hardened durasteel and cannibalized battle droid tech used to replace the substandard older parts originally installed by Imperial med teams.
- Increased weight, durability and servo motors give Valance more strength than the average humanoid.
- Built-in respirator can supplement lung function to allow for ten or more minutes in a vacuum.

ARM/HAND

- Palm blaster (A.K.A. "hand cannon"), boosted by banned Trandoshan tech, produces blasts proportional in power to the length of recharging. Repeated use before recharging drains other vital systems. Gloves sport nanotech seams to disguise weapon.
- Replacement hydraulic arms ringed with heat-resistant alloy, strong enough to punch holes in stormtrooper armor.
- Upper arm scomp link for data connection to computer terminal.

ARM 2

- Hollow forearm houses space for future weapon upgrades, such as a vibroblade, grappling hook or concussion disc launcher.

SHINBONE BLADE

- Hidden compartment within artificial tibia conceals beskar-forged dagger. Mechanism is pressure-activated and disconnected from Valance's electronic systems, making the blade an effective last resort should his cyborg systems be otherwise incapacitated.

ORGANS

- Ryboarse-based synthetic cardiomuscular cybernetics reinforce and strengthen severely damaged organic heart.
- Power cell could theoretically create enough energy for a personal shield generator, should Valance ever afford the necessary components.
- Synthetic organ filters lactic acid and other poisons from his system, allowing for greater stamina.

LEGS/FEET

- Piston-powered robotic reli-limb can generate push to leap at greatly enhanced strength compared to an average human.
- Magnetic pods in feet--when activated, can assist in scaling metal surfaces or stabilizing in zero gravity.

NUTRITION SUPPLY

- Food and energy capsules: A combination of nutrients and medicines to keep the few remaining human organs functioning; some are flavored despite the limited ability to taste (due to neuro damage) as a reminder of what Beilert once enjoyed.

MEDPAC

- Specialized medpac includes injectable vials of bacta, adrenal strength, alacrity and stamina boosters and spare rechargeable power cells.

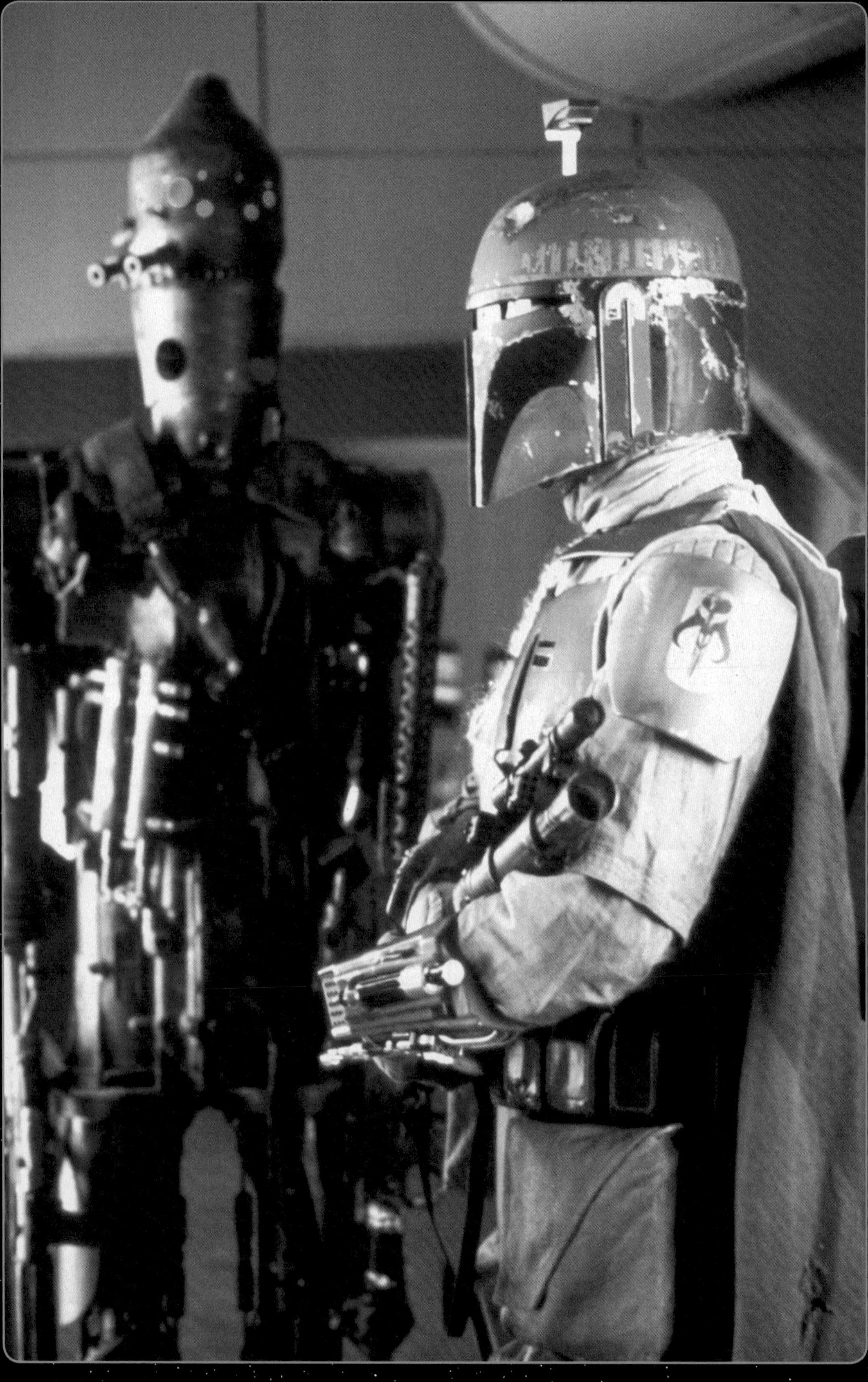

#1 Movie Variant

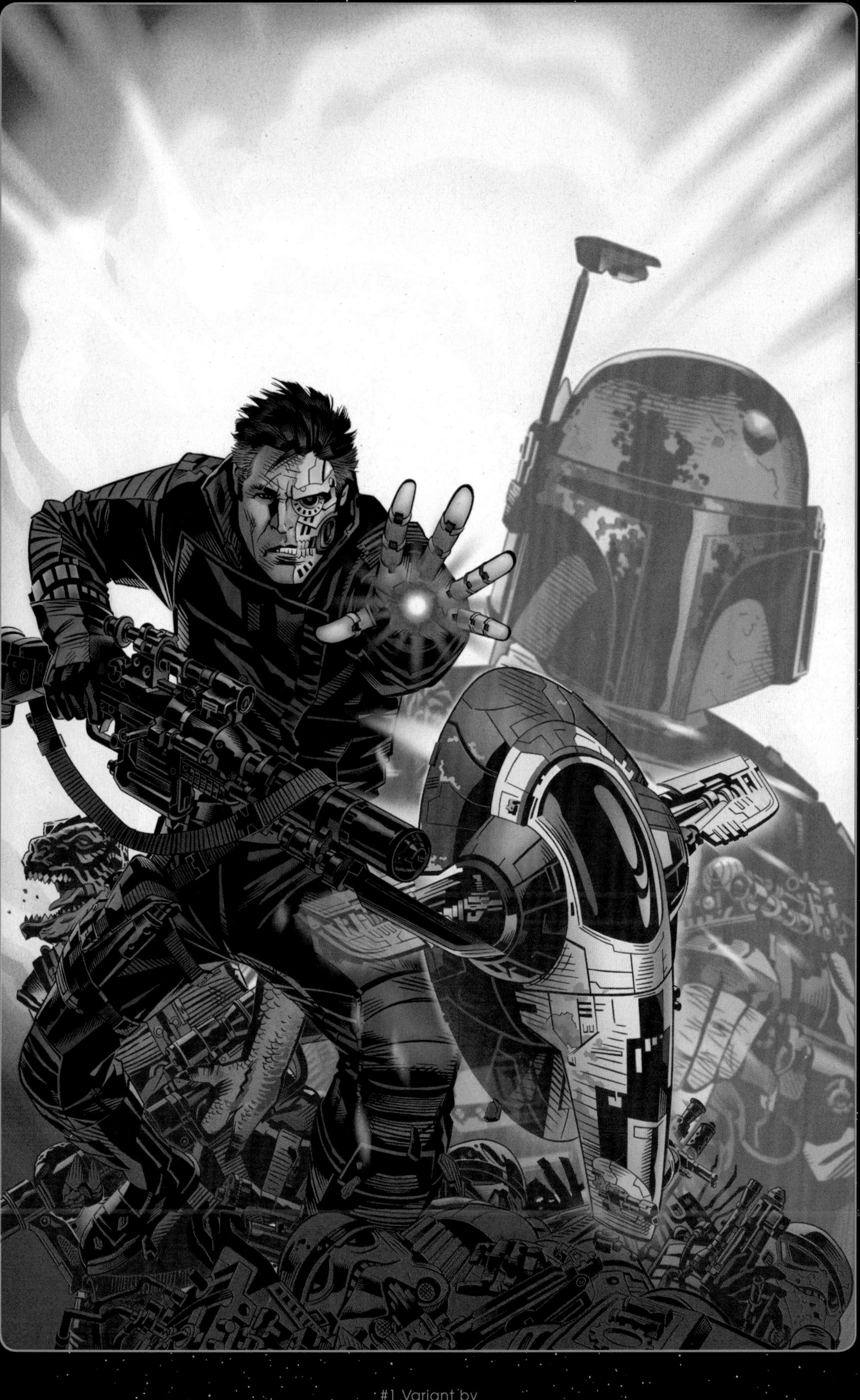

#1 Variant by
MICHAEL GOLDEN

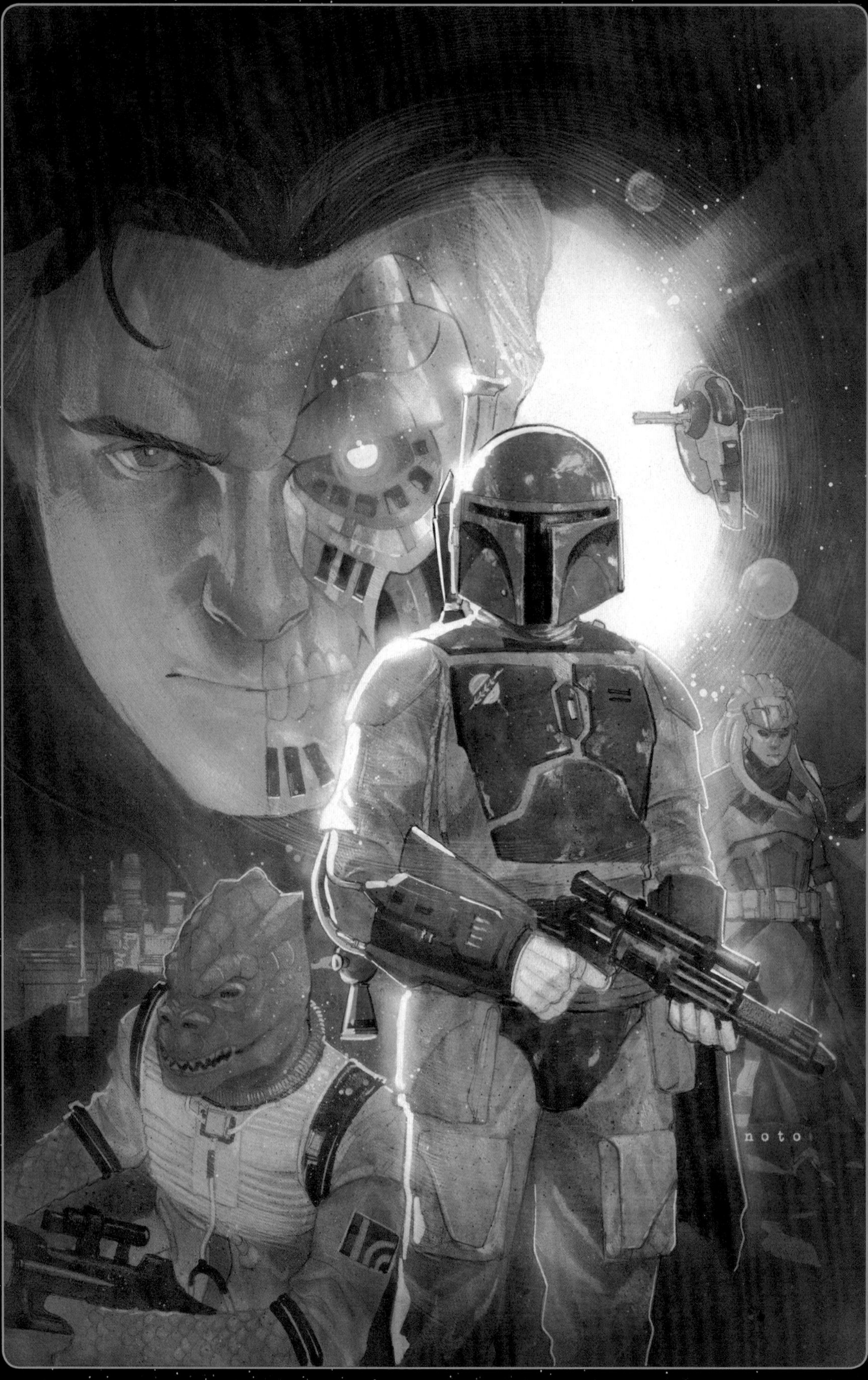
noto

#2 Variant by
PHIL NOTO

ROGUE ARCHAEOLOGIST DOCTOR APHRA THIEVES HER WAY ACROSS THE GALAXY!

STAR WARS: DOCTOR APHRA VOL. 1 – APHRA TPB
ISBN: 978-1302913212

STAR WARS: DOCTOR APHRA VOL. 2 – DOCTOR APHRA AND THE ENORMOUS PROFIT TPB
ISBN: 978-1302907631

STAR WARS: DOCTOR APHRA VOL. 3 – REMASTERED TPB
ISBN: 978-1302911522

STAR WARS: DOCTOR APHRA VOL. 4 – THE CATASTROPHE CON TPB
ISBN: 978-1302911539

STAR WARS: DOCTOR APHRA VOL. 5 – WORST AMONG EQUALS TPB
ISBN: 978-1302914875

STAR WARS: DOCTOR APHRA VOL. 6 – UNSPEAKABLE REBEL SUPERWEAPON TPB
ISBN: 978-1302914882

FOLLOW THE ADVENTURES OF LUKE, HAN AND LEIA IN THESE

STAR WARS™

COLLECTED EDITIONS!

START HERE

**Star Wars Vol. 1:
Skywalker Strikes**

ISBN 978-0-7851-9213-8

**Star Wars Vol. 2:
Showdown on the Smuggler's Moon**

ISBN 978-0-7851-9214-5

**Star Wars:
Vader Down**

ISBN 978-0-7851-9789-8

**Star Wars Vol. 3:
Rebel Jail**

ISBN 978-0-7851-9983-0

**Star Wars Vol. 4:
Last Flight of the Harbinger**

ISBN 978-0-7851-9984-7

**Star Wars Vol. 5:
Yoda's Secret War**

ISBN 978-1-302-90265-0

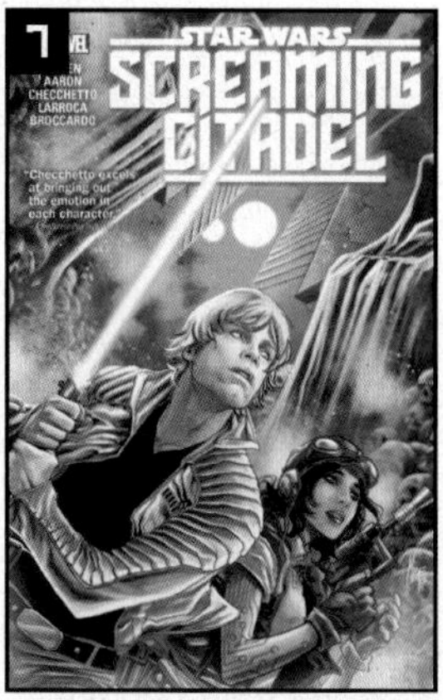
7
STAR WARS
SCREAMING CITADEL

Star Wars:
The Screaming Citadel
ISBN 978-1-302-90678-8

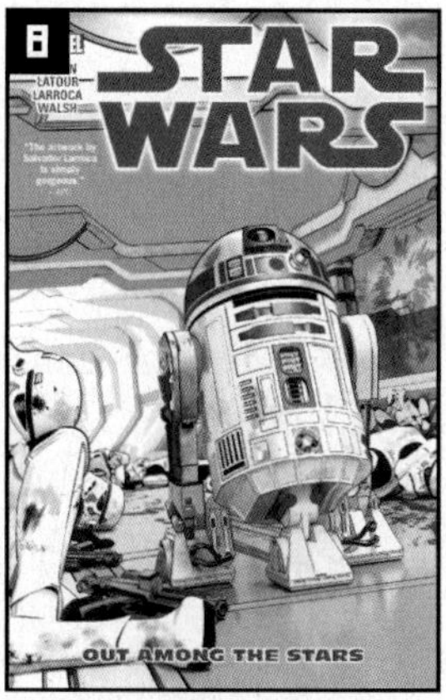
8
STAR WARS
OUT AMONG THE STARS

Star Wars Vol. 6:
Out Among the Stars
ISBN 978-1-302-90553-8

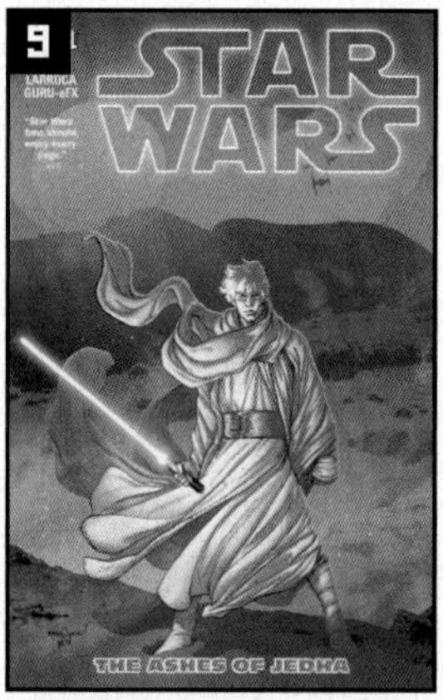
9
STAR WARS
THE ASHES OF JEDHA

Star Wars Vol. 7:
The Ashes of Jedha
ISBN 978-1-302-91052-5

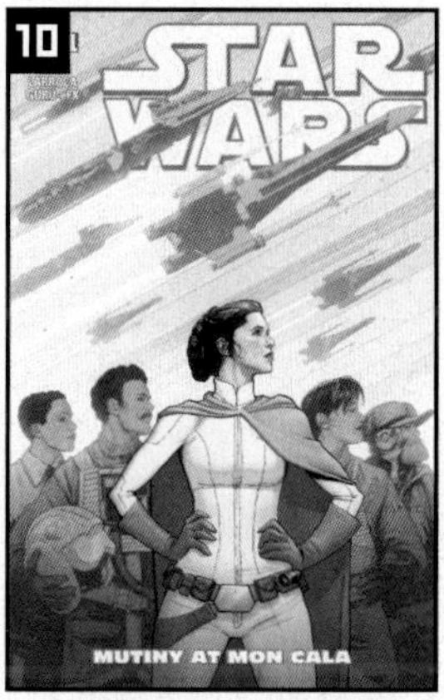
10
STAR WARS
MUTINY AT MON CALA

Star Wars Vol. 8:
Mutiny at Mon Cala
ISBN 978-1-302-91053-2

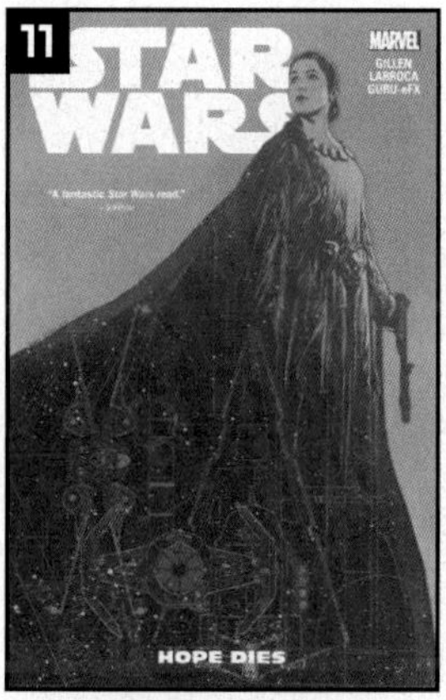
11
STAR WARS
MARVEL
GILLEN
LARROCA
GURU-eFX
HOPE DIES

Star Wars Vol. 9:
Hope Dies
ISBN 978-1-302-91054-9

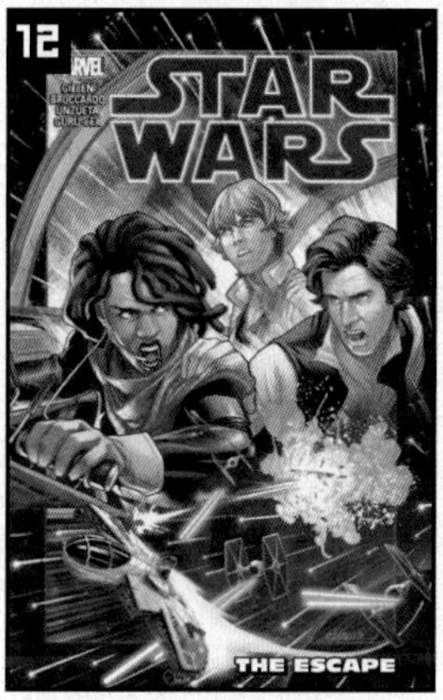
12
STAR WARS
THE ESCAPE

Star Wars Vol. 10:
The Escape
ISBN 978-1-302-91449-3

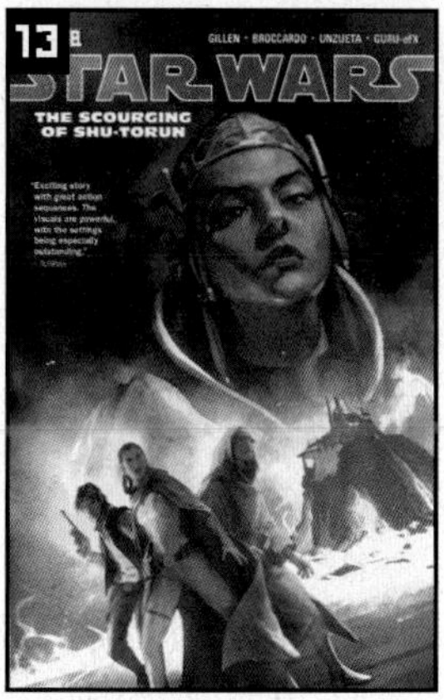
13
GILLEN · BROCCARDO · UNZUETA · GURU-eFX
STAR WARS
THE SCOURGING OF SHU-TORUN

Star Wars Vol. 11:
The Scourging of Shu-Torun
ISBN 978-1-302-91450-9

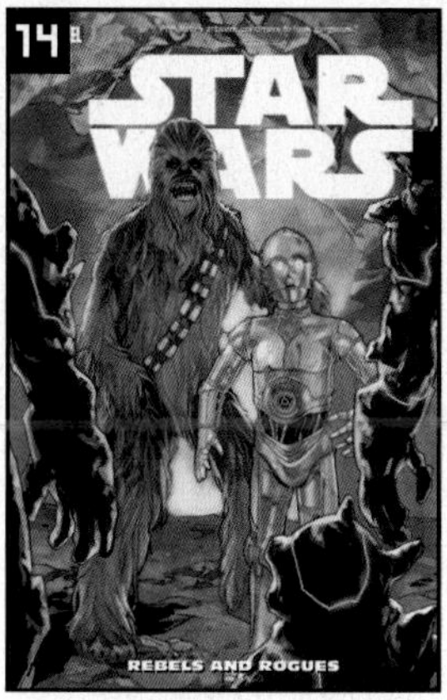
14
STAR WARS
REBELS AND ROGUES

Star Wars Vol. 12:
Rebels and Rogues
ISBN 978-1-302-91451-6

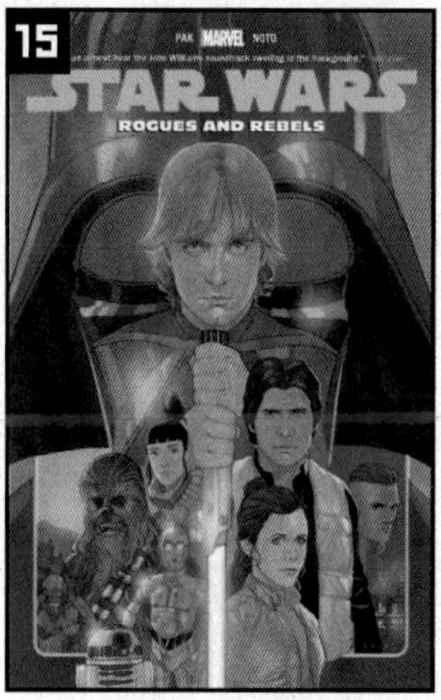
15
PAK MARVEL NOTO
STAR WARS
ROGUES AND REBELS

Star Wars Vol. 13:
Rogues and Rebels
ISBN 978-1-302-91450-9